THE
GOOD NEWS
CHILDREN'S
BIBLE

THE GOOD NEWS CHILDREN'S BIBLE

Passages selected from
Good News Bible in Today's English Version

Illustrated by Guido Bertello
Additional illustrations by Gordon King

THE BIBLE SOCIETIES

COLLINS

Old Testament passages first published by
Bible Societies and Collins in the Good News Bible 1976
New Testament passages originally published by
Fontana Books in "Good News for Modern Man" 1968

The Good News Bible was first published for children as
The Children's Bible (Collins 1978)
This revised edition was first published by
The Bible Societies and Collins in 1986
Reprinted 1990
Bible text Old Testament copyright © American Bible Society,
New York, 1976
Bible text New Testament copyright © American Bible Society,
New York, 1966, 1971, 1976

Illustrations copyright © William Collins Sons and Company
Limited, 1976, 1978, 1986
Illustrations by Guido Bertello
Additional illustrations on pages 14–15, 17, 163, 167, 239, 303,
307 and 314 by Gordon King

Introductory material and Bible helps copyright © British and
Foreign Bible Society, 1986

Permission to use any part of the British Edition should be
requested from:
The British and Foreign Bible Society (Publishing Division)
Stonehill Green, Westlea, Swindon SN5 7DG

British Library Cataloguing in Publication Data
[Bible. *English. Today's English. Selections. 1986*]
    The Children's Bible: passages
    selected from Good News Bible in Today's
    English Version.
    1. Bible stories, English
    I. Good News Bible
    220.9'505   BS551.2

    ISBN 0 00 107192 0 Collins
    ISBN 0 564 05573 5 Bible Society

Designed and phototypeset by
Nuprint Services, 30b Station Road, Harpenden, Herts AL5 4SE
Printed and bound in Hong Kong
Production arranged by Angus Hudson Ltd, London NW1 7QX

Foreword

To many people the Bible is the most important and precious book they will ever own. The first part of the Bible is called the Old Testament, and it begins with the wonderful story of how God created the earth and all the people, plants, and animals that live on it.

The Old Testament continues with the history of the ancient Jews (or Hebrews), God's special people. This is quite amazing, telling us how God looked for them, chose them, and watched over them through all their difficulties.

We are told about the prophets, the people God sent to bring us his messages. God spoke to us through them and many are sure that his words are relevant and of great value today. The prophets spoke of the coming of the special person who would be the Messiah or Saviour, as the Jews called him.

The stories about Jesus in the New Testament tell of his life on earth, of his healing and teaching, and of his close followers, the disciples. We read too of his death, of his coming back to life, and how he was taken by God into heaven. The New Testament also tells how Jesus' teaching led to the formation of the early Christian church.

Many people believe the Bible can tell us all we need to know to live a happy and fulfilled life here on earth. It can also help us to understand about the eternal life which belief in Jesus Christ offers. If you treasure your Bible, read it, and think about it regularly you will become familiar with Jesus and have the opportunity to get to know our creator / God as your friend.

WENDY CRAIG

Contents

THE OLD TESTAMENT

1
This is God's world
Page 19

In the beginning; The story of creation; The garden of Eden; **Mankind goes wrong**; The first people disobey God; Cain and Abel; "What about your brother?" **God's judgement and mercy**; "Why did I make these people?" Noah; "Get in the boat!" Dry land appears; A promise and a sign;

2
The nation of Israel begins
Page 31

The father of nations; God's call to Abram; God commands Abraham to offer Isaac; Finding a wife for Isaac; **The rival brothers**; Esau and Jacob; Jacob tricks Isaac; Jacob's dream; Jacob wrestles with God; **Joseph**; Joseph and his brothers; Joseph in Egypt; Joseph amazes his brothers; Benjamin and the missing cup; Joseph explains who he is;

3
The great escape
Page 50

Slavery in Egypt; Cruel treatment in Egypt; Baby boys are murdered; **The great leader**; The birth of Moses; Moses escapes; God calls Moses; Moses and Aaron before the king of Egypt; **The Israelites sense freedom**; The first Passover; The Israelites leave Egypt; Crossing the Red Sea; The song of Moses; **The long journey**; Food in the desert; Water supplies in the desert; A terrifying sight on Mount Sinai; The Ten Commandments; Other rules that were added; The golden bull; The death of Moses;

4
Men of courage
Page 72

Entering the Promised Land; Joshua is told to be confident; Jericho; Joshua's final message; **Holding on to the land**; Gideon is called to rescue Israel; The altar of a false god; Victory; **Leader and prophet**; Promised to God before he was born; Samuel is dedicated to the Lord; Samuel hears God speak; We want a king; The Israelites get their first king; **David**; Ruth leaves home; Ruth works in the fields; Boaz marries Ruth; David is anointed as king; **David's adventures as a young man**; Goliath challenges the Israelites; David's courage; David and Goliath; David is presented to Saul; Saul becomes jealous of David; David at the court of King Saul; Jonathan helps David; The secret sign to escape; David gets his chance of revenge; Saul calls up the spirit of Samuel; Samuel's prediction comes true; David's lament for Saul and Jonathan;

5
Kings and prophets
Page 102

David the King; David does wrong; David tries to hide what he's done; David's plan; Nathan confronts David; Absalom rebels; David flees from Jerusalem; Absalom takes over Jerusalem; Absalom gets conflicting advice; David is warned and escapes; The two armies meet in battle; David is told about Absalom; **King Solomon;** David's last instructions to Solomon; Solomon prays for wisdom; An example of Solomon's wise judgements; Respect for Solomon grows; The visit of the queen of Sheba; Solomon builds the Temple; The house of God; **The prophets speak out for God;** Elijah and the prophets of Baal; The earthquake, the fire, and the whisper; A new prophet is called; Trouble over Naboth's vineyard; Elijah is taken up to heaven; Naaman is cured; **The prophets speak out against wrongdoing;** Do what is right; The rich and the poor; What God wants; Obeying God; God's love for his rebellious people; **The disobedient prophet;** Jonah runs away; "Man overboard!" Jonah gets a second chance; The truth comes out; **Hope and despair;** God calls another prophet; The Assyrians threaten Jerusalem; Death in the camp; A hope for peace; A frightening discovery; What the book said; Josiah attempts to renew the covenant; **All is still not well;** Jeremiah's call to be a prophet; A last desperate warning; God's new covenant; Jerusalem is destroyed;

6
The great promise
Page 145

Hope in despair; Ezekiel sees a vision of God; God calls Ezekiel to be a prophet; Sheep in need of a shepherd; The valley of dry bones; **Victory out of suffering;** Words of hope; God's suffering servant; Daniel's visions; The fiery furnace; The writing on the wall; Daniel explains the writing; Daniel in the pit of lions; **Freedom out of exile;** Incredible news; A dream come true; The flame burns again on the altar; Opposition; Rebuild the Temple; Nehemiah goes to Jerusalem; A night ride through the ruins; A sword in one hand and a trowel in the other; Plots against Nehemiah; The wall is finished; The covenant is renewed.

Contents

THE NEW TESTAMENT

1
When Jesus was young
Page 170

The prophet is born; His name is to be John; Zechariah's prophecy; **The first Christmas;** Mary receives amazing news; Mary visits Elizabeth; Mary's song of praise; Jesus is born; The news is given to the shepherds; **Gold, frankincense, and myrrh;** Visitors from the East; The escape to Egypt; The children are killed; It is safe to return; Jesus is given his name; Jesus is presented in the Temple; Jesus, aged twelve, in the Temple;

2
How Jesus lived
Page 186

John prepares the way; The preaching of John the Baptist; Jesus comes to be baptized; **Jesus begins his work;** Jesus is tempted; Jesus calls four fishermen; The wedding in Cana; **Jesus demonstrates God's power to the people;** A man with an evil spirit; Many diseases cured; Everyone is looking for Jesus; Jesus heals a dreaded skin-disease; Jesus heals a paralysed man; Jesus heals a blind beggar; **Jesus is concerned for people;** Jesus calls Matthew; Jesus has pity for the people; The question about fasting; Crowds of people struggle to get to Jesus; **A new family chosen by Jesus;** Jesus chooses the twelve apostles; Jesus' mother and brothers; Who is this man? Jesus is unwelcome at Nazareth; Women who followed Jesus; The would-be followers of Jesus; **The good news spreads;** Jairus' daughter; Jesus sends out the twelve apostles; Jesus feeds five thousand men; Jesus walks on water; Jesus in Gennesaret; A woman's faith; The Roman officer's servant; The widow's son; Jesus receives a message from prison; Jesus at the home of Simon the Pharisee; Humility and hospitality; Jesus and Zacchaeus; Jesus heals a man born blind;

3
Stories told by Jesus
Page 213

Stories about God's rule; The parable of the lost sheep; The parable of the lost coin; The parable of the lost son; **Stories about God's kingdom;** The parable of the weeds; The parable of the mustard seed; The parable of the yeast; The parable of the hidden treasure; The parable of the fine pearl; The parable of the net; The parable of the growing seed; The parable of the fig tree which did not grow fruit; The parable of the great feast; The parable of the sower; Jesus explains the parable; **Stories about keeping alert;** The parable of the ten girls; The parable of the three servants; Watchful servants; The parable of the tenants in the vineyard; **Stories about prayer;** The parable of the friend at midnight; The parable of the widow and the judge; The parable of the Pharisee and the tax collector; **Stories about what really matters;** The parable of the unforgiving servant; The parable of the rich fool; The rich man and Lazarus; **Things are not always what they seem;** The parable of the two sons; The parable of the good Samaritan; The story of the final judgement;

4
Jesus teaches
Page 232

The Sermon on the Mount; Providing the salt; Letting your light shine; Teaching about anger; Teaching about revenge; Love your enemies; Teaching about giving; Teaching about prayer; Riches in heaven; God and possessions; Judging others; Ask, seek, knock; The narrow gate; A tree and its fruit; I never knew you; The two house builders; Crowd reaction; **Jesus and people who kept the Law;** The Sadducees; The Pharisees; Blind guides! Nicodemus; **Jesus and people who broke the Law;** The Samaritan woman; The woman caught in adultery; **What sort of laws should we keep?** Things that make a person unclean; The question about paying taxes; The great commandment; Jesus heals on the Sabbath;

5
The road
to the cross
Page 248

The great discovery; Peter realizes who Jesus is; Jesus speaks about his suffering and death; The transfiguration; **Humility goes with greatness;** Who is the greatest? Whoever is not against us is for us; Jesus blesses little children; The rich man; The request of James and John; Jesus' love for Jerusalem; **Death will not be the end;** Jesus receives some sad news; Jesus makes promises; Jesus weeps; Lazarus come out! The plot against Jesus; **Jesus goes to Jerusalem;** Jesus warns his disciples what to expect; Jesus' triumphant entry into Jerusalem; Jesus goes to the Temple; What right have you to do these things? The widow's offering; Jesus talks about the destruction of the Temple;

6
How Jesus
died
Page 265

Jesus' enemies move against him; The plot against Jesus; Jesus in Bethany; Judas plots with the priests; **The Last Supper;** The upstairs room; Jesus washes his disciples' feet; Jesus predicts that he will be betrayed; Jesus the way to the Father; The promise of the Holy Spirit; The Lord's Supper; **Deserted by everyone;** Who will stand by Jesus? Jesus prays in Gethsemane; The arrest of Jesus; Jesus before the Council; Peter denies Jesus; Jesus is taken to Pilate; Jesus is sentenced to death; Judas' death; The soldiers make fun of Jesus;

Jesus is nailed to the cross; Jesus dies; Jesus is buried; The guard at the tomb;

7
The victory of Jesus
Page 283

The unbelievable surprise; The tomb is empty; Peter goes to see for himself; Mary sees Jesus; The report of the guards; The walk to Emmaus; The story is confirmed; Jesus and Thomas; Jesus appears to the seven disciples; Many others see Jesus; Jesus' last instructions; Jesus is taken up to heaven; **Jesus' followers make sense of it all;** God always had a plan; One in Christ; God puts us right with him; **The disciples are like new men;** The coming of the Holy Spirit; Peter's message; Life among the believers; **They could not be stopped;** Peter orders a man to walk; Peter's message in the Temple; Peter and John before the Council; Miracles and wonders; The apostles are arrested;

8
Belief in Jesus spreads around the world
Page 298

A new apostle is called; Saul tries to destroy the church; Drama on the road to Damascus; Saul changes sides; **The Gentiles are told the good news;** Thrown into prison; In Athens; The riot in Ephesus; **Paul continues his work from prison;** Arrested in the Temple; Paul faces a furious crowd; Paul gets his enemies quarrelling; The plot against Paul's life; Paul appeals to the Emperor; **The journey to Rome;** Paul sets sail; The ship is carried along by a fierce storm; Abandon ship! On Malta; In Rome; **Looking backward and forward;** Paul's suffering; A vision of Jesus in heaven; Worshipping Jesus in heaven; A prayer of praise.

Index of Jesus' miracles
Page 318

Index of Jesus' parables
Page 318

Index of Bible references
Page 319

What is the Bible?

A book?

Many people think of the Bible as one book. It is easy to see why this is. It is given to us between two covers and in every way looks like a book. But it is more than one book. The word "Bible" itself comes from the Greek "Biblia", which means "books". So the Bible is a collection of books. This is very important to remember. When we use the word "book" we imagine something written quite quickly, usually by one person or a small group. The Bible was not put together in this way. It contains writings by many different people, most of whom did not know each other. They lived in different places over a period of many, many years. And they originally wrote in at least three different languages, which have since been translated into English.

A collection of completely separate books?

As you might expect, the Bible contains many different kinds of books. Often they were written for different reasons and for different people. For example, some were written to record very important events, some were written as letters, and some as collections of songs and poems. You will probably recognize other types of writing as you read on. They all have a lot in common and they tell a continuing story. It was this that made people collect the books together and call them the "Bible".

This did not happen all at once. When Jesus lived in Israel, almost 2,000 years ago, a collection of books had for many years been thought of as "special". The religious leaders of that place thought that these books gave them an understanding of God and his love for people which made them greater than any other book. This collection now forms the Old Testament of the Bible.

The Old Testament was put together long before any of the New Testament books were written. Jesus often used parts of it in his teaching. After Jesus' life on earth the first Christians wrote about him and what his life meant. Later on the church leaders collected these writings together to form the New Testament. They believed that these writings were as special as those in the Old Testament.

The same as any other Bible?

This book has been put together especially for young readers. It is a selection of passages from many of the books of the Bible. The titles and introductions are not part of the Bible, but have been put in to help you. After each title you are given the name of the book of the Bible which the passage is taken from and two sets of numbers (e.g. Genesis 13.10–17). This is called a "reference", and it helps you to find the same passage in any complete Bible. First then, there is the name of the book, next there is the chapter, and then the verse, as explained below.

When the first books of the Bible were written they were called by the first word in them. Later on they were given new names, which told the readers more about the contents of the book. For example, the first book in the Bible is called "Genesis", which means "beginning". Sometimes the name of the book came from the person who is thought to have written it or put it together, and sometimes from the name of the people for whom it was written.

Later, the books of the Bible were divided into chapters. Then the chapters were divided up. These divisions were called "verses". They were added to help those who were copying out passages from the Bible by hand. These numbers ensured that they did not lose their place. The first number, then, tells you the chapter to turn to, and the second set of numbers tells you the verses to read.

By using the references you can find the same passage in any complete Bible. But you may find that slightly different words are used in each. This is because there are many different translations of the Bible. The books in the Bible were originally written in Hebrew, Aramaic, or Greek, which few people today would understand. So they have been translated into most modern languages. The Bible was first translated into English about five hundred years ago, and copies of old translations are still sold. Over recent years there have been modern translations and this book contains passages taken from the Good News Bible.

The Bible has sold more copies than any other book ever printed, and is still regularly the world's bestseller.

Names and places

Names used for the people of God in the Old Testament

The Hebrews   There is some mystery about where this name came from but, as you will see, Abraham became famous for taking a long journey and settling in another land. Many people think that the name "Hebrew" literally means "those from beyond" or "people from the other side". We do not know whether this means the other side of a river, mountains, or a desert. The people soon took on a different name, but Hebrew was still the name of the language they spoke.

The Israelites   This is the most common name used in the Old Testament for the descendants of Abraham who were linked to God by the covenant.

During his life, Jacob was given the name "Israel", which comes from two Hebrew words, "YSR" and "EL". "EL" was the word for God and "YSR" comes from a word meaning "to rule".

Jacob's descendants were known as the "Children of Israel", or "Israelites". This was the name used when they became a nation and founded a country.

The Jews   At first this name was used to describe just the Israelites who lived in Judah, but later it became the name for all of them. By the time the New Testament was written it was a common way of describing the people of Israel.

Names used for the land in which God's people lived

Canaan   This was the name used to describe the area of land where Abraham settled when he left his home in Mesopotamia.

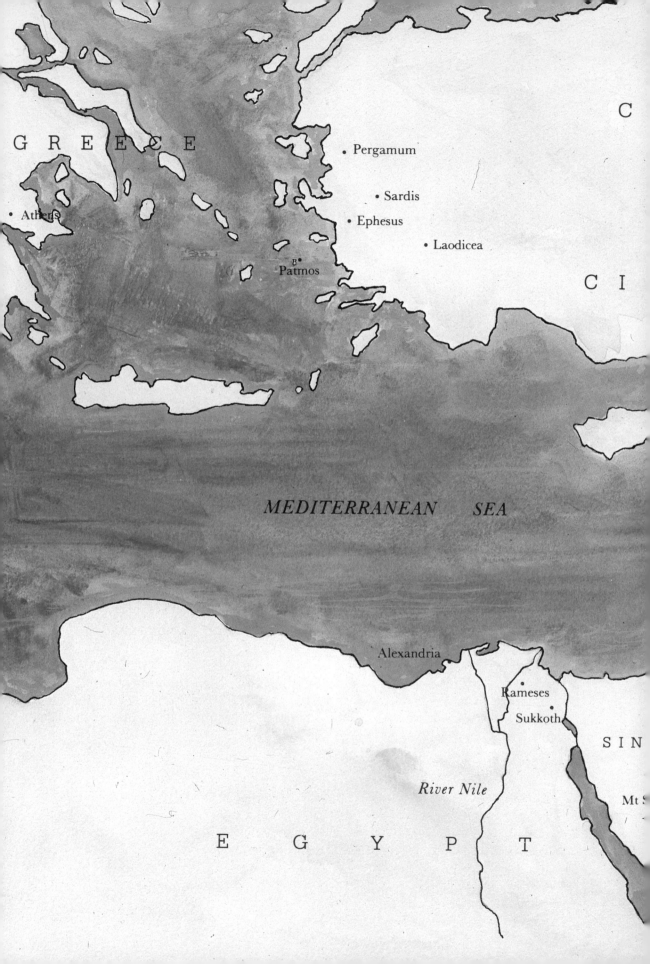

GREECE

• Athens

• Pergamum

• Sardis

• Ephesus

• Laodicea

E•
Patmos

C

CI

MEDITERRANEAN   SEA

Alexandria

• Rameses

Sukkoth

SIN

River Nile

Mt S

E   G   Y   P   T

P O N T U S

PADOCIA

MAP OF THE WORLD TODAY

CIA

MESOPOTAMIA

ASSYRIA

• Haran

• Nineveh

Euphrates

PHOENICIA

SYRIA

BANON

Sidon•

• Damascus

Tigris

Ur

yre•

• Caesarea Philippi

ernaum•

Cana•

Sea of Galilee

reth•

aria•

hiloh•

thel•

em•

• Jericho

BABYLONIA

• Bethlehem

eba•

Dead Sea

River Jordan

MOAB

80   160   Kilometers

SEA

Israel Gradually the other tribes in Canaan began to move away northwards and the Israelites started to take over the area. As they did this they gave their name to the land, and it became known as Israel.

Judah After the death of King Solomon the country split into two parts. The larger, northern part kept the name Israel, and the smaller, southern part became known as Judah.

Palestine This name originally came from the word "Philistine", which was the name of a group of people who once lived in the whole area. It was used by the Romans and the Greeks to describe the entire region around what had been called Israel and Judah. It also included areas where non-Jews lived.

It is important to know that the names Canaan, Israel, and Palestine roughly describe the same piece of land. The names are different because they suggest who was in control at the time. In the same way the names Hebrews, Israelites, and Jews all describe the same group of people.

Names used for the followers of Jesus in the New Testament

Disciples Religious teachers would gather people around them who would learn their teachings and pass them on to others. They were called "disciples". In the New Testament the word "disciples" is used of the followers of John the Baptist and of Jesus. It especially refers to Jesus' twelve closest followers.

Apostles This word means "messenger". It usually refers to the twelve men who Jesus chose to be his special followers and helpers. As he left this earth he told eleven of them to take his message to the world. These men became leaders of the first churches.

Christians At Antioch (a place in Syria) people began to call those who believed in Jesus Christ "Christians". At first it was used as a kind of nickname, but the name stuck, and is still used today to describe those who follow Jesus.

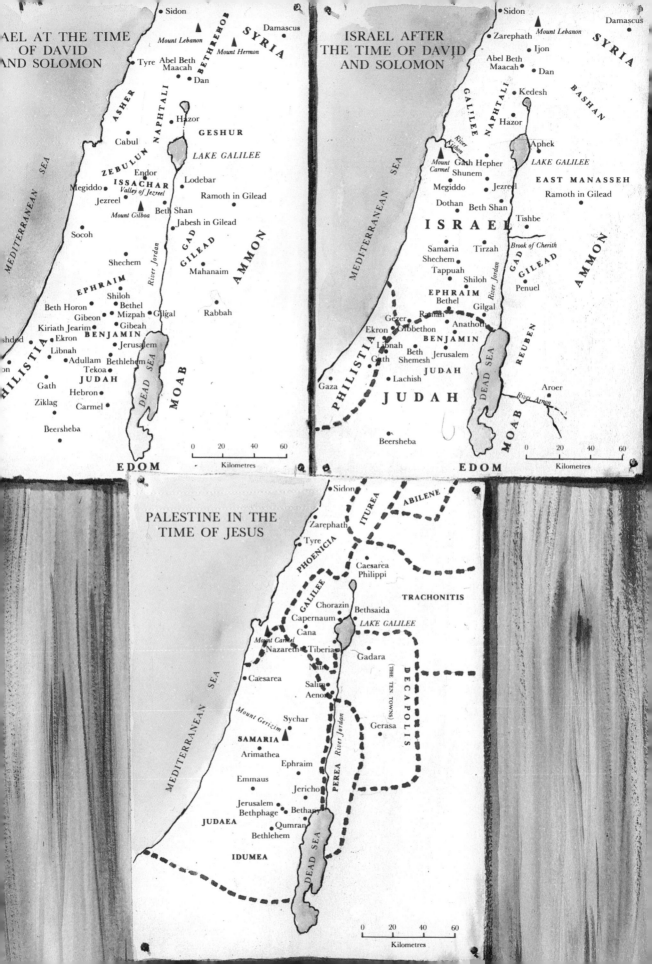

The Old Testament

I
This is
God's world

In the beginning

We can't imagine what it was like before people, the world, or the universe began. But that is where the story told in the Bible begins.

The Bible does not tell us exactly how the universe began, but it does say some very important things about why it was made.

The first book of the Bible is called Genesis and it tells us that the world is not an accident. God created it. God wanted it. God cares about it and everything in it.

Sometimes, when children ask their parents a difficult question, they are answered with a story. This happens with adults too. Genesis contains some stories which were first told long ago, so that people could learn from them.

These stories were very important to the people of Israel. You need to know something about them before you can understand the rest of the Bible.

The story of creation   Genesis 1.1—2.3

In the beginning, when God created the universe, the earth was formless and desolate. The raging ocean that covered everything was engulfed in total darkness, and the power of God was moving over the water. Then God commanded, "Let there be light"—and light appeared. God was pleased with what he saw. Then he separated the light from the darkness, and he named the light "Day" and the darkness "Night". Evening passed and morning came—that was the first day.

Then God commanded, "Let there be a dome to divide the water and to keep it in two separate places"—and it was done. So God made a dome, and it separated the water under it from the water above it. He named the dome "Sky." Evening passed and morning came—that was the second day.

Then God commanded, "Let the water below the sky come together in one place, so that the land will appear"—and it was done. He named the land "Earth," and the water which had come together he named "Sea." And God was pleased with what he saw. Then he commanded, "Let the earth produce all kinds of plants, those that bear grain and those that bear fruit"—and it was done. So the earth produced all kinds of plants, and God was pleased with what he saw. Evening passed and morning came—that was the third day.

Then God commanded, "Let lights appear in the sky to separate day from night and to show the time when days, years, and religious festivals begin; they will shine in the sky to give light to the earth"—and it was done. So God made the two larger lights, the sun to rule over the day and the moon to rule over the night; he also made the stars. He placed the lights in the sky to shine on the earth, to rule over the day and the night, and to separate light from darkness. And God was pleased with what he saw. Evening passed and morning came—that was the fourth day.

Then God commanded, "Let the water be filled with many kinds of living beings, and let the air be filled with birds." So God created the great sea-monsters, all kinds of creatures that live in the water, and all kinds of birds. And God was pleased with what he saw. He blessed them all and told the creatures that live in the water to reproduce, and to fill the sea, and he told the birds to increase in number. Evening passed and morning came—that was the fifth day.

Then God commanded, "Let the earth produce all kinds of animal life: domestic and wild, large and small"—and it was done. So God made them all, and he was pleased with what he saw.

Then God said, "And now we will make human beings; they will be like us and resemble us. They will have power over the fish, the birds, and all animals, domestic and wild, large and small." So God created human beings, making them to be like himself. He created them male and female, blessed them, and said, "Have many children, so that your descendants will live all over the earth and bring it under their control. I am putting you in charge of the fish, the birds, and all the wild animals. I have provided all kinds of grain and all kinds of fruit for you to eat; but for all the wild animals and for all the birds I have provided grass and leafy plants for food"—and it was done. God looked at everything he had made, and he was very pleased. Evening passed and morning came—that was the sixth day.

20

And so the whole universe was completed. By the seventh day God finished what he had been doing and stopped working. He blessed the seventh day and set it apart as a special day, because by that day he had completed his creation and stopped working.

The garden of Eden   Genesis 2.8–9, 15–17

The word "garden" brings a different picture to different people's minds.

Then the LORD God planted a garden in Eden, in the East, and there he put the man he had formed. He made all kinds of beautiful trees grow there and produce good fruit. In the middle of the garden stood the tree that gives life and the tree that gives knowledge of what is good and what is bad.

Then the LORD God placed the man in the Garden of Eden to cultivate it and guard it. He said to him, "You may eat the fruit of any tree in the garden, except the tree that gives knowledge of what is good and what is bad. You must not eat the fruit of that tree; if you do, you will die the same day."

Mankind goes wrong

The first people disobey God   Genesis 3.1–13, 22–23

For a long time people have asked this question: "If God made a good world which he was very pleased with, where do bad things come from?" This story gives an answer.

Now the snake was the most cunning animal that the LORD God had made. The snake asked the woman, "Did God really tell you not to eat fruit from any tree in the garden?"

"We may eat the fruit of any tree in the garden," the woman answered, "except the tree in the middle of it. God told us not to eat the fruit of that tree or even touch it; if we do, we will die."

The snake replied, "That's not true; you will not die. God said that, because he knows that when you eat it you will be like God and know what is good and what is bad."

The woman saw how beautiful the tree was and how good its fruit would be to eat, and she thought how wonderful it would be to become wise. So she took some of the fruit and ate it. Then she gave some to her husband, and he also ate it. As soon as they had eaten it, they were given

understanding and realized that they were naked; so they sewed fig leaves together and covered themselves.

That evening they heard the LORD God walking in the garden, and they hid from him among the trees. But the LORD God called out to the man, "Where are you?"

He answered, "I heard you in the garden; I was afraid and hid from you, because I was naked."

"Who told you that you were naked?" God asked. "Did you eat the fruit that I told you not to eat?"

The man answered, "The woman you put here with me gave me the fruit, and I ate it."

The LORD God asked the woman, "Why did you do this?"

She replied, "The snake tricked me into eating it."

Then the LORD God said, "Now the man has become like one of us and has knowledge of what is good and what is bad. He must not be allowed to take fruit from the tree that gives life, eat it, and live for ever." So the LORD God sent him out of the Garden of Eden and made him cultivate the soil from which he had been formed.

Cain and Abel   Genesis 4.2–7

"The man" in the previous section is now called "Adam". This Hebrew name means "mankind". "The woman" is called "Eve", which sounds like the Hebrew for "living". Adam and Eve refused to do things God's way. Instead, they chose their own way, and in the next story we can begin to see what happens when they do this. Cain and Abel are Adam and Eve's children.

Abel became a shepherd, but Cain was a farmer. After some time, Cain brought some of his harvest and gave it as an offering to the LORD. Then Abel brought the first lamb born to one of his sheep, killed it, and gave the best parts of it as an offering. The LORD was pleased with Abel and his offering, but he rejected Cain and his offering. Cain became furious, and he scowled in anger. Then the LORD said to Cain, "Why are you angry? Why that scowl on your face? If you had done the right thing, you would be smiling; but because you have done evil, sin is crouching at your door. It wants to rule you, but you must overcome it."

"What about your brother?"   Genesis 4.8–14, 16

The book of Genesis does not tell us why God refused Cain's offering, but it does tell us what Cain did.

Then Cain said to his brother Abel, "Let's go out in the fields." When they were out in the fields, Cain turned on his brother and killed him.

The LORD asked Cain, "Where is your brother Abel?"

He answered, "I don't know. Am I supposed to take care of my brother?"

Then the LORD said, "Why have you done this terrible thing? Your brother's blood is crying out to me from the ground, like a voice calling for revenge. You are placed under a curse and can no longer farm the soil. It has soaked up your brother's blood as if it had opened its mouth to receive it when you killed him. If you try to grow crops, the soil will not produce anything; you will be a homeless wanderer on the earth."

And Cain said to the LORD, "This punishment is too hard for me to bear. You are driving me off the land and away from your presence. I will be a homeless wanderer on the earth, and anyone who finds me will kill me."

And Cain went away from the LORD's presence and lived in a land called "Wandering," which is east of Eden.

God's judgement and mercy

"Why did I make these people?"   Genesis 6.5–8

God became very upset because people did not live in the way he wanted them to. They could hurt each other and God's world.

When the LORD saw how wicked everyone on earth was and how evil their thoughts were all the time, he was sorry that he had ever made them and put them on the earth. He was so filled with regret that he said, "I will wipe out these people I have created, and also the animals and the birds, because I am sorry that I made any of them." But the LORD was pleased with Noah.

Noah   Genesis 6.9–22

God had a plan to rescue the only man who did not do bad things. His plan involved an amazing building job for Noah.

This is the story of Noah. He had three sons, Shem, Ham, and Japheth. Noah had no faults and was the only good man of his time. He lived in fellowship with God, but everyone else was evil in God's sight, and violence had spread everywhere. God looked at the world and saw that it was evil, for the people were all living evil lives.

25

God said to Noah, "I have decided to put an end to all mankind. I will destroy them completely, because the world is full of their violent deeds. Build a boat for yourself out of good timber; make rooms in it and cover it with tar inside and out. Make it 133 metres long, 22 metres wide, and 13 metres high. Make a roof for the boat and leave a space of 44 centimetres between the roof and the sides. Build it with three decks and put a door in the side. I am going to send a flood on the earth to destroy every living being. Everything on the earth will die, but I will make a covenant with you. Go into the boat with your wife, your sons, and their wives. Take into the boat with you a male and a female of every kind of animal and of every kind of bird, in order to keep them alive. Take along all kinds of food for you and for them." Noah did everything that God commanded.

"Get in the boat!"   Genesis 7.1–5, 7–10, 11–24

Many ancient stories tell of a great flood. But the one in the Bible is the only one which tells us that it was God's way of rescuing the world from doing wrong, or evil.

The LORD said to Noah, "Go into the boat with your whole family; I have found that you are the only one in all the world who does what is right. Take with you seven pairs of each kind of ritually clean animal, but only one pair of each kind of unclean animal. Take also seven pairs of each kind of bird. Do this so that every kind of animal and bird will be kept alive to reproduce again on the earth. Seven days from now I am going to send rain that will fall for forty days and nights, in order to destroy all the living beings that I have made." And Noah did everything that the LORD commanded.

He and his wife, and his sons and their wives, went into the boat to escape the flood. A male and a female of every kind of animal and bird, whether ritually clean or unclean, went into the boat with Noah, as God had commanded. Seven days later the flood came.

...All the outlets of the vast body of water beneath the earth burst open, all the floodgates of the sky were opened, and rain fell on the earth for forty days and nights. On that same day Noah and his wife went into the boat with their three sons, Shem, Ham, and Japheth, and their wives. With them went every kind of animal, domestic and wild, large and small, and every kind of bird. A male and a female of each kind of living being went into the boat with Noah, as God had commanded. Then the LORD shut the door behind Noah.

The flood continued for forty days, and the water became deep enough for the boat to float. The water became deeper, and the boat drifted on the surface. It became so deep that it covered the highest mountains; it went on rising until it was about seven metres above the tops of the

mountains. Every living being on the earth died—every bird, every animal, and every person. Everything on earth that breathed died. The LORD destroyed all living beings on the earth—human beings, animals, and birds. The only ones left were Noah and those who were with him in the boat. The water did not start going down for a hundred and fifty days.

Dry land appears   Genesis 8.1–12, 13–22

God had not forgotten Noah and all the animals with him in the boat; he caused a wind to blow, and the water started going down. The outlets of the water beneath the earth and the floodgates of the sky were closed. The rain stopped, and the water gradually went down for a hundred and fifty days. On the seventeenth day of the seventh month the boat came to rest on a mountain in the Ararat range. The water kept going down, and on the first day of the tenth month the tops of the mountains appeared.

After forty days Noah opened a window and sent out a raven. It did not come back, but kept flying around until the water was completely gone. Meanwhile, Noah sent out a dove to see if the water had gone down, but since the water still covered all the land, the dove did not find a place to alight. It flew back to the boat, and Noah reached out and took it in. He waited another seven days and sent out the dove again. It returned to him in the evening with a fresh olive leaf in its beak. So Noah knew that the water had gone down. Then he waited another seven days and sent out the dove once more; this time it did not come back.

...On the first day of the first month, the water was gone. Noah removed the covering of the boat, looked round, and saw that the ground was getting dry. By the twenty-seventh day of the second month the earth was completely dry.

God said to Noah, "Go out of the boat with your wife, your sons, and their wives. Take all the birds and animals out with you, so that they may reproduce and spread over all the earth." So Noah went out of the boat with his wife, his sons, and their wives. All the animals and birds went out of the boat in groups of their own kind.

Noah built an altar to the LORD; he took one of each kind of ritually clean animal and bird, and burnt them whole as a sacrifice on the altar. The odour of the sacrifice pleased the LORD, and he said to himself, "Never again will I put the earth under a curse because of what man does; I know that from the time he is young his thoughts are evil. Never again will I destroy all living beings, as I have done this time. As long as the world exists, there will be a time for planting and a time for harvest. There will always be cold and heat, summer and winter, day and night."

A promise and a sign   Genesis 9.8–17

The word "covenant" means a solemn agreement between God and his people. Often when a covenant was made, something was given to everyone to remind them of what had happened. The reminder given here was a very special one that we still see today.

God said to Noah and his sons, "I am now making my covenant with you and with your descendants, and with all living beings—all birds and all animals—everything that came out of the boat with you. With these words I make my covenant with you: I promise that never again will all living beings be destroyed by a flood; never again will a flood destroy the earth. As a sign of this everlasting covenant which I am making with you and with all living beings, I am putting my bow in the clouds. It will be the sign of my covenant with the world. Whenever I cover the sky with clouds and the rainbow appears, I will remember my promise to you and to all the animals that a flood will never again destroy all living beings. When the rainbow appears in the clouds, I will see it and remember the everlasting covenant between me and all living beings on earth. That is the sign of the promise which I am making to all living beings."

2
The nation of Israel begins

All the stories we have read so far happened in a place called Mesopotamia. Today this is part of Iraq. Look at the map at the beginning of the book to see exactly where it is.

The stories in this chapter are about Abraham and the members of his family who lived soon after him. They show us how people began to see what God was like and how he wanted them to live.

The father of nations

God's call to Abram   Genesis 12.1–7

Like almost everyone else living at the time, the people in Mesopotamia believed in many gods, such as the gods of the sun, the moon, and the stars. Abram saw things differently. There was one true God ("The LORD" as the Bible puts it) who created the sun, moon, and stars and whose power reaches everywhere. He told Abram to leave where he lived in Mesopotamia and set out on a great adventure, with nothing to hope in but God's promise.

The LORD said to Abram, "Leave your country, your relatives, and your father's home, and go to a land that I am going to show you. I will give you many descendants, and they will become a great nation. I will bless you and make your name famous, so that you will be a blessing.
I will bless those who bless you,
But I will curse those who curse you.
And through you I will bless all the nations."

When Abram was seventy-five years old, he started out from Haran, as the LORD had told him to do; and Lot went with him. Abram took his wife Sarai, his nephew Lot, and all the wealth and all the slaves they had acquired in Haran, and they started out for the land of Canaan.

When they arrived in Canaan, Abram travelled through the land until he came to the sacred tree of Moreh, the holy place at Shechem. (At that time the Canaanites were still living in the land.) The LORD appeared to Abram and said to him, "This is the country that I am going to give to your descendants." Then Abram built an altar there to the LORD, who had appeared to him.

Abram and his household reached the land of Canaan (later called Israel) safely. God had protected him. He had also said, "I will give you many descendants", and even told him to change his name to Abraham, so that it sounded like "ancestor of many nations". It was many years before Abraham and his wife Sarah had a son.

God commands Abraham to offer Isaac   Genesis 22.1–18

In Mesopotamia, where Abraham had come from, there was a custom where people sometimes sacrificed their children to the gods. They thought it was a way of giving thanks for the gift of children and making sure they had many more. So Abraham would not be surprised then when God asked him to sacrifice Isaac. But the Lord was really testing how much faith Abraham had. Abraham had enough faith in God to be prepared to sacrifice his son. In this way God taught the Israelites that he did not want this kind of sacrifice.

Some time later God tested Abraham; he called to him, "Abraham!" And Abraham answered, "Yes, here I am!"

"Take your son," God said, "your only son, Isaac, whom you love so much, and go to the land of Moriah. There on a mountain that I will show you, offer him as a sacrifice to me."

Early the next morning Abraham cut some wood for the sacrifice, loaded his donkey, and took Isaac and two servants with him. They started out for the place that God had told him about. On the third day Abraham saw the place in the distance. Then he said to the servants, "Stay here with the donkey. The boy and I will go over there and worship, and then we will come back to you."

Abraham made Isaac carry the wood for the sacrifice, and he himself carried a knife and live coals for starting the fire. As they walked along together, Isaac said, "Father!"

He answered, "Yes, my son?"

Isaac asked, "I see that you have the coals and the wood, but where is the lamb for the sacrifice?"

Abraham answered, "God himself will provide one." And the two of them walked on together.

When they came to the place which God had told him about, Abraham built an altar and arranged the wood on it. He tied up his son and placed him on the altar, on top of the wood. Then he picked up the knife to kill him. But the angel of the LORD called to him from heaven, "Abraham, Abraham!"

He answered, "Yes, here I am."

"Don't hurt the boy or do anything to him," he said. "Now I know that you honour and obey God, because you have not kept back your only son from me."

Abraham looked round and saw a ram caught in a bush by its horns. He went and got it and offered it as a burnt-offering instead of his son. Abraham named that place "The LORD Provides." And even today people say, "On the LORD's mountain he provides."

The angel of the LORD called to Abraham from heaven a second time, "I make a vow by my own name—the LORD is speaking—that I will richly bless you. Because you did this and did not keep back your only son from me, I promise that I will give you as many descendants as there are stars in the sky or grains of sand along the seashore. Your descendants will conquer their enemies. All the nations will ask me to bless them as I have blessed your descendants—all because you obeyed my command."

Finding a wife for Isaac   Genesis 24.1–28

It was the custom for fathers to arrange marriages for their children. Abraham asks his servant to do this for him and asks him to make him a promise. The servant shows that the promise cannot be changed by placing his hand between Abraham's thighs.

Abraham was now very old, and the LORD had blessed him in everything he did. He said to his oldest servant, who was in charge of all that he had, "Place your hand between my thighs and make a vow. I want you to make a vow in the name of the LORD, the God of heaven and earth, that you will not choose a wife for my son from the people here in Canaan. You must go back to the country where I was born and get a wife for my son Isaac from among my relatives."

But the servant asked, "What if the girl will not leave home to come with me to this land? Shall I send your son back to the land you came from?"

Abraham answered, "Make sure that you don't send my son back there! The LORD, the God of heaven, brought me from the home of my father and from the land of my relatives, and he solemnly promised me that he would give this land to my descendants. He will send his angel before you, so that you can get a wife there for my son. If the girl is not willing to come with you, you will be free from this promise. But you must not under any circumstances take my son back there." So the servant put his hand between the thighs of Abraham, his master, and made a vow to do what Abraham had asked.

The servant, who was in charge of Abraham's property, took ten of his master's camels and went to the city where Nahor had lived in northern Mesopotamia. When he arrived, he made the camels kneel down at the well outside the city. It was late afternoon, the time when women came out to get water. He prayed, "LORD, God of my master Abraham, give me success today and keep your promise to my master. Here I am at the well where the young women of the city will be coming to get water. I will say to one of them, 'Please, lower your jar and let me have a drink.' If she says, 'Drink, and I will also bring water for your camels,' may she be the one that you have chosen for your servant Isaac. If this happens, I will know that you have kept your promise to my master."

Before he had finished praying, Rebecca arrived with a water-jar on her shoulder. She was the daughter of Bethuel, who was the son of Abraham's brother Nahor and his wife Milcah. She was a very beautiful young girl and still a virgin. She went down to the well, filled her jar, and came back. The servant ran to meet her and said, "Please give me a drink of water from your jar."

She said, "Drink, sir," and quickly lowered her jar from her shoulder and held it while he drank. When he had finished, she said, "I will also bring water for your camels and let them have all they want." She quickly emptied her jar into the animals' drinking-trough and ran to the well to get more water, until she had watered all his camels. The man kept watching her in silence, to see if the LORD had given him success.

When she had finished, the man took an expensive gold ring and put it in her nose and put two large gold bracelets on her arms. He said, "Please tell me who your father is. Is there room in his house for my men and me to spend the night?"

"My father is Bethuel son of Nahor and Milcah," she answered. "There is plenty of straw and fodder at our house, and there is a place for you to stay."

Then the man knelt down and worshipped the LORD. He said, "Praise the LORD, the God of my master Abraham, who has faithfully kept his promise to my master. The LORD has led me straight to my master's relatives."

The girl ran to her mother's house and told the whole story.

The rival brothers

Esau and Jacob   Genesis 25.24–34

Rebecca travelled to Canaan and married Isaac. Later on, she gave birth to twin boys. According to the customs of those times the son who was born first usually became head of the family after his father died, and inherited two-thirds of the family's property. He made all the important decisions.

The time came for her to give birth, and she had twin sons. The first one was reddish, and his skin was like a hairy robe, so he was named Esau. The second one was born holding on tightly to the heel of Esau, so he was named Jacob. Isaac was sixty years old when they were born.

The boys grew up, and Esau became a skilled hunter, a man who loved the outdoor life, but Jacob was a quiet man who stayed at home. Isaac preferred Esau, because he enjoyed eating the animals Esau killed, but Rebecca preferred Jacob.

One day while Jacob was cooking some bean soup, Esau came in from hunting. He was hungry and said to Jacob, "I'm starving; give me some of that red stuff"...

Jacob answered, "I will give it to you if you give me your rights as the first-born son."

Esau said, "All right! I am about to die; what good will my rights do me then?"

Jacob answered, "First make a vow that you will give me your rights."

Esau made the vow and gave his rights to Jacob. Then Jacob gave him some bread and some of the soup. He ate and drank and then got up and left. That was all Esau cared about his rights as the first-born son.

Jacob tricks Isaac   Genesis 27.1–41

Isaac thought he was about to die. It was very important for him to bless his son before he did so. If he did this, his son would be recognized as the one who would receive what God had promised to give to Isaac's descendants.

Isaac was now old and had become blind. He sent for his elder son Esau and said to him, "My son!"

"Yes," he answered.

Isaac said, "You see that I am old and may die soon. Take your bow and arrows, go out into the country, and kill an animal for me. Cook me some of that tasty food that I like, and bring it to me. After I have eaten it, I will give you my final blessing before I die."

While Isaac was talking to Esau, Rebecca was listening. So when Esau went out to hunt, she said to Jacob, "I have just heard your father say to Esau, 'Bring me an animal and cook it for me. After I have eaten it, I will give you my blessing in the presence of the LORD before I die.' Now, my son," Rebecca continued, "listen to me and do what I say. Go to the flock and pick out two fat young goats, so that I can cook them and make some of that food your father likes so much. You can take it to him to eat, and he will give you his blessing before he dies."

But Jacob said to his mother, "You know that Esau is a hairy man, but I have smooth skin. Perhaps my father will touch me and find out that I am deceiving him; in this way I will bring a curse on myself instead of a blessing."

His mother answered, "Let any curse against you fall on me, my son; just do as I say, and go and get the goats for me." So he went to get them and brought them to her, and she cooked the kind of food that his father liked. Then she took Esau's best clothes, which she kept in the house, and put them on Jacob. She put the skins of the goats on his arms and on the hairless part of his neck. She handed him the tasty food, together with the bread she had baked.

Then Jacob went to his father and said, "Father!"

"Yes," he answered. "Which of my sons are you?"

Jacob answered, "I am your elder son Esau; I have done as you told me. Please sit up and eat some of the meat that I have brought you, so that you can give me your blessing."

Isaac said, "How did you find it so quickly, my son?"

Jacob answered, "The LORD your God helped me to find it."

Isaac said to Jacob, "Please come closer so that I can touch you. Are you really Esau?" Jacob moved closer to his father, who felt him and said, "Your voice sounds like Jacob's voice, but your arms feel like Esau's arms." He did not recognize Jacob, because his arms were hairy like Esau's. He was about to give him his blessing, but asked again, "Are you really Esau?"

"I am," he answered.

Isaac said, "Bring me some of the meat. After I have eaten it, I will give you my blessing." Jacob brought it to him, and he also brought him some wine to drink. Then his father said to him, "Come closer and kiss me, my son." As he came up to kiss him, Isaac smelt his clothes—so he gave him his blessing. He said, "The pleasant smell of my son is like the smell of a field which the LORD has blessed. May God give you dew from heaven and make your fields fertile! May he give you plenty of corn and wine! May nations be your servants, and may peoples bow down before you. May you rule over all your relatives, and may your mother's descendants bow down before you. May those who curse you be cursed, and may those who bless you be blessed."

Isaac finished giving his blessing, and as soon as Jacob left, his brother Esau came in from hunting. He also cooked some tasty food and took it to his father. He said, "Please, father, sit up and eat some of the meat that I have brought you, so that you can give me your blessing."

"Who are you?" Isaac asked.

"Your elder son Esau," he answered.

Isaac began to tremble and shake all over, and he asked, "Who was it, then, who killed an animal and brought it to me? I ate it just before you came. I gave him my final blessing, and so it is his for ever."

When Esau heard this, he cried out loudly and bitterly and said, "Give me your blessing also, father!"

Isaac answered, "Your brother came and deceived me. He has taken away your blessing."

Esau said, "This is the second time that he has cheated me. No wonder his name is Jacob. He took my rights as the first-born son, and now he has taken away my blessing. Haven't you saved a blessing for me?"

Isaac answered, "I have already made him master over you, and I have made all his relatives his slaves. I have given him corn and wine. Now there is nothing that I can do for you, my son!"

Esau continued to plead with his father: "Have you only one blessing, father? Bless me too, father!" He began to cry.

Then Isaac said to him,
  "No dew from heaven for you,
  No fertile fields for you.
  You will live by your sword,
  But be your brother's slave.
  Yet when you rebel,
  You will break away from his control."

Esau hated Jacob, because his father had given Jacob the blessing. He thought, "The time to mourn my father's death is near; then I will kill Jacob."

40

Jacob's dream   Genesis 28.11–22

Rebecca heard of Esau's plan to kill Jacob. So she persuaded Jacob to run away to her brother's home. It was a long way away, and she thought Jacob would be safe there.

At sunset he came to a holy place and camped there. He lay down to sleep, resting his head on a stone. He dreamt that he saw a stairway reaching from earth to heaven, with angels going up and coming down on it. And there was the LORD standing beside him. "I am the LORD, the God of Abraham and Isaac," he said. "I will give to you and to your descendants this land on which you are lying. They will be as numerous as the specks of dust on the earth. They will extend their territory in all directions, and through you and your descendants I will bless all the nations. Remember, I will be with you and protect you wherever you go, and I will bring you back to this land. I will not leave you until I have done all that I have promised you."

Jacob woke up and said, "The LORD is here! He is in this place, and I didn't know it!" He was afraid and said, "What a terrifying place this is! It must be the house of God; it must be the gate that opens into heaven."

Jacob got up early next morning, took the stone that was under his head, and set it up as a memorial. Then he poured olive-oil on it to dedicate it to God. He named the place Bethel. (The town there was once known as Luz.) Then Jacob made a vow to the LORD: "If you will be with me and protect me on the journey I am making and give me food and clothing, and if I return safely to my father's home, then you will be my God. This memorial stone which I have set up will be the place where you are worshipped, and I will give you a tenth of everything you give me."

Jacob wrestles with God   Genesis 32.24–31

Jacob arrived safely at his uncle's house. He married his uncle's daughters, Leah and Rachel, had children, and became rich. At last Jacob decided to return to the land he had been born in and see his brother Esau. Jacob was frightened about meeting Esau because of the things that had happened before. He and his family started the journey, but as he prepared to meet his brother he stayed behind, alone.

Then a man came and wrestled with him until just before daybreak. When the man saw that he was not winning the struggle, he struck Jacob on the hip, and it was thrown out of joint. The man said, "Let me go; daylight is coming."

"I won't, unless you bless me," Jacob answered.

" What is your name?" the man asked.

"Jacob," he answered.

The man said, "Your name will no longer be Jacob. You have struggled with God and with men, and you have won; so your name will be Israel."

Jacob said, "Now tell me your name."

But he answered, "Why do you want to know my name?" Then he blessed Jacob.

Jacob said, "I have seen God face to face, and I am still alive"; so he named the place Peniel. The sun rose as Jacob was leaving Peniel, and he was limping because of his hip.

Joseph

Joseph and his brothers   Genesis 37.1–35

The twin brothers met again and they lived in peace. This is the story of Jacob's family. Joseph was Jacob's favourite son. Joseph had a dream and told his brothers about it. By telling everyone about his dream, Joseph was really saying, "God is telling you this", because dreams were seen as messages from God.

Jacob continued to live in the land of Canaan, where his father had lived, and this is the story of Jacob's family.

Joseph, a young man of seventeen, took care of the sheep and goats with his brothers, the sons of Bilhah and Zilpah, his father's concubines. He brought bad reports to his father about what his brothers were doing.

Jacob loved Joseph more than all his other sons, because he had been born to him when he was old. He made a long robe with full sleeves for him. When his brothers saw that their father loved Joseph more than he loved them, they hated their brother so much that they would not speak to him in a friendly manner.

One night Joseph had a dream, and when he told his brothers about it, they hated him even more. He said, "Listen to the dream I had. We were all in the field tying up sheaves of wheat, when my sheaf got up and stood up straight. Yours formed a circle round mine and bowed down to it."

"Do you think you are going to be a king and rule over us?" his brothers asked. So they hated him even more because of his dreams and because of what he said about them.

Then Joseph had another dream and said to his brothers, "I had another dream, in which I saw the sun, the moon, and eleven stars bowing down to me."

He also told the dream to his father, and his father scolded him: "What kind of a dream is that? Do you think that your mother, your brothers, and I are going to come and bow down to you?" Joseph's brothers were jealous of him, but his father kept thinking about the whole matter.

One day when Joseph's brothers had gone to Shechem to take care of their father's flock, Jacob said to Joseph, "I want you to go to Shechem, where your brothers are taking care of the flock."

Joseph answered, "I am ready."

His father said, "Go and see if your brothers are safe and if the flock is all right; then come back and tell me." So his father sent him on his way from the Valley of Hebron.

Joseph arrived at Shechem and was wandering about in the country when a man saw him and asked him, "What are you looking for?"

"I am looking for my brothers, who are taking care of their flock," he answered. "Can you tell me where they are?"

The man said, "They have already left. I heard them say that they were going to Dothan." So Joseph went after his brothers and found them at Dothan.

They saw him in the distance, and before he reached them, they plotted against him and decided to kill him. They said to one another, "Here comes that dreamer. Come on now, let's kill him and throw his body into one of the dry wells. We can say that a wild animal killed him. Then we will see what becomes of his dreams."

Reuben heard them and tried to save Joseph. "Let's not kill him," he said. "Just throw him into this well in the wilderness, but don't hurt him." He said this, planning to save him from them and send him back to his father. When Joseph came up to his brothers, they ripped off his long robe with full sleeves. Then they took him and threw him into the well, which was dry.

While they were eating, they suddenly saw a group of Ishmaelites travelling from Gilead to Egypt. Their camels were loaded with spices and resins. Judah said to his brothers, "What will we gain by killing our brother and covering up the murder? Let's sell him to these Ishmaelites. Then we won't have to hurt him; after all, he is our brother, our own flesh and blood." His brothers agreed, and when some Midianite traders came by, the brothers pulled Joseph out of the well and sold him for twenty pieces of silver to the Ishmaelites, who took him to Egypt.

When Reuben came back to the well and found that Joseph was not there, he tore his clothes in sorrow. He returned to his brothers and said, "The boy is not there! What am I going to do?"

Then they killed a goat and dipped Joseph's robe in its blood. They took the robe to their father and said, "We found this. Does it belong to your son?"

He recognized it and said, "Yes, it is his! Some wild animal has killed him. My son Joseph has been torn to pieces!" Jacob tore his clothes in sorrow and put on sackcloth. He mourned for his son a long time. All his sons and daughters came to comfort him, but he refused to be comforted and said, "I will go down to the world of the dead still mourning for my son." So he continued to mourn for his son Joseph.

Joseph in Egypt   Genesis 41.17–46

Many things happened to Joseph in Egypt. He was in prison for a time, though he did not deserve to be. But his talent for explaining the meaning of dreams made him famous, and he was set free to try to explain a dream for the king of Egypt.

The king said, "I dreamt that I was standing on the bank of the Nile, when seven cows, fat and sleek, came up out of the river and began feeding on the grass. Then seven other cows came up which were thin and bony. They were the poorest cows I have ever seen anywhere in Egypt. The thin cows ate up the fat ones, but no one would have known it, because they looked just as bad as before. Then I woke up. I also dreamt that I saw seven ears of corn which were full and ripe, growing on one stalk. Then seven ears of corn sprouted, thin and scorched by the desert wind, and the thin ears of corn swallowed the full ones. I told the dreams to the magicians, but none of them could explain them to me."

Joseph said to the king, "The two dreams mean the same thing; God has told you what he is going to do. The seven fat cows are seven years, and the seven full ears of corn are also seven years; they have the same meaning. The seven thin cows which came up later and the seven thin ears of corn scorched by the desert wind are seven years of famine. It is just as I told you—God has shown you what he is going to do. There will be seven years of great plenty in all the land of Egypt. After that, there will be seven years of famine, and all the good years will be forgotten, because the famine will ruin the country. The time of plenty will be entirely forgotten, because the famine which follows will be so terrible. The repetition of your dream means that the matter is fixed by God and that he will make it happen in the near future.

"Now you should choose some man with wisdom and insight and put him in charge of the country. You must also appoint other officials and

44

take a fifth of the crops during the seven years of plenty. Order them to collect all the food during the good years that are coming, and give them authority to store up corn in the cities and guard it. The food will be a reserve supply for the country during the seven years of famine which are going to come on Egypt. In this way the people will not starve."

The king and his officials approved this plan, and he said to them, "We will never find a better man than Joseph, a man who has God's spirit in him." The king said to Joseph, "God has shown you all this, so it is obvious that you have greater wisdom and insight than anyone else. I will put you in charge of my country, and all my people will obey your orders. Your authority will be second only to mine. I now appoint you governor over all Egypt." The king removed from his finger the ring engraved with the royal seal and put it on Joseph's finger. He put a fine linen robe on him, and placed a gold chain round his neck. He gave him the second royal chariot to ride in, and his guard of honour went ahead of him and cried out, "Make way! Make way!" And so Joseph was appointed governor over all Egypt. The king said to him, "I am the king—and no one in all Egypt shall so much as lift a hand or a foot without your permission." He gave Joseph the Egyptian name Zaphenath Paneah, and he gave him a wife, Asenath, the daughter of Potiphera, a priest in the city of Heliopolis.

Joseph amazes his brothers   Genesis 43.29–34

Joseph's brothers went to Egypt to buy food but they did not recognize him. Joseph pretended to think they were spies. He told them that they could not buy any more food unless they brought their youngest brother, Benjamin, with them. At last things were so bad that Jacob let Benjamin go, even though he was frightened that he would never see him again.

When Joseph saw his brother Benjamin, he said, "So this is your youngest brother, the one you told me about. God bless you, my son." Then Joseph left suddenly, because his heart was full of tender feelings for his brother. He was about to break down, so he went to his room and cried. After he had washed his face, he came out, and controlling himself, he ordered the meal to be served. Joseph was served at one table and his brothers at another. The Egyptians who were eating there were served separately, because they considered it beneath their dignity to eat with Hebrews. The brothers had been seated at table, facing Joseph, in the order of their age from the eldest to the youngest. When they saw how they had been seated, they looked at one another in amazement. Food was served to them from Joseph's table, and Benjamin was served five times as much as the rest of them. So they ate and drank with Joseph until they were drunk.

Benjamin and the missing cup   Genesis 44.1–34

Joseph commanded the servant in charge of his house, "Fill the men's sacks with as much food as they can carry, and put each man's money in the top of his sack. Put my silver cup in the top of the youngest brother's sack, together with the money for his corn." He did as he was told. Early in the morning the brothers were sent on their way with their donkeys. When they had gone only a short distance from the city, Joseph said to the servant in charge of his house, "Hurry after those men. When you catch up with them, ask them, 'Why have you paid back evil for good? Why did you steal my master's silver cup? It is the one he drinks from, the one he uses for divination. You have committed a serious crime!'"

When the servant caught up with them, he repeated these words. They answered him, "What do you mean, sir, by talking like this? We swear that we have done no such thing. You know that we brought back to you from the land of Canaan the money we found in the top of our sacks. Why then should we steal silver or gold from your master's house? Sir, if any one of us is found to have it, he will be put to death, and the rest of us will become your slaves."

He said, "I agree; but only the one who has taken the cup will become my slave, and the rest of you can go free." So they quickly lowered their sacks to the ground, and each man opened his sack. Joseph's servant searched carefully, beginning with the eldest and ending with the youngest, and the cup was found in Benjamin's sack. The brothers tore their clothes in sorrow, loaded their donkeys, and returned to the city.

When Judah and his brothers came to Joseph's house, he was still there. They bowed down before him, and Joseph said, "What have you done? Didn't you know that a man in my position could find you out by practising divination?"

"What can we say to you, sir?" Judah answered. "How can we argue? How can we clear ourselves? God has uncovered our guilt. All of us are now your slaves and not just the one with whom the cup was found."

Joseph said, "Oh, no! I would never do that! Only the one who had the cup will be my slave. The rest of you may go back safe and sound to your father."

Judah went up to Joseph and said, "Please, sir, allow me to speak with you freely. Don't be angry with me; you are like the king himself. Sir, you asked us, 'Have you got a father or another brother?' We answered, 'We have a father who is old and a younger brother, born to him in his old age. The boy's brother is dead, and he is the only one of his mother's children still alive; his father loves him very much.' Sir, you told us to bring him here, so that you could see him, and we answered that the boy could not leave his father; if he did, his father would die. Then you said,

'You will not be admitted to my presence again unless your youngest brother comes with you.'

"When we went back to our father, we told him what you had said. Then he told us to return and buy a little food. We answered, 'We cannot go; we will not be admitted to the man's presence unless our youngest brother is with us. We can go only if our youngest brother goes also.' Our father said to us, 'You know that my wife Rachel bore me only two sons. One of them has already left me. He must have been torn to pieces by wild animals, because I have not seen him since he left. If you take this one from me now and something happens to him, the sorrow you would cause me would kill me, old as I am.'

"And now, sir," Judah continued, "if I go back to my father without the boy, as soon as he sees that the boy is not with me, he will die. His life is wrapped up with the life of the boy, and he is so old that the sorrow we would cause him would kill him. What is more, I pledged my life to my father for the boy. I told him that if I did not bring the boy back to him, I would bear the blame all my life. And now, sir, I will stay here as your slave in place of the boy; let him go back with his brothers. How can I go back to my father if the boy is not with me? I cannot bear to see this disaster come upon my father."

Joseph explains who he is   Genesis 45.1–20, 25–28; 46.5–7

Joseph was no longer able to control his feelings in front of his servants, so he ordered them all to leave the room. No one else was with him when Joseph told his brothers who he was. He cried with such loud sobs that the Egyptians heard it, and the news was taken to the king's palace. Joseph said to his brothers, "I am Joseph. Is my father still alive?" But when his brothers heard this, they were so terrified that they could not answer. Then Joseph said to them, "Please come closer." They did, and he said, "I am your brother Joseph, whom you sold into Egypt. Now do not be upset or blame yourselves because you sold me here. It was really God who sent me ahead of you to save people's lives. This is only the second year of famine in the land; there will be five more years in which there will be neither ploughing nor reaping. God sent me ahead of you to rescue you in this amazing way and to make sure that you and your descendants survive. So it was not really you who sent me here, but God. He has made me the king's highest official. I am in charge of his whole country; I am the ruler of all Egypt.

"Now hurry back to my father and tell him that this is what his son Joseph says: 'God has made me ruler of all Egypt; come to me without delay. You can live in the region of Goshen, where you can be near me—you, your children, your grandchildren, your sheep, your goats, your cattle, and everything else that you have. If you are in Goshen, I can take care of you. There will still be five years of famine; and I do not want you, your family, and your livestock to starve.'"

Joseph continued, "Now all of you, and you too, Benjamin, can see that I am really Joseph. Tell my father how powerful I am here in Egypt and tell him about everything that you have seen. Then hurry and bring him here."

He threw his arms round his brother Benjamin and began to cry; Benjamin also cried as he hugged him. Then, still weeping, he embraced each of his brothers and kissed them. After that, his brothers began to talk with him.

When the news reached the palace that Joseph's brothers had come, the king and his officials were pleased. He said to Joseph, "Tell your brothers to load their animals and to return to the land of Canaan. Let them get their father and their families and come back here. I will give them the best land in Egypt, and they will have more than enough to live on. Tell them also to take wagons with them from Egypt for their wives and small children and to bring their father with them. They are not to worry about leaving their possessions behind; the best in the whole land of Egypt will be theirs" ...

They left Egypt and went back home to their father Jacob in Canaan. "Joseph is still alive!" they told him. "He is the ruler of all Egypt!" Jacob was stunned and could not believe them.

But when they told him all that Joseph had said to them, and when he saw the wagons which Joseph had sent to take him to Egypt, he recovered from the shock. "My son Joseph is still alive!" he said. "This is all I could ask for! I must go and see him before I die" ...

Jacob set out from Beersheba. His sons put him, their small children, and their wives in the wagons which the king of Egypt had sent. They took their livestock and the possessions they had acquired in Canaan and went to Egypt. Jacob took all his descendants with him: his sons, his grandsons, his daughters, and his granddaughters.

3
The great
escape

Today it is hard to imagine what it is like to become a slave and to lose all your freedom. But there have been times when countries have made whole groups of people into slaves. This is what happened to Joseph's descendants, who became known as the "Israelites".

Slavery in Egypt

Egypt was a very powerful nation. Escaping from slavery seemed to be impossible for the Israelites.

Cruel treatment in Egypt   Exodus 1.1–14

When Jacob and the rest of Joseph's family arrived in Egypt, the king gave them part of the land to live in. But later on things did not go so well.

The sons of Jacob who went to Egypt with him, each with his family, were Reuben, Simeon, Levi, Judah, Issachar, Zebulun, Benjamin, Dan, Naphtali, Gad, and Asher. The total number of these people directly descended from Jacob was seventy. His son Joseph was already in Egypt. In the course of time Joseph, his brothers, and all the rest of that generation died, but their descendants, the Israelites, had many children and became so numerous and strong that Egypt was filled with them.

Then, a new king, who knew nothing about Joseph, came to power in Egypt. He said to his people, "These Israelites are so numerous and strong that they are a threat to us. In case of war they might join our enemies in order to fight against us, and might escape from the country. We must find some way to keep them from becoming even more numerous." So the Egyptians put slave-drivers over them to crush their spirits with hard labour. The Israelites built the cities of Pithom and Rameses to serve as supply centres for the king. But the more the Egyptians oppressed the Israelites, the more they increased in number and the further they spread through the land. The Egyptians came to fear the Israelites and made their lives miserable by forcing them into cruel slavery. They made them work on their building projects and in their fields, and they had no mercy on them.

Baby boys are murdered   Exodus 1.15–22

"Hebrew" is another name for "Israelite". A midwife is someone who helps when a baby is being born.

Then the king of Egypt spoke to Shiphrah and Puah, the two midwives who helped the Hebrew women. "When you help the Hebrew women give birth," he said to them, "kill the baby if it is a boy; but if it is a girl, let it live." But the midwives feared God and so did not obey the king; instead, they let the boys live. So the king sent for the midwives and asked them, "Why are you doing this? Why are you letting the boys live?"

They answered, "The Hebrew women are not like Egyptian women; they give birth easily, and their babies are born before either of us gets there." Because the midwives feared God, he was good to them and gave them families of their own. And the Israelites continued to increase and become strong. Finally the king issued a command to all his people: "Take every new-born Hebrew boy and throw him into the Nile, but let all the girls live."

The great leader

The birth of Moses   Exodus 2.1–10

Moses became one of the most important people in the history of Israel. But he nearly died when he was a baby.

During this time a man from the tribe of Levi married a woman of his own tribe, and she bore him a son. When she saw what a fine baby he was, she hid him for three months. But when she could not hide him any longer, she took a basket made of reeds and covered it with tar to make it watertight. She put the baby in it and then placed it in the tall grass at the edge of the river. The baby's sister stood some distance away to see what would happen to him.

The king's daughter came down to the river to bathe, while her servants walked along the bank. Suddenly she noticed the basket in the tall grass and sent a slave-girl to get it. The princess opened it and saw a baby boy. He was crying, and she felt sorry for him. "This is one of the Hebrew babies," she said.

Then his sister asked her, "Shall I go and call a Hebrew woman to act as a wet-nurse?"

"Please do," she answered. So the girl went and brought the baby's own mother. The princess told the woman, "Take this baby and nurse him for me, and I will pay you." So she took the baby and nursed him. Later, when the child was old enough, she took him to the king's daughter, who adopted him as her own son. She said to herself, "I pulled him out of the water, and so I name him Moses."

Moses escapes Exodus 2.11–25

Moses was brought up as an Egyptian. The first time he tried to help his own people everything went wrong.

The name "Gershom" sounds like the Hebrew for foreigner.

When Moses had grown up, he went out to visit his people, the Hebrews, and he saw how they were forced to do hard labour. He even saw an Egyptian kill a Hebrew, one of Moses' own people. Moses looked all round, and when he saw that no one was watching, he killed the Egyptian and hid his body in the sand. The next day he went back and saw two Hebrew men fighting. He said to the one who was in the wrong, "Why are you beating up a fellow-Hebrew?"

The man answered, "Who made you our ruler and judge? Are you going to kill me just as you killed that Egyptian?" Then Moses was afraid and said to himself, "People have found out what I have done." When the king heard about what had happened, he tried to have Moses killed, but Moses fled and went to live in the land of Midian.

One day, when Moses was sitting by a well, seven daughters of Jethro, the priest of Midian, came to draw water and fill the troughs for their father's sheep and goats. But some shepherds drove Jethro's daughters away. Then Moses went to their rescue and watered their animals for them. When they returned to their father, he asked, "Why have you come back so early today?"

"An Egyptian rescued us from the shepherds," they answered, "and he even drew water for us and watered our animals."

"Where is he?" he asked his daughters. "Why did you leave the man out there? Go and invite him to eat with us."

So Moses agreed to live there, and Jethro gave him his daughter Zipporah in marriage, who bore him a son. Moses said to himself, "I am a foreigner in this land, and so I name him Gershom."

Years later the king of Egypt died, but the Israelites were still groaning under their slavery and cried out for help. Their cry went up to God, who heard their groaning and remembered his covenant with Abraham, Isaac, and Jacob. He saw the slavery of the Israelites and was concerned for them.

God calls Moses   Exodus 3.1–17; 4.10–16

Although God can do things without help, he often uses people to help him. God used Moses in a very special way. This is the story of how God asked Moses to help him.

The Egyptians believed there were many gods, and they all had different names. Because of this Moses wanted to know God's name.

One day while Moses was taking care of the sheep and goats of his father-in-law Jethro, the priest of Midian, he led the flock across the desert and came to Sinai, the holy mountain. There the angel of the LORD appeared to him as a flame coming from the middle of a bush. Moses saw that the bush was on fire but that it was not burning up. "This is strange," he thought. "Why isn't the bush burning up? I will go closer and see."

When the LORD saw that Moses was coming closer, he called to him from the middle of the bush and said, "Moses! Moses!"

He answered, "Yes, here I am."

God said, "Do not come any closer. Take off your sandals, because you are standing on holy ground. I am the God of your ancestors, the God of Abraham, Isaac, and Jacob." So Moses covered his face, because he was afraid to look at God.

Then the LORD said, "I have seen how cruelly my people are being treated in Egypt; I have heard them cry out to be rescued from their slave-drivers. I know all about their sufferings, and so I have come down to rescue them from the Egyptians and to bring them out of Egypt to a spacious land, one which is rich and fertile and in which the Canaanites, the Hittites, the Amorites, the Perizzites, the Hivites, and the Jebusites now live. I have indeed heard the cry of my people, and I see how the Egyptians are oppressing them. Now I am sending you to the king of Egypt so that you can lead my people out of his country."

But Moses said to God, "I am nobody. How can I go to the king and bring the Israelites out of Egypt?"

God answered, "I will be with you, and when you bring the people out of Egypt, you will worship me on this mountain. That will be the proof that I have sent you."

But Moses replied, "When I go to the Israelites and say to them, 'The God of your ancestors sent me to you,' they will ask me, 'What is his name?' So what can I tell them?"

God said, "I am who I am. This is what you must say to them: 'The one who is called I AM has sent me to you.' Tell the Israelites that I, the

LORD, the God of their ancestors, the God of Abraham, Isaac, and Jacob, have sent you to them. This is my name for ever; this is what all future generations are to call me. Go and gather the leaders of Israel together and tell them that I, the LORD, the God of their ancestors, the God of Abraham, Isaac, and Jacob, appeared to you. Tell them that I have come to them and have seen what the Egyptians are doing to them. I have decided that I will bring them out of Egypt, where they are being treated cruelly, and will take them to a rich and fertile land—the land of the Canaanites, the Hittites, the Amorites, the Perizzites, the Hivites, and the Jebusites..."

But Moses said, "No, LORD, don't send me. I have never been a good speaker, and I haven't become one since you began to speak to me. I am a poor speaker, slow and hesitant."

The LORD said to him, "Who gives man his mouth? Who makes him deaf or dumb? Who gives him sight or makes him blind? It is I, the LORD. Now, go! I will help you to speak, and I will tell you what to say."

But Moses answered, "No, Lord, please send someone else."

At this the LORD became angry with Moses and said, "What about your brother Aaron, the Levite? I know that he can speak well. In fact, he is now coming to meet you and will be glad to see you. You can speak to him and tell him what to say. I will help both of you to speak, and I will tell you both what to do. He will be your spokesman and speak to the people for you. Then you will be like God, telling him what to say."

Moses and Aaron before the king of Egypt   Exodus 5.1–9

Moses and Aaron left Midian and went to Egypt to do what God had told them. The Egyptians, like everyone else, thought that the most powerful countries had the most powerful gods. The Israelites were a nation of slaves, so the Egyptians thought the God of Israel was very weak and could easily be ignored.

Then Moses and Aaron went to the king of Egypt and said, "The LORD, the God of Israel, says, 'Let my people go, so that they can hold a festival in the desert to honour me.'"

"Who is the LORD?" the king demanded. "Why should I listen to him and let Israel go? I do not know the LORD; and I will not let Israel go."

Moses and Aaron replied, "The God of the Hebrews has revealed himself to us. Allow us to travel for three days into the desert to offer sacrifices to the LORD our God. If we don't do so, he will kill us with disease or by war."

The king said to Moses and Aaron, "What do you mean by making the

people neglect their work? Get those slaves back to work! You people have become more numerous than the Egyptians. And now you want to stop working!"

That same day the king commanded the Egyptian slave-drivers and the Israelite foremen: "Stop giving the people straw for making bricks. Make them go and find it for themselves. But still require them to make the same number of bricks as before, not one brick less. They haven't enough work to do, and that is why they keep asking me to let them go and offer sacrifices to their God! Make these men work harder and keep them busy, so that they won't have time to listen to a pack of lies."

The Israelites sense freedom

The first Passover   Exodus 12.1–14

The Egyptians would not let the Israelites go, and they suffered many troubles. During the final plague the eldest son in each Egyptian family died, but the Israelite families were "passed over". This event became known as the "Passover". Today the descendants of the Israelites celebrate the Passover every year to help them remember what God did. The Last Supper, which Jesus had with his disciples the night before he died, was part of these Passover celebrations. This tells us about the first Passover.

The LORD spoke to Moses and Aaron in Egypt: "This month is to be the first month of the year for you. Give these instructions to the whole community of Israel: On the tenth day of this month each man must choose either a lamb or a young goat for his household. If his family is too small to eat a whole animal, he and his next-door neighbour may share an animal, in proportion to the number of people and the amount that each person can eat. You may choose either a sheep or a goat, but it must be a one-year-old male without any defects. Then, on the evening of the fourteenth day of the month, the whole community of Israel will kill the animals. The people are to take some of the blood and put it on the door-posts and above the doors of the houses in which the animals are to be eaten. That night the meat is to be roasted, and eaten with bitter herbs and with bread made without yeast. Do not eat any of it raw or boiled, but eat it roasted whole, including the head, the legs, and the internal organs. You must not leave any of it until morning; if any is left over, it must be burnt. You are to eat it quickly, for you are to be dressed for travel, with your sandals on your feet and your stick in your hand. It is the Passover Festival to honour me, the LORD.

"On that night I will go through the land of Egypt, killing every first-born male, both human and animal, and punishing all the gods of Egypt. I am the LORD. The blood on the door-posts will be a sign to mark the houses in which you live. When I see the blood, I will pass over you and will not harm you when I punish the Egyptians. You must celebrate this day as a religious festival to remind you of what I, the LORD, have done. Celebrate it for all time to come."

The Israelites leave Egypt   Exodus 12.37–42

Now the Israelites were ready to leave. In desperation after the plagues, the king of Egypt let them go. They needed to leave quickly and they needed some food. So they took bread dough made without yeast. It could be cooked quickly because it did not need time to rise, and it made what was called "unleavened" bread. Even today, unleavened bread is used by Jews (the descendants of the Israelites) in the Passover celebration. It reminds them of the speed with which their ancestors left Egypt.

The Israelites set out on foot from Rameses for Sukkoth. There were about six hundred thousand men, not counting women and children. A large number of other people and many sheep, goats, and cattle also went with them. They baked unleavened bread from the dough that they had brought out of Egypt, for they had been driven out of Egypt so suddenly that they did not have time to get their food ready or to prepare leavened dough.

The Israelites had lived in Egypt for 430 years. On the day the 430 years ended, all the tribes of the LORD's people left Egypt. It was a night when the LORD kept watch to bring them out of Egypt; this same night is dedicated to the LORD for all time to come as a night when the Israelites must keep watch.

Crossing the Red Sea   Exodus 14.5–31

So the journey to their new home began. At times it was quite dramatic. Even today nobody really knows how this amazing event happened. For the Israelites it was a clear sign that God was with them.

When the king of Egypt was told that the people had escaped, he and his officials changed their minds and said, "What have we done? We have let the Israelites escape, and we have lost them as our slaves!" The king got his war chariot and his army ready. He set out with all his chariots, including the six hundred finest, commanded by their officers. The LORD made the king stubborn, and he pursued the Israelites, who were leaving triumphantly. The Egyptian army, with all the horses, chariots, and drivers, pursued them and caught up with them where they were camped by the Red Sea near Pi Hahiroth and Baal Zephon.

When the Israelites saw the king and his army marching against them, they were terrified and cried out to the LORD for help. They said to Moses, "Weren't there any graves in Egypt? Did you have to bring us out here in the desert to die? Look what you have done by bringing us out of Egypt! Didn't we tell you before we left that this would happen? We told you to leave us alone and let us go on being slaves of the Egyptians. It would be better to be slaves there than to die here in the desert."

Moses answered, "Don't be afraid! Stand your ground, and you will see what the LORD will do to save you today; you will never see these Egyptians again. The LORD will fight for you, and there is no need for you to do anything."

The LORD said to Moses, "Why are you crying out for help? Tell the people to move forward. Lift up your stick and hold it out over the sea. The water will divide, and the Israelites will be able to walk through the sea on dry ground. I will make the Egyptians so stubborn that they will go in after them, and I will gain honour by my victory over the king, his army, his chariots, and his drivers. When I defeat them, the Egyptians will know that I am the LORD."

The angel of God, who had been in front of the army of Israel, moved and went to the rear. The pillar of cloud also moved until it was between the Egyptians and the Israelites. The cloud made it dark for the Egyptians, but gave light to the people of Israel, and so the armies could not come near each other all night.

Moses held out his hand over the sea, and the LORD drove the sea back with a strong east wind. It blew all night and turned the sea into dry land. The water was divided, and the Israelites went through the sea on dry ground, with walls of water on both sides. The Egyptians pursued them and went after them into the sea with all their horses, chariots, and drivers. Just before dawn the LORD looked down from the pillar of fire and cloud at the Egyptian army and threw them into a panic. He made the wheels of their chariots get stuck, so that they moved with great difficulty. The Egyptians said, "The LORD is fighting for the Israelites against us. Let's get out of here!"

The LORD said to Moses, "Hold out your hand over the sea, and the water will come back over the Egyptians and their chariots and drivers." So Moses held out his hand over the sea, and at daybreak the water returned to its normal level. The Egyptians tried to escape from the water, but the LORD threw them into the sea. The water returned and covered the chariots, the drivers, and all the Egyptian army that had followed the Israelites into the sea; not one of them was left. But the

Israelites walked through the sea on dry ground, with walls of water on both sides.

On that day the LORD saved the people of Israel from the Egyptians, and the Israelites saw them lying dead on the seashore. When the Israelites saw the great power with which the LORD had defeated the Egyptians, they stood in awe of the LORD; and they had faith in the LORD and in his servant Moses.

The song of Moses   Exodus 15.1–3

Here is part of the song that Moses sang to celebrate the Israelites' escape from the Egyptians.

Then Moses and the Israelites sang this song to the LORD:
   "I will sing to the LORD, because he has won a glorious victory;
      he has thrown the horses and their riders into the sea.
   The LORD is my strong defender;
      he is the one who has saved me.
   He is my God, and I will praise him,
      my father's God, and I will sing about his greatness.
   The LORD is a warrior;
      the LORD is his name."

The long journey

The Israelites had wanted to be free for a long time. But they were not really prepared for the problems of the journey. The area they had to cross was mostly desert, and it took them a long time to reach the land which God had promised them.

Food in the desert   Exodus 16.2–3, 9–16

Quails are birds which regularly migrate over this area. We are not sure what the "thin and flaky" substance was. In fact the Israelites called it "manna", which sounds like the Hebrew words for "What is it?" Whatever it was, the Israelites thanked God that it kept them alive.

There in the desert they all complained to Moses and Aaron and said to them, "We wish that the LORD had killed us in Egypt. There we could at least sit down and eat meat and as much other food as we wanted. But you have brought us out into this desert to starve us all to death" ...

Moses said to Aaron, "Tell the whole community to come and stand

before the LORD, because he has heard their complaints." As Aaron spoke to the whole community, they turned towards the desert, and suddenly the dazzling light of the LORD appeared in a cloud. The LORD said to Moses, "I have heard the complaints of the Israelites. Tell them that at twilight they will have meat to eat, and in the morning they will have all the bread they want. Then they will know that I, the LORD, am their God."

In the evening a large flock of quails flew in, enough to cover the camp, and in the morning there was dew all round the camp. When the dew evaporated, there was something thin and flaky on the surface of the desert. It was as delicate as frost. When the Israelites saw it, they didn't know what it was and asked each other, "What is it?"

Moses said to them, "This is the food that the LORD has given you to eat. The LORD has commanded that each of you is to gather as much of it as he needs, two litres for each member of his household."

Water supplies in the desert   Exodus 17.1–6

The whole Israelite community left the desert of Sin, moving from one place to another at the command of the LORD. They made camp at Rephidim, but there was no water there to drink. They complained to Moses and said, "Give us water to drink."

Moses answered, "Why are you complaining? Why are you putting the LORD to the test?"

But the people were very thirsty and continued to complain to Moses. They said, "Why did you bring us out of Egypt? To kill us and our children and our livestock with thirst?"

Moses prayed earnestly to the LORD and said, "What can I do with these people? They are almost ready to stone me."

The LORD said to Moses, "Take some of the leaders of Israel with you, and go on ahead of the people. Take along the stick with which you struck the Nile. I will stand before you on a rock at Mount Sinai. Strike the rock, and water will come out of it for the people to drink." Moses did so in the presence of the leaders of Israel.

A terrifying sight on Mount Sinai   Exodus 19.16–20

If God was to go on working through the Israelites, he wanted them to love and trust him. They were to show this by keeping his laws or "commandments". The Israelites camped on Mount Sinai while the covenant (agreement) (see page 66) was made. While they were there they saw a great example of God's power. You can see where Mount Sinai is on the map on page 15.

On the morning of the third day there was thunder and lightning, a thick cloud appeared on the mountain, and a very loud trumpet blast was heard. All the people in the camp trembled with fear. Moses led them out of the camp to meet God, and they stood at the foot of the mountain. The whole of Mount Sinai was covered with smoke, because the LORD had come down on it in fire. The smoke went up like the smoke of a furnace, and all the people trembled violently. The sound of the trumpet became louder and louder. Moses spoke, and God answered him with thunder. The LORD came down on the top of Mount Sinai and called Moses to the top of the mountain.

The Ten Commandments   Exodus 20.1–17

Just as a modern agreement has "terms" (things which each side agrees to do) so did the covenant between God and the Israelites. God gave Ten Commandments which the Israelites had to keep. In return he promised they would be his special people. He would give them a land to live in, and he would protect them from their enemies. The Israelites met many people who worshipped idols. Idols were statues of gods which people believed had special power.

God spoke, and these were his words: "I am the LORD your God who brought you out of Egypt, where you were slaves.

"Worship no god but me.

"Do not make for yourselves images of anything in heaven or on earth or in the water under the earth. Do not bow down to any idol or worship it, because I am the LORD your God and I tolerate no rivals. I bring punishment on those who hate me and on their descendants down to the third and fourth generation. But I show my love to thousands of generations of those who love me and obey my laws.

"Do not use my name for evil purposes, for I, the LORD your God, will punish anyone who misuses my name.

"Observe the Sabbath and keep it holy. You have six days in which to do your work, but the seventh day is a day of rest dedicated to me. On that day no one is to work—neither you, your children, your slaves, your animals, nor the foreigners who live in your country. In six days I, the LORD, made the earth, the sky, the sea, and everything in them, but on the seventh day I rested. That is why I, the LORD, blessed the Sabbath and made it holy.

"Respect your father and your mother, so that you may live a long time in the land that I am giving you.

"Do not commit murder.

"Do not commit adultery.

"Do not steal.

"Do not accuse anyone falsely.

"Do not desire another man's house; do not desire his wife, his slaves, his cattle, his donkeys, or anything else that he owns."

Other rules that were added   Leviticus 19.1, 13–18

Although the Ten Commandments were the terms of the covenant, other laws were given to the Israelites later on. They often gave more details on how to obey the Ten Commandments. Here are some examples.

The LORD told Moses...

"Do not take advantage of anyone or rob him. Do not hold back the wages of someone you have hired, not even for one night. Do not curse a deaf man or put something in front of a blind man so as to make him stumble over it. Obey me; I am the LORD your God.

"Be honest and just when you make decisions in legal cases; do not show favouritism to the poor or fear the rich. Do not spread lies about anyone, and when someone is on trial for his life, speak out if your testimony can help him. I am the LORD.

"Do not bear a grudge against anyone, but settle your differences with him, so that you will not commit a sin because of him. Do not take revenge on anyone or continue to hate him, but love your neighbour as you love yourself. I am the LORD."

The golden bull   Exodus 32.1–20

It was not long before the Israelites broke the first commandment. It is sometimes hard to worship God when you cannot see him. The Israelites had to learn to do this.

When the people saw that Moses had not come down from the mountain but was staying there a long time, they gathered round Aaron and said to him, "We do not know what has happened to this man Moses, who led us out of Egypt; so make us a god to lead us."

Aaron said to them, "Take off the gold earrings which your wives, your sons, and your daughters are wearing, and bring them to me." So all the people took off their gold earrings and brought them to Aaron. He took the earrings, melted them, poured the gold into a mould, and made a gold bull-calf.

The people said, "Israel, this is our god, who led us out of Egypt!"

Then Aaron built an altar in front of the gold bull and announced, "Tomorrow there will be a festival to honour the LORD." Early the next morning they brought some animals to burn as sacrifices and others to eat as fellowship-offerings. The people sat down to a feast, which turned into an orgy of drinking and sex.

The LORD said to Moses, "Go back down at once, because your people, whom you led out of Egypt, have sinned and rejected me. They have already left the way that I commanded them to follow; they have made a bull-calf out of melted gold and have worshipped it and offered sacrifices

to it. They are saying that this is their god, who led them out of Egypt. I know how stubborn these people are. Now, don't try to stop me. I am angry with them, and I am going to destroy them. Then I will make you and your descendants into a great nation."

But Moses pleaded with the LORD his God and said, "LORD, why should you be so angry with your people, whom you rescued from Egypt with great might and power? Why should the Egyptians be able to say that you led your people out of Egypt, planning to kill them in the mountains and destroy them completely? Stop being angry; change your mind and do not bring this disaster on your people. Remember your servants Abraham, Isaac, and Jacob. Remember the solemn promise you made to them to give them as many descendants as there are stars in the sky and to give their descendants all that land you promised would be their possession for ever." So the LORD changed his mind and did not bring on his people the disaster he had threatened.

Moses went back down the mountain, carrying the two stone tablets with the commandments written on both sides. God himself had made the tablets and had engraved the commandments on them.

Joshua heard the people shouting and said to Moses, "I hear the sound of battle in the camp."

Moses said, "That doesn't sound like a shout of victory or a cry of defeat; it's the sound of singing."

When Moses came close enough to the camp to see the bull-calf and to see the people dancing, he was furious. There at the foot of the mountain, he threw down the tablets he was carrying and broke them. He took the bull-calf which they had made, melted it, ground it into fine powder, and mixed it with water. Then he made the people of Israel drink it.

The death of Moses   Deuteronomy 34.1–12

Moses led the Israelites until they reached the edge of the Promised Land (the land God had promised them).

By this time he was an old man, but he was allowed to see the land before he died.

Moses went up from the plains of Moab to Mount Nebo, to the top of Mount Pisgah east of Jericho, and there the LORD showed him the whole land: the territory of Gilead as far north as the town of Dan; the entire territory of Naphtali; the territories of Ephraim and Manasseh; the territory of Judah as far west as the Mediterranean Sea; the southern part of Judah; and the plain that reaches from Zoar to Jericho, the city of palm-trees. Then the LORD said to Moses, "This is the land that I promised Abraham, Isaac, and Jacob I would give to their descendants. I have let you see it, but I will not let you go there.''

So Moses, the LORD's servant, died there in the land of Moab, as the LORD had said he would. The LORD buried him in a valley in Moab, opposite the town of Bethpeor, but to this day no one knows the exact place of his burial. Moses was a hundred and twenty years old when he died; he was as strong as ever, and his eyesight was still good. The people of Israel mourned for him for thirty days in the plains of Moab.

Joshua son of Nun was filled with wisdom, because Moses had appointed him to be his successor. The people of Israel obeyed Joshua and kept the commands that the LORD had given them through Moses.

There has never been a prophet in Israel like Moses; the LORD spoke with him face to face. No other prophet has ever done miracles and wonders like those that the LORD sent Moses to perform against the king of Egypt, his officials, and the entire country. No other prophet has been able to do the great and terrifying things that Moses did in the sight of all Israel.

4
Men of courage

When Moses died the Israelites were on the borders of the Promised Land. At first they could only settle in some parts of the land, but gradually they came to own more and more of it. Again and again they were attacked by other tribes who did not want them to stay. The stories in this chapter are about men who are remembered for their courage. They led the Israelites in times of danger and difficulty. Often such courage brought victory, even when the enemy seemed much stronger.

Entering the Promised Land

Joshua is told to be confident   Joshua 1.1–9

Joshua was chosen to be the leader after Moses died, and he took the Israelites into the Promised Land. Once again, God told Joshua how important it was to keep the Law.

After the death of the LORD's servant Moses, the LORD spoke to Moses' helper, Joshua son of Nun. He said, "My servant Moses is dead. Get ready now, you and all the people of Israel, and cross the River Jordan into the land that I am giving them. As I told Moses, I have given you and all my people the entire land that you will be marching over. Your borders will reach from the desert in the south to the Lebanon Mountains in the north; from the great River Euphrates in the east, through the Hittite country, to the Mediterranean Sea in the west. Joshua, no one will be able to defeat you as long as you live. I will be with you as I was with Moses. I will always be with you; I will never abandon you. Be determined and confident, for you will be the leader of these people as they occupy this land which I promised their ancestors. Just be determined, be confident; and make sure that you obey the whole Law that my servant Moses gave you. Do not neglect any part of it and you will succeed wherever you go. Be sure that the book of the Law is always read in your worship. Study it day and night, and make sure that you obey everything written in it. Then you will be prosperous and successful. Remember that I have commanded you to be determined and confident! Don't be afraid or discouraged, for I, the LORD your God, am with you wherever you go."

Jericho   Joshua 6.1–7, 12–13, 15–16, 20

Joshua led the people of Israel across the River Jordan into Canaan. Then they had to pass a town called Jericho. The Israelites had already found that the people of Jericho were scared of them. So they prepared for battle, carrying the Covenant Box at the head of the army. It was a gold-covered wooden box fixed to two poles. It contained the Ten Commandments, written on two pieces of stone. Notice what an important part the Covenant Box plays in the story. This box reminded the people of God's covenant and showed he was with them. If the Covenant Box was carried before the army into battle everyone would understand that the Israelites were trusting God for victory.

The gates of Jericho were kept shut and guarded to keep the Israelites out. No one could enter or leave the city. The LORD said to Joshua, "I am putting into your hands Jericho, with its king and all its brave soldiers. You and your soldiers are to march round the city once a day for six days. Seven priests, each carrying a trumpet, are to go in front of the Covenant Box. On the seventh day you and your soldiers are to march round the city seven times while the priests blow the trumpets. Then they are to sound one long note. As soon as you hear it, all the men are to give a loud shout, and the city walls will collapse. Then the whole army will go straight into the city."

Joshua called the priests and said to them, "Take the Covenant Box, and seven of you go in front of it, carrying trumpets." Then he ordered his men to start marching round the city, with an advance guard going on ahead of the LORD's Covenant Box...

Joshua got up early the next morning, and for the second time the priests and soldiers marched round the city in the same order as the day before: first, the advance guard; next, the seven priests blowing the seven trumpets; then, the priests carrying the LORD's Covenant Box; and finally, the rearguard. All this time the trumpets were sounding...

On the seventh day they got up at daybreak and marched seven times round the city in the same way—this was the only day that they marched round it seven times. The seventh time round, when the priests were about to sound the trumpets, Joshua ordered his men to shout, and he said, "The LORD has given you the city! . . ."

So the priests blew the trumpets. As soon as the men heard it, they gave a loud shout, and the walls collapsed. Then all the army went straight up the hill into the city and captured it.

Joshua's final message   Joshua 24.14–24

When news spread that Jericho had been conquered by the small Israelite army, the tribes around became very frightened. With Joshua as their leader the Israelites had many victories, but even after this they were not completely loyal to the Lord. At the end of his life, Joshua had to issue a strong challenge about keeping the covenant.

"Now then," Joshua continued, "honour the LORD and serve him sincerely and faithfully. Get rid of the gods which your ancestors used to worship in Mesopotamia and in Egypt, and serve only the LORD. If you are not willing to serve him, decide today whom you will serve, the gods your ancestors worshipped in Mesopotamia or the gods of the Amorites, in whose land you are now living. As for my family and me, we will serve the LORD."

The people replied, "We would never leave the LORD to serve other gods! The LORD our God brought our fathers and us out of slavery in Egypt, and we saw the miracles that he performed. He kept us safe wherever we went among all the nations through which we passed. As we advanced into this land, the LORD drove out all the Amorites who lived here. So we also will serve the LORD; he is our God."

Joshua said to the people, "But you may not be able to serve the LORD. He is a holy God and will not forgive your sins. He will tolerate no rivals, and if you leave him to serve foreign gods, he will turn against you and punish you. He will destroy you, even though he was good to you before."

The people said to Joshua, "No! We *will* serve the LORD."

Joshua said to them, "You are your own witnesses to the fact that you have chosen to serve the LORD."

"Yes," they said, "we are witnesses."

"Then get rid of those foreign gods that you have," he demanded, "and pledge your loyalty to the LORD, the God of Israel."

74

The people then said to Joshua, "We will serve the LORD our God. We will obey his commands."

Holding on to the land

Gideon is called to rescue Israel   Judges 6.1–16

The Israelites went back to worshipping other gods after Joshua's death.

Once again the people of Israel sinned against the LORD, so he let the people of Midian rule them for seven years. The Midianites were stronger than Israel, and the people of Israel hid from them in caves and other safe places in the hills. Whenever the Israelites sowed any seed, the Midianites would come with the Amalekites and the desert tribes and attack them. They would camp on the land and destroy the crops as far south as the area round Gaza. They would take all the sheep, cattle, and donkeys, and leave nothing for the Israelites to live on. They would come with their livestock and tents, as thick as locusts. They and their camels were too many to count. They came and devastated the land, and Israel was helpless against them.

Then the people of Israel cried out to the LORD for help against the Midianites, and he sent them a prophet who brought them this message from the LORD, the God of Israel: "I brought you out of slavery in Egypt. I rescued you from the Egyptians and from the people who fought against you here in this land. I drove them out as you advanced, and I gave you their land. I told you that I am the LORD your God and that you should not worship the gods of the Amorites, whose land you are now living in. But you did not listen to me."

Then the LORD's angel came to the village of Ophrah and sat under the oak-tree that belonged to Joash, a man of the clan of Abiezer. His son Gideon was threshing some wheat secretly in a wine-press, so that the Midianites would not see him. The LORD's angel appeared to him there and said, "The LORD is with you, brave and mighty man!"

Gideon said to him, "If I may ask, sir, why has all this happened to us if the LORD is with us? What about all the wonderful things that our fathers told us the LORD used to do—how he brought them out of Egypt? The LORD has abandoned us and left us to the mercy of the Midianites."

Then the LORD ordered him, "Go with all your great strength and rescue Israel from the Midianites. I myself am sending you."

Gideon replied, "But LORD, how can I rescue Israel? My clan is the weakest in the tribe of Manasseh, and I am the least important member of my family.''

The LORD answered, "You can do it because I will help you. You will crush the Midianites as easily as if they were only one man.''

The altar of a false god   Judges 6.25–32

That night the LORD told Gideon, "Take your father's bull and another bull seven years old, tear down your father's altar to Baal, and cut down the symbol of the goddess Asherah, which is beside it. Build a well-constructed altar to the LORD your God on top of this mound. Then take the second bull and burn it whole as an offering, using for firewood the symbol of Asherah you have cut down.'' So Gideon took ten of his servants and did what the LORD had told him. He was too afraid of his family and the people of the town to do it by day, so he did it at night.

When the people of the town got up early the next morning, they found that the altar to Baal and the symbol of Asherah had been cut down, and that the second bull had been burnt on the altar that had been built there. They asked each other, "Who did this?'' They investigated and found out that Gideon son of Joash had done it. Then they said to Joash, "Bring your son out here, so that we can kill him! He tore down the altar to Baal and cut down the symbol of Asherah beside it.''

But Joash said to all those who confronted him, "Are you standing up for Baal? Are you defending him? Anyone who stands up for him will be killed before morning. If Baal is a god, let him defend himself. It is his altar that was torn down.'' From then on Gideon was known as Jerubbaal, because Joash said, "Let Baal defend himself; it is his altar that was torn down.''

Victory   Judges 7.1–21

It was important for everyone to know that it was God who gave the victory.

One day Gideon and all his men got up early and camped beside the Spring of Harod. The Midianite camp was in the valley to the north of them by Moreh Hill.

The LORD said to Gideon, "The men you have are too many for me to give them victory over the Midianites. They might think that they had won by themselves, and so give me no credit. Announce to the people, 'Anyone who is afraid should go back home, and we will stay here at Mount Gilead.'" So twenty-two thousand went back, but ten thousand stayed.

Then the LORD said to Gideon, "You still have too many men. Take them down to the water, and I will separate them for you there. If I tell you a man should go with you, he will go. If I tell you a man should not go with you, he will not go." Gideon took the men down to the water, and the LORD said to him, "Separate everyone who laps up the water with his tongue like a dog, from everyone who gets down on his knees to drink." There were three hundred men who scooped up water in their hands and lapped it; all the others got down on their knees to drink. The LORD said to Gideon, "I will rescue you and give you victory over the Midianites with the three hundred men who lapped the water. Tell everyone else to go home." So Gideon sent all the Israelites home, except the three hundred, who kept all the supplies and trumpets. The Midianite camp was below them in the valley.

That night the LORD commanded Gideon, "Get up and attack the camp; I am giving you victory over it. But if you are afraid to attack, go down to the camp with your servant Purah. You will hear what they are saying, and then you will have the courage to attack." So Gideon and his servant Purah went down to the edge of the enemy camp. The Midianites, the Amalekites, and the desert tribesmen were spread out in the valley like a swarm of locusts, and they had as many camels as there were grains of sand on the seashore.

When Gideon arrived, he heard a man telling a friend about a dream. He was saying, "I dreamt that a loaf of barley bread rolled into our camp and hit a tent. The tent collapsed and lay flat on the ground."

His friend replied, "It's the sword of the Israelite, Gideon son of Joash! It can't mean anything else! God has given him victory over Midian and our whole army!"

When Gideon heard about the man's dream and what it meant, he fell to his knees and worshipped the LORD. Then he went back to the Israelite camp and said, "Get up! The LORD is giving you victory over the Midianite army!" He divided his three hundred men into three groups and gave each man a trumpet and a jar with a torch inside it. He told them, "When I get to the edge of the camp, watch me, and do what I do. When my group and I blow our trumpets, then you blow yours all round the camp and shout, 'For the LORD and for Gideon!'"

Gideon and his hundred men came to the edge of the camp a short while before midnight, just after the guard had been changed. Then they blew the trumpets and broke the jars they were holding, and the other two groups did the same. They all held the torches in their left hands, the trumpets in their right, and shouted, "A sword for the LORD and for Gideon!" Every man stood in his place round the camp, and the whole enemy army ran away yelling.

Leader and prophet

Men like Joshua and Gideon were really soldiers. Good fighters were important, but a group of people called "prophets" were also becoming important. The prophet's job was to give the people God's message for them. Samuel was one of the first prophets. He led the people until Israel had its first king.

Promised to God before he was born   1 Samuel 1.9–20

The story of Samuel's birth is rather unusual. To the Israelites, having children was a sign of God's blessing. It was a great disgrace to be unable to have any. Hannah had no children. This made her sad, especially when the whole family travelled to Shiloh, where the Covenant Box was kept. They went there each year to make sacrifices.

One day, after they had finished their meal in the house of the LORD at Shiloh, Hannah got up. She was deeply distressed, and she cried bitterly as she prayed to the LORD. Meanwhile, Eli the priest was sitting in his place by the door. Hannah made a solemn promise: "Almighty LORD, look at me, your servant! See my trouble and remember me! Don't forget me! If you give me a son, I promise that I will dedicate him to you for his whole life and that he will never have his hair cut."

Hannah continued to pray to the LORD for a long time, and Eli watched her lips. She was praying silently; her lips were moving, but she made no sound. So Eli thought that she was drunk, and said to her, "Stop making a drunken show of yourself! Stop your drinking and sober up!"

"No, I'm not drunk, sir," she answered. "I haven't been drinking! I am desperate, and I have been praying, pouring out my troubles to the LORD. Don't think I am a worthless woman. I have been praying like this because I'm so miserable."

"Go in peace," Eli said, "and may the God of Israel give you what you have asked him for."

"May you always think kindly of me," she replied. Then she went away, ate some food, and was no longer sad.

The next morning Elkanah and his family got up early, and after worshipping the LORD, they went back home to Ramah. Elkanah had intercourse with his wife Hannah, and the LORD answered her prayer. So it was that she became pregnant and gave birth to a son. She named him Samuel, and explained, "I asked the LORD for him."

Samuel is dedicated to the Lord   1 Samuel 1.24–28

Hannah promised that her son would never have his hair cut. This seems strange to us now, but then it showed everyone that he was a Nazirite. The Nazirites were people who had made a special vow to dedicate themselves to God.

After she had weaned him, she took him to Shiloh, taking along a three-year-old bull, ten kilogrammes of flour, and a leather bag full of wine. She took Samuel, young as he was, to the house of the LORD at Shiloh. After they had killed the bull, they took the child to Eli. Hannah said to him, "Excuse me, sir. Do you remember me? I am the woman you saw standing here, praying to the LORD. I asked him for this child, and he gave me what I asked for. So I am dedicating him to the LORD. As long as he lives, he will belong to the LORD."

Then they worshipped the LORD there.

Samuel hears God speak   1 Samuel 3.1–21

Samuel, like many prophets, could remember when he first heard God calling him.

In those days, when the boy Samuel was serving the LORD under the direction of Eli, there were very few messages from the LORD, and visions from him were quite rare. One night Eli, who was now almost blind, was sleeping in his own room; Samuel was sleeping in the sanctuary, where the sacred Covenant Box was. Before dawn, while the lamp was still burning, the LORD called Samuel. He answered, "Yes, sir!" and ran to Eli and said, "You called me, and here I am."

But Eli answered, "I didn't call you; go back to bed." So Samuel went back to bed.

The LORD called Samuel again. The boy did not know that it was the LORD, because the LORD had never spoken to him before. So he got up, went to Eli, and said, "You called me, and here I am."

But Eli answered, "My son, I didn't call you; go back to bed."

The LORD called Samuel a third time; he got up, went to Eli, and said, "You called me, and here I am."

Then Eli realized that it was the LORD who was calling the boy, so he said to him, "Go back to bed; and if he calls you again, say, 'Speak, LORD, your servant is listening.'" So Samuel went back to bed.

The LORD came and stood there, and called as he had before, "Samuel! Samuel!"

Samuel answered, "Speak; your servant is listening."

The Lord said to him, "Some day I am going to do something to the people of Israel that is so terrible that everyone who hears about it will be stunned. On that day I will carry out all my threats against Eli's family, from beginning to end. I have already told him that I am going to punish his family for ever because his sons have spoken evil things against me. Eli knew they were doing this, but he did not stop them. So I solemnly declare to the family of Eli that no sacrifice or offering will ever be able to remove the consequences of this terrible sin."

Samuel stayed in bed until morning; then he got up and opened the doors of the house of the LORD. He was afraid to tell Eli about the vision. Eli called him, "Samuel, my boy!"

"Yes, sir," answered Samuel.

"What did the LORD tell you?" Eli asked. "Don't keep anything from me. God will punish you severely if you don't tell me everything he said."

So Samuel told him everything; he did not keep anything back. Eli said, "He is the LORD; he will do whatever seems best to him."

As Samuel grew up, the LORD was with him and made everything that Samuel said come true. So all the people of Israel, from one end of the country to the other, knew that Samuel was indeed a prophet of the LORD. The LORD continued to reveal himself at Shiloh, where he had appeared to Samuel and had spoken to him. And when Samuel spoke, all Israel listened.

"We want a king" 1 Samuel 8.1–22

One of the big differences between the Israelites and most of the other nations was that the Israelites did not have a king. Men like Joshua and Gideon led the people for a time, and when they died the nation asked God to give them another leader. Sometimes this system seemed to bring the Israelites victory and at other times defeat.

Many people thought that if they had a king they would be more united, stronger, and better able to fight off attack.

The writer of the book of Samuel was quite certain that the defeats were because of the Israelites' sins, rather than because their leaders had let them down.

When Samuel grew old, he made his sons judges in Israel. The elder son was named Joel and the younger one Abijah; they were judges in Beersheba. But they did not follow their father's example; they were interested only in making money, so they accepted bribes and did not decide cases honestly.

Then all the leaders of Israel met together, went to Samuel in Ramah, and said to him, "Look, you are getting old and your sons don't follow your example. So then, appoint a king to rule over us, so that we will have a king, as other countries have." Samuel was displeased with their request for a king; so he prayed to the LORD, and the LORD said, "Listen to everything the people say to you. You are not the one they have rejected; I am the one they have rejected as their king. Ever since I brought them out of Egypt, they have turned away from me and worshipped other gods; and now they are doing to you what they have always done to me. So then, listen to them, but give them strict warnings and explain how their kings will treat them."

Samuel told the people who were asking him for a king everything that the LORD had said to him. "This is how your king will treat you," Samuel explained. "He will make soldiers of your sons; some of them will serve in his war chariots, others in his cavalry, and others will run before his chariots. He will make some of them officers in charge of a thousand men, and others in charge of fifty men. Your sons will have to plough his fields, harvest his crops, and make his weapons and the equipment for his chariots. Your daughters will have to make perfumes for him and work as his cooks and his bakers. He will take your best fields, vineyards, and olive-groves, and give them to his officials. He will take a tenth of your corn and of your grapes for his court officers and other officials. He will take your servants and your best cattle and donkeys, and make them work for him. He will take a tenth of your flocks. And you yourselves will become his slaves. When that time comes, you will complain bitterly because of your king, whom you yourselves chose, but the LORD will not listen to your complaints."

The people paid no attention to Samuel, but said, "No! We want a king, so that we will be like other nations, with our own king to rule us and to lead us out to war and to fight our battles." Samuel listened to everything they said and then went and told the LORD. The LORD answered, "Do what they want and give them a king." Then Samuel told all the men of Israel to go back home.

The Israelites get their first king   1 Samuel 10.17–25

Samuel called the people together for a religious gathering at Mizpah and said to them, "The LORD, the God of Israel, says, 'I brought you out of Egypt and rescued you from the Egyptians and all the other peoples who were oppressing you. I am your God, the one who rescues you from all your troubles and difficulties, but today you have rejected me and have asked me to give you a king. Very well, then, gather yourselves before the LORD by tribes and by clans.'"

Then Samuel made each tribe come forward, and the LORD picked the tribe of Benjamin. Then Samuel made the families of the tribe of Benjamin come forward, and the family of Matri was picked out. Then the men of the family of Matri came forward, and Saul son of Kish was picked out. They looked for him, but when they could not find him, they asked the LORD, "Is there still someone else?"

The LORD answered, "Saul is over there, hiding behind the supplies."

So they ran and brought Saul out to the people, and they could see that he was a head taller than anyone else. Samuel said to the people, "Here is the man the LORD has chosen! There is no one else among us like him."

All the people shouted, "Long live the king!"

Samuel explained to the people the rights and duties of a king, and then wrote them in a book, which he deposited in a holy place. Then he sent everyone home.

84

David

The Israelites' first king, Saul, turned out to be a great disappointment. Their second king was David and he was, and still is, looked upon as the greatest king they ever had. He was the most successful at encouraging the people to keep the covenant. The country grew in size and importance during his reign. Long after he died, some of the prophets hoped that his descendants would provide a new hope for Israel. The New Testament points out that Mary's husband, Joseph, was directly descended from David. But to begin David's story we have to go back to something that happened before he was born.

Ruth leaves home   Ruth 1.1–19

Not many Israelites ever left the land of Israel and it was unusual for them to marry people from other countries.

Long ago, in the days before Israel had a king, there was a famine in the land. So a man named Elimelech, who belonged to the clan of Ephrath and who lived in Bethlehem in Judah, went with his wife Naomi and their two sons Mahlon and Chilion to live for a while in the country of Moab. While they were living there, Elimelech died, and Naomi was left alone with her two sons, who married Moabite girls, Orpah and Ruth. About ten years later Mahlon and Chilion also died, and Naomi was left all alone, without husband or sons.

Some time later Naomi heard that the LORD had blessed his people by giving them a good harvest; so she got ready to leave Moab with her daughters-in-law. They started out together to go back to Judah, but on the way she said to them, "Go back home and stay with your mothers. May the LORD be as good to you as you have been to me and to those who have died. And may the LORD make it possible for each of you to marry again and have a home."

So Naomi kissed them good-bye. But they started crying and said to her, "No! We will go with you to your people."

"You must go back, my daughters," Naomi answered. "Why do you want to come with me? Do you think I could have sons again for you to marry? Go back home, for I am too old to get married again. Even if I thought there was still hope, and so got married tonight and had sons, would you wait until they had grown up? Would this keep you from marrying someone else? No, my daughters, you know that's impossible. The LORD has turned against me, and I feel very sorry for you."

Again they started crying. Then Orpah kissed her mother-in-law good-bye and went back home, but Ruth held on to her. So Naomi said to her,

"Ruth, your sister-in-law has gone back to her people and to her god. Go back home with her."

But Ruth answered, "Don't ask me to leave you! Let me go with you. Wherever you go, I will go; wherever you live, I will live. Your people will be my people, and your God will be my God. Wherever you die, I will die, and that is where I will be buried. May the LORD's worst punishment come upon me if I let anything but death separate me from you!"

When Naomi saw that Ruth was determined to go with her, she said nothing more.

They went on until they came to Bethlehem.

Ruth works in the fields   Ruth 2.1–3, 14–16

Naomi and Ruth arrived in Bethlehem like refugees, with almost nothing. It was the custom to allow poor people to pick up the corn which got left behind at harvest time.

Naomi had a relative named Boaz, a rich and influential man who belonged to the family of her husband Elimelech. One day Ruth said to Naomi, "Let me go to the fields to gather the corn that the harvest workers leave. I am sure to find someone who will let me work with him."

Naomi answered, "Go ahead, my daughter."

So Ruth went out to the fields and walked behind the workers, picking up the corn which they left. It so happened that she was in a field that belonged to Boaz...

At meal-time Boaz said to Ruth, "Come and have a piece of bread, and dip it in the sauce." So she sat with the workers, and Boaz passed some roasted grain to her. She ate until she was satisfied, and she still had some food left over.

After she had left to go on picking up corn, Boaz ordered the workers, "Let her pick it up even where the bundles are lying, and don't say anything to stop her. Besides that, pull out some corn from the bundles and leave it for her to pick up."

Boaz marries Ruth   Ruth 4.13–22

The writers of history in the Bible were interested in family trees. They recorded this one to show that the greatest of the Israelite kings was partly descended from a foreigner. Although the Israelites were special people, this did not mean that others had no part in God's plan.

Boaz took Ruth home as his wife. The LORD blessed her, and she became pregnant and had a son. The women said to Naomi, "Praise the LORD! He has given you a grandson today to take care of you. May the boy become famous in Israel! Your daughter-in-law loves you, and has done more for you than seven sons. And now she has given you a grandson, who will bring new life to you and give you security in your old age." Naomi took the child, held him close, and took care of him.

The women of the neighbourhood named the boy Obed. They told everyone, "A son has been born to Naomi!"

Obed became the father of Jesse, who was the father of David.

This is the family line from Perez to David: Perez, Hezron, Ram, Amminadab, Nahshon, Salmon, Boaz, Obed, Jesse, David.

David is anointed as king   1 Samuel 16.1–13

Saul had disobeyed God's commands, and so Samuel was ordered to anoint his successor in secret.

The LORD said to Samuel, "How long will you go on grieving over Saul? I have rejected him as king of Israel. But now get some olive-oil and go to Bethlehem, to a man named Jesse, because I have chosen one of his sons to be king."

"How can I do that?" Samuel asked. "If Saul hears about it, he will kill me!"

The LORD answered, "Take a calf with you and say that you are there to offer a sacrifice to the LORD. Invite Jesse to the sacrifice, and I will tell you what to do. You will anoint as king the man I tell you to."

Samuel did what the LORD told him to do and went to Bethlehem, where the city leaders came trembling to meet him and asked, "Is this a peaceful visit, seer?"

"Yes," he answered. "I have come to offer a sacrifice to the LORD. Purify yourselves and come with me." He also told Jesse and his sons to purify themselves, and he invited them to the sacrifice.

When they arrived, Samuel saw Jesse's son Eliab and said to himself, "This man standing here in the LORD's presence is surely the one he has chosen." But the LORD said to him, "Pay no attention to how tall and handsome he is. I have rejected him, because I do not judge as man judges. Man looks at the outward appearance, but I look at the heart."

Then Jesse called his son Abinadab and brought him to Samuel. But Samuel said, "No, the LORD hasn't chosen him either." Jesse then brought Shammah. "No, the LORD hasn't chosen him either," Samuel said. In this way Jesse brought seven of his sons to Samuel. And Samuel said to him, "No, the LORD hasn't chosen any of these." Then he asked him, "Have you any more sons?"

Jesse answered, "There is still the youngest, but he is out taking care of the sheep."

"Tell him to come here," Samuel said. "We won't offer the sacrifice until he comes." So Jesse sent for him. He was a handsome, healthy young man, and his eyes sparkled. The LORD said to Samuel, "This is the one—anoint him!" Samuel took the olive-oil and anointed David in front of his brothers. Immediately the spirit of the LORD took control of David and was with him from that day on. Then Samuel returned to Ramah.

David's adventures as a young man

Goliath challenges the Israelites   1 Samuel 17.2–11

Saul and the Israelites assembled and camped in the Valley of Elah, where they got ready to fight the Philistines. The Philistines lined up on one hill and the Israelites on another, with a valley between them.

A man named Goliath, from the city of Gath, came out from the Philistine camp to challenge the Israelites. He was nearly three metres tall and wore bronze armour that weighed about fifty-seven kilogrammes and a bronze helmet. His legs were also protected by bronze armour, and he carried a bronze javelin slung over his shoulder. His spear was as thick as the bar on a weaver's loom, and its iron head weighed about seven kilogrammes. A soldier walked in front of him carrying his shield. Goliath stood and shouted at the Israelites, "What are you doing there, lined up for battle? I am a Philistine, you slaves of Saul! Choose one of your men to fight me. If he wins and kills me, we will be your slaves; but if I win and kill him, you will be our slaves. Here and now I challenge the Israelite army. I dare you to pick someone to fight me!" When Saul and his men heard this, they were terrified.

David's courage   1 Samuel 17.12–40

David was the son of Jesse, who was an Ephrathite from Bethlehem in Judah. Jesse had eight sons, and at the time Saul was king, he was already a very old man. His three eldest sons had gone with Saul to war. The eldest was Eliab, the next was Abinadab, and the third was Shammah. David was the youngest son, and while the three eldest brothers stayed with Saul, David would go back to Bethlehem from time to time, to take care of his father's sheep.

Goliath challenged the Israelites every morning and evening for forty days.

One day Jesse said to David, "Take ten kilogrammes of this roasted grain and these ten loaves of bread, and hurry with them to your brothers in the camp. And take these ten cheeses to the commanding officer. Find out how your brothers are getting on and bring back something to show that you saw them and that they are well. King Saul, your brothers, and all the other Israelites are in the Valley of Elah fighting the Philistines."

David got up early the next morning, left someone else in charge of the sheep, took the food, and went as Jesse had told him to. He arrived at the camp just as the Israelites were going out to their battle line, shouting the war-cry. The Philistine and the Israelite armies took up positions for battle, facing each other. David left the food with the officer in charge of the supplies, ran to the battle line, went to his brothers, and asked how they were getting on. As he was talking to them, Goliath came forward and challenged the Israelites as he had done before. And David heard him. When the Israelites saw Goliath, they ran away in terror. "Look at him!" they said to each other. "Listen to his challenge! King Saul has promised to give a big reward to the man who kills him; the king will also give him his daughter to marry and will not require his father's family to pay taxes."

David asked the men who were near him, "What will the man get who kills this Philistine and frees Israel from this disgrace? After all, who is this heathen Philistine to defy the army of the living God?" They told him what would be done for the man who killed Goliath.

Eliab, David's eldest brother, heard David talking to the men. He was angry with David and said, "What are you doing here? Who is taking care of those sheep of yours out there in the wilderness? You cheeky brat, you! You just came to watch the fighting!"

"Now what have I done?" David asked. "Can't I even ask a question?" He turned to another man and asked him the same question, and every time he asked, he got the same answer.

Some men heard what David had said, and they told Saul, who sent for him. David said to Saul, "Your Majesty, no one should be afraid of this Philistine! I will go and fight him."

"No," answered Saul. "How could you fight him? You're just a boy, and he has been a soldier all his life!"

"Your Majesty," David said, "I take care of my father's sheep. Whenever a lion or a bear carries off a lamb, I go after it, attack it, and rescue the lamb. And if the lion or bear turns on me, I grab it by the throat and beat it to death. I have killed lions and bears, and I will do the same to this heathen Philistine, who has defied the army of the living God. The LORD has saved me from lions and bears; he will save me from this Philistine."

"All right," Saul answered. "Go, and the LORD be with you." He gave his own armour to David for him to wear: a bronze helmet, which he put on David's head, and a coat of armour. David strapped Saul's sword over the armour and tried to walk, but he couldn't, because he wasn't used to wearing them. "I can't fight with all this," he said to Saul. "I'm not used to it." So he took it all off. He took his shepherd's stick and then picked up five smooth stones from the stream and put them in his bag. With his sling ready, he went out to meet Goliath.

David and Goliath   1 Samuel 17.41–54

The Philistine started walking towards David, with his shield-bearer walking in front of him. He kept coming closer, and when he got a good look at David, he was filled with scorn for him because he was just a nice, good-looking boy. He said to David, "What's that stick for? Do you think I'm a dog?" And he called down curses from his god on David. "Come on," he challenged David, "and I will give your body to the birds and animals to eat."

David answered, "You are coming against me with sword, spear, and javelin, but I come against you in the name of the LORD Almighty, the God of the Israelite armies, which you have defied. This very day the LORD will put you in my power; I will defeat you and cut off your head. And I will give the bodies of the Philistine soldiers to the birds and animals to eat. Then the whole world will know that Israel has a God, and everyone here will see that the LORD does not need swords or spears to save his people. He is victorious in battle, and he will put all of you in our power."

Goliath started walking towards David again, and David ran quickly towards the Philistine battle line to fight him. He put his hand into his bag and took out a stone, which he slung at Goliath. It hit him on the forehead and broke his skull, and Goliath fell face downwards on the ground. And so, without a sword, David defeated and killed Goliath with a sling and a stone! He ran to him, stood over him, took Goliath's sword out of its sheath, and cut off his head and killed him.

When the Philistines saw that their hero was dead, they ran away. The men of Israel and Judah shouted and ran after them, pursuing them all the way to Gath and to the gates of Ekron. The Philistines fell wounded all along the road that leads to Shaaraim, as far as Gath and Ekron. When the Israelites came back from pursuing the Philistines, they looted their camp. David picked up Goliath's head and took it to Jerusalem, but he kept Goliath's weapons in his own tent.

David is presented to Saul   1 Samuel 17.55 — 18.5

When Saul saw David going out to fight Goliath, he asked Abner, the commander of his army, "Abner, whose son is he?"

"I have no idea, Your Majesty," Abner answered.

"Then go and find out," Saul ordered.

So when David returned to camp after killing Goliath, Abner took him to Saul. David was still carrying Goliath's head. Saul asked him, "Young man, whose son are you?"

"I am the son of your servant Jesse from Bethlehem," David answered.

Saul and David finished their conversation. After that, Saul's son Jonathan was deeply attracted to David and came to love him as much as he loved himself. Saul kept David with him from that day on and did not let him go back home. Jonathan swore eternal friendship with David because of his deep affection for him. He took off the robe he was wearing and gave it to David, together with his armour and also his sword, bow, and belt. David was successful in all the missions on which Saul sent him, and so Saul made him an officer in his army. This pleased all of Saul's officers and men.

Saul becomes jealous of David   1 Samuel 18.6–16

As David was returning after killing Goliath and as the soldiers were coming back home, women from every town in Israel came out to meet King Saul. They were singing joyful songs, dancing, and playing tambourines and lyres. In their celebration the women sang, "Saul has killed thousands, but David tens of thousands." Saul did not like this, and he became very angry. He said, "For David they claim tens of thousands, but only thousands for me. They will be making him king next!" And so he was jealous and suspicious of David from that day on.

The next day an evil spirit from God suddenly took control of Saul, and he raved in his house like a madman. David was playing the harp, as he did every day, and Saul was holding a spear. "I'll pin him to the wall," Saul said to himself, and he threw the spear at him twice; but David dodged each time.

Saul was afraid of David because the LORD was with David but had abandoned him. So Saul sent him away and put him in command of a thousand men. David led his men in battle and was successful in all he did, because the LORD was with him. Saul noticed David's success and became even more afraid of him. But everyone in Israel and Judah loved David because he was such a successful leader.

94

David at the court of King Saul

Jonathan helps David   1 Samuel 20.1–23

Jonathan was Saul's son. He would have expected to be king after his father. Since Saul was so jealous of David, it is surprising that Jonathan and David were such good friends. David had already run and hidden from Saul before.

"What have I done?" David asked. "What crime have I committed? What wrong have I done to your father to make him want to kill me?" ·

Jonathan answered, "God forbid that you should die! My father tells me everything he does, important or not, and he would not hide this from me. It isn't true!"

But David answered, "Your father knows very well how much you like me, and he has decided not to let you know what he plans to do, because you would be deeply hurt. I swear to you by the living LORD that I am only a step away from death!"

Jonathan said, "I'll do anything you want."

"Tomorrow is the New Moon Festival," David replied, "and I am supposed to eat with the king. But if it's all right with you, I will go and hide in the fields until the evening of the day after tomorrow. If your father notices that I am not at table, tell him that I begged your permission to hurry home to Bethlehem, since it's the time for the annual sacrifice there for my whole family. If he says, 'All right,' I will be safe; but if he becomes angry, you will know that he is determined to harm me. Please do me this favour, and keep the sacred promise you made to me. But if I'm guilty, kill me yourself! Why take me to your father to be killed?"

"Don't even think such a thing!" Jonathan answered. "If I knew for certain that my father was determined to harm you, wouldn't I tell you?"

David then asked, "Who will let me know if your father answers you angrily?"

"Let's go out to the fields," Jonathan answered. So they went, and Jonathan said to David, "May the LORD God of Israel be our witness! At this time tomorrow and on the following day I will question my father. If his attitude towards you is good, I will send you word. If he intends to harm you, may the LORD strike me dead if I don't let you know about it and get you safely away. May the LORD be with you as he was with my father! And if I remain alive, please keep your sacred promise and be loyal to me; but if I die, show the same kind of loyalty to my family for ever. And when the LORD has completely destroyed all your enemies, may our promise to each other still be unbroken. If it is broken, the LORD will punish you."

Once again Jonathan made David promise to love him, for Jonathan loved David as much as he loved himself. Then Jonathan said to him, "Since tomorrow is the New Moon Festival, your absence will be noticed if you aren't at the meal. The day after tomorrow your absence will be noticed even more; so go to the place where you hid the other time, and hide behind the pile of stones there. I will then shoot three arrows at it, as though it were a target. Then I will tell my servant to go and find them. And if I tell him, 'Look, the arrows are on this side of you; get them,' that means that you are safe and can come out. I swear by the living LORD that you will be in no danger. But if I tell him, 'The arrows are on the other side of you,' then leave, because the LORD is sending you away. As for the promise we have made to each other, the LORD will make sure that we will keep it for ever."

The secret sign to escape   1 Samuel 20.24–41

So David hid in the fields. At the New Moon Festival, King Saul came to the meal and sat in his usual place by the wall. Abner sat next to him, and Jonathan sat opposite him. David's place was empty, but Saul said nothing that day, because he thought, "Something has happened to him, and he is not ritually pure." On the following day, the day after the New Moon Festival, David's place was still empty, and Saul asked Jonathan, "Why didn't David come to the meal either yesterday or today?"

Jonathan answered, "He begged me to let him go to Bethlehem. 'Please let me go,' he said, 'because our family is celebrating the sacrificial feast in town, and my brother ordered me to be there. So then, if you are my friend, let me go and see my relatives.' That is why he isn't in his place at your table."

Saul was furious with Jonathan and said to him, "How rebellious and faithless your mother was! Now I know you are taking sides with David and are disgracing yourself and that mother of yours! Don't you realize that as long as David is alive, you will never be king of this country? Now go and bring him here—he must die!"

"Why should he die?" Jonathan replied. "What has he done?"

At that, Saul threw his spear at Jonathan to kill him, and Jonathan realized that his father was really determined to kill David. Jonathan got up from the table in a rage and ate nothing that day—the second day of the New Moon Festival. He was deeply distressed about David, because Saul had insulted him. The following morning Jonathan went to the fields to meet David, as they had agreed. He took a young boy with him

96

and said to him, "Run and find the arrows I'm going to shoot." The boy ran, and Jonathan shot an arrow beyond him. When the boy reached the place where the arrow had fallen, Jonathan shouted to him, "The arrow is further on! Don't just stand there! Hurry up!" The boy picked up the arrow and returned to his master, not knowing what it all meant; only Jonathan and David knew. Jonathan gave his weapons to the boy and told him to take them back to the town.

After the boy had left, David got up from behind the pile of stones, fell on his knees and bowed with his face to the ground three times. Both he and Jonathan were crying as they kissed each other; David's grief was even greater than Jonathan's.

David gets his chance of revenge   1 Samuel 26.1–25

Saul went on trying to kill David. But David had been anointed as Saul's successor by the prophet Samuel and was very popular with the people. What happened next tempted David to take a short cut to power by doing something very wrong.

Some men from Ziph came to Saul at Gibeah and told him that David was hiding on Mount Hachilah at the edge of the Judaean wilderness. Saul went at once with three thousand of the best soldiers in Israel to the wilderness of Ziph to look for David, and camped by the road on Mount Hachilah. David was still in the wilderness, and when he learnt that Saul had come to look for him, he sent spies and found out that Saul was indeed there. He went at once and located the exact place where Saul and Abner son of Ner, commander of Saul's army, slept. Saul slept inside the camp, and his men camped round him.

Then David asked Ahimelech the Hittite, and Abishai the brother of Joab (their mother was Zeruiah), "Which of you two will go to Saul's camp with me?"

"I will," Abishai answered.

So that night David and Abishai entered Saul's camp and found Saul sleeping in the centre of the camp with his spear stuck in the ground near his head. Abner and the troops were sleeping round him. Abishai said to David, "God has put your enemy in your power tonight. Now let me plunge his own spear through him and pin him to the ground with just one blow—I won't have to strike twice!"

But David said, "You must not harm him! The LORD will certainly punish whoever harms his chosen king. By the living LORD," David continued, "I know that the LORD himself will kill Saul, either when his time comes to die a natural death or when he dies in battle. The LORD forbid that I should try to harm the one whom the LORD has made king!

Let's take his spear and his water jar, and go." So David took the spear and the water jar from just beside Saul's head, and he and Abishai left. No one saw it or knew what had happened or even woke up—they were all sound asleep, because the LORD had sent a heavy sleep on them all.

Then David crossed over to the other side of the valley to the top of the hill, a safe distance away, and shouted to Saul's troops and to Abner, "Abner! Can you hear me?"

"Who is that shouting and waking up the king?" Abner asked.

David answered, "Abner, aren't you the greatest man in Israel? So why aren't you protecting your master, the king? Just now someone entered the camp to kill your master. You failed in your duty, Abner! I swear by the living LORD that all of you deserve to die, because you have not protected your master, whom the LORD made king. Look! Where is the king's spear? Where is the water jar that was beside his head?"

Saul recognized David's voice and asked, "David, is that you, my son?"

"Yes, Your Majesty," David answered. And he added, "Why, sir, are you still pursuing me, your servant? What have I done? What crime have I committed? Your Majesty, listen to what I have to say. If it is the LORD who has turned you against me, an offering to him will make him change his mind; but if men have done it, may the LORD's curse fall on them. For they have driven me out from the LORD's land to a country where I can only worship foreign gods. Don't let me be killed on foreign soil, away from the LORD. Why should the king of Israel come to kill a flea like me? Why should he hunt me down like a wild bird?"

Saul answered, "I have done wrong. Come back, David, my son! I will never harm you again, because you have spared my life tonight. I have been a fool! I have done a terrible thing!"

David replied, "Here is your spear, Your Majesty. Let one of your men come over and get it. The LORD rewards those who are faithful and righteous. Today he put you in my power, but I did not harm you, whom the LORD made king. Just as I have spared your life today, may the LORD do the same to me and free me from all troubles!"

Saul said to David, "God bless you, my son! You will succeed in everything you do!"

So David went on his way, and Saul returned home.

Saul calls up the spirit of Samuel   1 Samuel 28.3–25

What Saul did here was not allowed by God. There was little comfort for Saul when he broke this law.

Now Samuel had died, and all the Israelites had mourned for him and had buried him in his own city of Ramah. Saul had forced all the fortune-tellers and mediums to leave Israel.

The Philistine troops assembled and camped near the town of Shunem; Saul gathered the Israelites and camped at Mount Gilboa. When Saul saw the Philistine army, he was terrified, and so he asked the LORD what to do. But the LORD did not answer him at all, either by dreams or by the use of Urim and Thummim or by prophets. Then Saul ordered his officials, "Find me a woman who is a medium, and I will go and consult her."

"There is one in Endor," they answered.

So Saul disguised himself; he put on different clothes, and after dark he went with two of his men to see the woman. "Consult the spirits for me and tell me what is going to happen," he said to her. "Call up the spirit of the man I name."

The woman answered, "Surely you know what King Saul has done, how he forced the fortune-tellers and mediums to leave Israel. Why, then, are you trying to trap me and get me killed?"

Then Saul made a sacred vow. "By the living LORD I promise that you will not be punished for doing this," he told her.

"Whom shall I call up for you?" the woman asked.

"Samuel," he answered.

When the woman saw Samuel, she screamed and said to Saul, "Why have you tricked me? You are King Saul!"

"Don't be afraid!" the king said to her. "What do you see?"

"I see a spirit coming up from the earth," she answered.

"What does it look like?" he asked.

"It's an old man coming up," she answered. "He is wearing a cloak."

Then Saul knew that it was Samuel, and he bowed to the ground in respect.

Samuel said to Saul, "Why have you disturbed me? Why did you make me come back?"

Saul answered, "I am in great trouble! The Philistines are at war with me, and God has abandoned me. He doesn't answer me any more, either by prophets or by dreams. And so I have called you, for you to tell me what I must do."

Samuel said, "Why do you call me when the LORD has abandoned you and become your enemy? The LORD has done to you what he told you through me: he has taken the kingdom away from you and given it to David instead. You disobeyed the LORD's command and did not completely destroy the Amalekites and all they had. That is why the LORD is doing this to you now. He will hand you and Israel over to the Philistines. Tomorrow you and your sons will join me, and the LORD will also hand the army of Israel over to the Philistines."

At once Saul fell down and lay stretched out on the ground, terrified by what Samuel had said. He was weak, because he had not eaten anything all day and all night. The woman went over to him and saw that he was terrified, so she said to him, "Please, sir, I risked my life by doing what you asked. Now please do what I ask. Let me prepare some food for you. You must eat so that you will be strong enough to travel."

Saul refused and said he would not eat anything. But his officers also urged him to eat. He finally gave in, got up from the ground, and sat on the bed. The woman quickly killed a calf which she had been fattening. Then she took some flour, prepared it, and baked some bread without yeast. She set the food before Saul and his officers, and they ate it. And they left that same night.

Samuel's prediction comes true   1 Samuel 31.1–6

The Philistines fought a battle against the Israelites on Mount Gilboa. Many Israelites were killed there, and the rest of them, including King Saul and his sons, fled. But the Philistines caught up with them and killed three of Saul's sons, Jonathan, Abinadab, and Malchishua. The fighting was heavy round Saul, and he himself was hit by enemy arrows and badly wounded. He said to the young man carrying his weapons, "Draw your sword and kill me, so that these godless Philistines won't gloat over me and kill me." But the young man was too terrified to do it. So Saul took his own sword and threw himself on it. The young man saw that Saul was dead, so he too threw himself on his own sword and died with Saul. And that is how Saul, his three sons, and the young man died; all of Saul's men died that day.

David's lament for Saul and Jonathan
2 Samuel 1.17–18, 19–27

David wrote many songs and poems. This is one of his saddest. It is full of praise, even for Saul, who had tried to kill him.

David sang this lament for Saul and his son Jonathan, and ordered it to be taught to the people of Judah...

"On the hills of Israel our leaders are dead!
   The bravest of our soldiers have fallen!
Do not announce it in Gath
   or in the streets of Ashkelon.
Do not make the women of Philistia glad;
   do not let the daughters of pagans rejoice.

"May no rain or dew fall on Gilboa's hills;
   may its fields be always barren!
For the shields of the brave lie there in disgrace;
   the shield of Saul is no longer polished with oil.
Jonathan's bow was deadly,
   the sword of Saul was merciless,
   striking down the mighty, killing the enemy.

"Saul and Jonathan, so wonderful and dear;
   together in life, together in death;
   swifter than eagles, stronger than lions.

"Women of Israel, mourn for Saul!
   He clothed you in rich scarlet dresses
   and adorned you with jewels and gold.

"The brave soldiers have fallen,
   they were killed in battle.
   Jonathan lies dead in the hills.

"I grieve for you, my brother Jonathan;
   how dear you were to me!...

"The brave soldiers have fallen,
   their weapons abandoned and useless."

5
Kings and prophets

Times changed. The Israelites now controlled most of Canaan. They lived in walled cities and Jerusalem became the capital city of Israel. But neighbouring tribes and foreign countries still caused trouble. Many Israelites were still tempted to worship idols, and the prophets often had to remind the people—and even their king—about the covenant with God.

David the king

Saul had not been a popular king. He did not have everyone's whole-hearted support. When David became king he managed to unite many of the people who had argued before. David's army was well-organized and this helped the Israelites to form their own country. Now that the country was growing and becoming strong, David spent his time in a palace in the new capital city, Jerusalem, and not camping with his soldiers.

David does wrong   2 Samuel 11.1–5

Although David is seen as the greatest king of Israel he was not perfect, and the Bible does not try to cover up his weaknesses.

The following spring, at the time of the year when kings usually go to war, David sent out Joab with his officers and the Israelite army; they defeated the Ammonites and besieged the city of Rabbah. But David himself stayed in Jerusalem.

One day, late in the afternoon, David got up from his nap and went to the palace roof. As he walked about up there, he saw a woman having a bath. She was very beautiful. So he sent a messenger to find out who she was, and learnt that she was Bathsheba, the daughter of Eliam and the wife of Uriah the Hittite. David sent messengers to fetch her; they brought her to him and he made love to her. (She had just finished her monthly ritual of purification.) Then she went back home. Afterwards she discovered that she was pregnant and sent a message to David to tell him.

David tries to hide what he has done   2 Samuel 11.6–13

Bathsheba's husband, Uriah, was a soldier in David's army. The army was on a campaign, living in tents. The Law said that, if this was so, soldiers must not go home to be with their wives.

David then sent a message to Joab: "Send me Uriah the Hittite." So Joab sent him to David. When Uriah arrived, David asked him if Joab and the troops were well, and how the fighting was going. Then he said to Uriah, "Go home and rest a while." Uriah left, and David sent a present to his home. But Uriah did not go home; instead he slept at the palace gate with the king's guards. When David heard that Uriah had not gone home, he asked him, "You have just returned after a long absence; why didn't you go home?"

Uriah answered, "The men of Israel and Judah are away at the war, and the Covenant Box is with them; my commander Joab and his officers are camping out in the open. How could I go home, eat and drink, and sleep with my wife? By all that's sacred, I swear that I could never do such a thing!"

So David said, "Then stay here the rest of the day, and tomorrow I'll send you back." So Uriah stayed in Jerusalem that day and the next. David invited him to supper and made him drunk. But again that night Uriah did not go home; instead he slept on his blanket in the palace guardroom.

David's plan   2 Samuel 11.14–21, 25–27

David plans to kill Uriah so that he can marry Bathsheba.

The next morning David wrote a letter to Joab and sent it by Uriah. He wrote: "Put Uriah in the front line, where the fighting is heaviest, then retreat and let him be killed." So while Joab was besieging the city, he sent Uriah to a place where he knew the enemy was strong. The enemy troops came out of the city and fought Joab's forces; some of David's officers were killed, and so was Uriah.

Then Joab sent a report to David telling him about the battle, and he instructed the messenger, "After you have told the king all about the battle, he may get angry and ask you, 'Why did you go so near the city to fight them? Didn't you realize that they would shoot arrows from the walls? Don't you remember how Abimelech son of Gideon was killed? It was at Thebez, where a woman threw a millstone down from the wall and killed him. Why, then, did you go so near the wall?' If the king asks you this, tell him, 'Your officer Uriah was also killed'"...

David said to the messenger, "Encourage Joab and tell him not to be upset, since you never can tell who will die in battle. Tell him to launch a stronger attack on the city and capture it."

When Bathsheba heard that her husband had been killed, she mourned for him. When the time of mourning was over, David sent for her to come to the palace; she became his wife and bore him a son. But the LORD was not pleased with what David had done.

Nathan confronts David   2 Samuel 12.1–15

In many countries what David had done would have been allowed. A king could take what he wanted. But not in Israel. The king, like anyone else, must obey God's Law.

Nathan, in his job as a prophet, made David condemn himself.

The LORD sent the prophet Nathan to David. Nathan went to him and said, "There were two men who lived in the same town; one was rich and the other poor. The rich man had many cattle and sheep, while the poor man had only one lamb, which he had bought. He took care of it, and it grew up in his home with his children. He would feed it with some of his own food, let it drink from his cup, and hold it in his lap. The lamb was like a daughter to him. One day a visitor arrived at the rich man's home. The rich man didn't want to kill one of his own animals to prepare a meal for him; instead, he took the poor man's lamb and cooked a meal for his guest."

David was very angry with the rich man and said, "I swear by the living LORD that the man who did this ought to die! For having done such a cruel thing, he must pay back four times as much as he took."

"You are that man," Nathan said to David. "And this is what the LORD God of Israel says: 'I made you king of Israel and rescued you from Saul. I gave you his kingdom and his wives; I made you king over Israel and Judah. If this had not been enough, I would have given you twice as much. Why, then, have you disobeyed my commands? Why did you do this evil thing? You had Uriah killed in battle; you let the Ammonites kill him, and then you took his wife! Now, in every generation some of your descendants will die a violent death because you have disobeyed me and have taken Uriah's wife. I swear to you that I will cause someone from your own family to bring trouble on you. You will see it when I take your wives from you and give them to another man; and he will have intercourse with them in broad daylight. You sinned in secret, but I will make this happen in broad daylight for all Israel to see.'"

"I have sinned against the LORD," David said.

Nathan replied, "The LORD forgives you; you will not die. But because you have shown such contempt for the LORD in doing this, your child will die." Then Nathan went home.

Absalom rebels   2 Samuel 15.1–6, 12

Absalom was one of David's grown-up sons.

After this, Absalom provided a chariot and horses for himself, and an escort of fifty men. He would get up early and go and stand by the road at the city gate. Whenever someone came there with a dispute that he wanted the king to settle, Absalom would call him over and ask him where he was from. And after the man had told him what tribe he was from, Absalom would say, "Look, the law is on your side, but there is no representative of the king to hear your case." And he would add, "How I wish I were a judge! Then anyone who had a dispute or a claim could come to me, and I would give him justice." When the man approached Absalom to bow down before him, Absalom would reach out, take hold of him, and kiss him. Absalom did this with every Israelite who came to the king for justice, and so he won their loyalty...

And while he was offering sacrifices, Absalom also sent to the town of Gilo for Ahithophel, who was one of King David's advisers. The plot against the king gained strength, and Absalom's followers grew in number.

David flees from Jerusalem   2 Samuel 15.13–23

A messenger reported to David, "The Israelites are pledging their loyalty to Absalom."

So David said to all his officials who were with him in Jerusalem, "We must get away at once if we want to escape from Absalom! Hurry! Or else he will soon be here and defeat us and kill everyone in the city!"

"Yes, Your Majesty," they answered. "We are ready to do whatever you say." So the king left, accompanied by all his family and officials, except for ten concubines, whom he left behind to take care of the palace.

As the king and all his men were leaving the city, they stopped at the last house. All his officials stood next to him as the royal bodyguard passed by in front of him. The six hundred soldiers who had followed him from Gath also passed by, and the king said to Ittai, their leader, "Why are you going with us? Go back and stay with the new king. You are a foreigner, a refugee away from your own country. You have lived here only a short time, so why should I make you wander round with me? I don't even know where I'm going. Go back and take your fellow-countrymen with you—and may the LORD be kind and faithful to you."

But Ittai answered, "Your Majesty, I swear to you in the LORD's name that I will always go with you wherever you go, even if it means death."

"Fine!" David answered. "March on!" So Ittai went on with all his men and their dependants. The people cried loudly as David's followers left. The king crossed the brook of Kidron, followed by his men, and together they went out towards the wilderness.

Absalom takes over Jerusalem   2 Samuel 16.15–20, 23

While David was leaving Jerusalem, Absalom was making plans to enter it.

Absalom and all the Israelites with him entered Jerusalem, and Ahithophel was with them. When Hushai, David's trusted friend, met Absalom, he shouted, "Long live the king! Long live the king!"

"What has happened to your loyalty to your friend David?" Absalom asked him. "Why didn't you go with him?"

Hushai answered, "How could I? I am on the side of the one chosen by the LORD, by these people, and by all the Israelites. I will stay with you. After all, whom should I serve, if not my master's son? As I served your father, so now I will serve you."

Then Absalom turned to Ahithophel and said, "Now that we are here, what do you advise us to do?" ...

Any advice that Ahithophel gave in those days was accepted as though it were the very word of God; both David and Absalom followed it.

Absalom gets conflicting advice   2 Samuel 17.1–14

Not long after that, Ahithophel said to Absalom, "Let me choose twelve thousand men, and tonight I will set out after David. I will attack him while he is tired and discouraged. He will be frightened, and all his men will run away. I will kill only the king and then bring back all his men to you, like a bride returning to her husband. You want to kill only one man; the rest of the people will be safe." This seemed like good advice to Absalom and all the Israelite leaders.

Absalom said, "Now call Hushai, and let us hear what he has to say." When Hushai arrived, Absalom said to him, "This is the advice that Ahithophel has given us; shall we follow it? If not, you tell us what to do."

Hushai answered, "The advice Ahithophel gave you this time is no good. You know that your father David and his men are hard fighters and that they are as fierce as a mother bear robbed of her cubs. Your father is an experienced soldier and does not stay with his men at night. Just now he is probably hiding in a cave or some other place. As soon as David attacks your men, whoever hears about it will say that your men have been defeated. Then even the bravest men, as fearless as lions, will be afraid because everyone in Israel knows that your father is a great soldier and that his men are hard fighters. My advice is that you bring all the Israelites together from one end of the country to the other, as many as the grains of sand on the seashore, and that you lead them personally in battle. We will find David wherever he is, and attack him before he knows what's happening. Neither he nor any of his men will survive. If he retreats into a city, our people will all bring ropes and just pull the city into the valley below. Not a single stone will be left there on top of the hill."

Absalom and all the Israelites said, "Hushai's advice is better than Ahithophel's." The LORD had decided that Ahithophel's good advice would not be followed, so that disaster would come on Absalom.

David is warned and escapes   2 Samuel 17.15–23

Then Hushai told the priests Zadok and Abiathar what advice he had given to Absalom and the Israelite leaders and what advice Ahithophel had given. Hushai added, "Quick, now! Send a message to David not to spend the night at the river crossings in the wilderness, but to cross the Jordan at once, so that he and his men won't all be caught and killed."

Abiathar's son Jonathan and Zadok's son Ahimaaz were waiting at the spring of Enrogel, on the outskirts of Jerusalem, because they did not dare to be seen entering the city. A servant-girl would regularly go and tell them what was happening, and then they would go and tell King David. But one day a boy happened to see them, and he told Absalom; so they hurried off to hide in the house of a certain man in Bahurim. He had a well near his house, and they got down into it. The man's wife took a covering, spread it over the opening of the well and scattered grain over it, so that no one would notice anything. Absalom's officials came to the house and asked the woman, "Where are Ahimaaz and Jonathan?"

"They crossed the river," she answered.

The men looked for them but could not find them, and so they returned to Jerusalem. After they left, Ahimaaz and Jonathan came up out of the well and went and reported to King David. They told him what Ahithophel had planned against him and said, "Hurry up and cross the river." So David and his men started crossing the Jordan, and by daybreak they had all gone across.

When Ahithophel saw that his advice had not been followed, he saddled his donkey and went back to his own city. After putting his affairs in order, he hanged himself. He was buried in the family grave.

The two armies meet in battle
2 Samuel 17.24, 27, 28–29; 18.1–18

David had reached the town of Mahanaim by the time Absalom and the Israelites had crossed the Jordan…

When David arrived at Mahanaim, he was met by Shobi son of Nahash … and by Machir son of Ammiel, … and by Barzillai…

They brought bowls, clay pots, and bedding, and also food for David and his men: wheat, barley, meal, roasted grain, beans, peas, honey, cheese, cream, and some sheep. They knew that David and his men would be hungry, thirsty, and tired in the wilderness…

King David brought all his men together, divided them into units of a thousand and of a hundred, and placed officers in command of them. Then he sent them out in three groups, with Joab and Joab's brother Abishai and Ittai from Gath, each in command of a group. And the king said to his men, "I will go with you myself."

"You mustn't go with us," they answered. "It won't make any difference to the enemy if the rest of us turn and run, or even if half of us are killed; but you are worth ten thousand of us. It will be better if you stay here in the city and send us help."

"I will do whatever you think best," the king answered. Then he stood by the side of the gate as his men marched out in units of a thousand and of a hundred. He gave orders to Joab, Abishai, and Ittai: "For my sake don't harm the young man Absalom." And all the troops heard David give this command to his officers.

David's army went out into the countryside and fought the Israelites in the forest of Ephraim. The Israelites were defeated by David's men; it was a terrible defeat, with twenty thousand men killed that day. The fighting spread over the countryside, and more men died in the forest than were killed in battle.

Suddenly Absalom met some of David's men. Absalom was riding a mule, and as it went under a large oak-tree, Absalom's head got caught in the branches. The mule ran on and Absalom was left hanging in mid air. One of David's men saw him and reported to Joab, "Sir, I saw Absalom hanging in an oak-tree!"

Joab answered, "If you saw him, why didn't you kill him on the spot? I myself would have given you ten pieces of silver and a belt."

But the man answered, "Even if you gave me a thousand pieces of silver, I wouldn't lift a finger against the king's son. We all heard the king command you and Abishai and Ittai, 'For my sake don't harm the young man Absalom.' But if I had disobeyed the king and killed Absalom, the king would have heard about it—he hears about everything—and you would not have defended me."

"I'm not going to waste any more time with you," Joab said. He took three spears and plunged them into Absalom's chest while he was still alive, hanging in the oak-tree. Then ten of Joab's soldiers closed in on Absalom and finished killing him.

Joab ordered the trumpet to be blown to stop the fighting, and his troops came back from pursuing the Israelites. They took Absalom's body, threw it into a deep pit in the forest, and covered it with a huge pile of stones. All the Israelites fled, each man to his own home.

During his lifetime Absalom had built a monument for himself in King's Valley, because he had no son to keep his name alive. So he named it after himself, and to this day it is known as Absalom's Monument.

David is told about Absalom   2 Samuel 18.19–33

Then Ahimaaz son of Zadok said to Joab, "Let me run to the king with the good news that the LORD has saved him from his enemies."

"No," Joab said, "today you will not take any good news. Some other day you may do so, but not today, for the king's son is dead." Then he said to his Sudanese slave, "Go and tell the king what you have seen." The slave bowed and ran off.

Ahimaaz insisted, "I don't care what happens; please let me take the news also."

"Why do you want to do it, my son?" Joab asked. "You will get no reward for it."

"Whatever happens," Ahimaaz said again, "I want to go."

"Then go," Joab said. So Ahimaaz ran off down the road through the Jordan Valley, and soon he passed the slave.

David was sitting in the space between the inner and outer gates of the city. The watchman went up to the top of the wall and stood on the roof of the gateway; he looked out and saw a man running alone. He called down and told the king, and the king said, "If he is alone, he is bringing good news." The runner came nearer and nearer.

Then the watchman saw another man running alone, and he called down to the gatekeeper, "Look! There's another man running!"

The king answered, "This one also is bringing good news."

The watchman said, "I can see that the first man runs like Ahimaaz."

"He's a good man," the king said, "and he is bringing good news."

Ahimaaz called out a greeting to the king, threw himself down to the ground before him, and said, "Praise the LORD your God, who has given you victory over the men who rebelled against Your Majesty!"

"Is the young man Absalom safe?" the king asked.

Ahimaaz answered, "Sir, when your officer Joab sent me, I saw a great commotion, but I couldn't tell what it was."

"Stand over there," the king said; and he went over and stood there.

Then the Sudanese slave arrived and said to the king, "I have good news for Your Majesty! Today the LORD has given you victory over all who rebelled against you!"

"Is the young man Absalom safe?" the king asked.

The slave answered, "I wish that what has happened to him would happen to all your enemies, sir, and to all who rebel against you."

The king was overcome with grief. He went up to the room over the gateway and wept. As he went, he cried, "O my son! My son Absalom! Absalom, my son! If only I had died in your place, my son! Absalom, my son!"

King Solomon

David had been known as a hard fighter. When he died he left a strong, thriving kingdom to his son, Solomon. Solomon became famous for his wisdom. He governed the country in peace for the whole of his reign and became very rich.

David's last instructions to Solomon   1 Kings 2.1–4

When David was about to die, he called his son Solomon and gave him his last instructions: "My time to die has come. Be confident and determined, and do what the LORD your God orders you to do. Obey all his laws and commands, as written in the Law of Moses, so that wherever you go you may prosper in everything you do. If you obey him, the LORD will keep the promise he made when he told me that my descendants would rule Israel as long as they were careful to obey his commands faithfully with all their heart and soul..."

Solomon prays for wisdom   1 Kings 3.5–15

That night the LORD appeared to him in a dream and asked him, "What would you like me to give you?"

Solomon answered, "You always showed great love for my father David, your servant, and he was good, loyal, and honest in his relations with you. And you have continued to show him your great and constant love by giving him a son who today rules in his place. O LORD God, you have let me succeed my father as king, even though I am very young and don't know how to rule. Here I am among the people you have chosen to be your own, a people who are so many that they cannot be counted. So give me the wisdom I need to rule your people with justice and to know the difference between good and evil. Otherwise, how would I ever be able to rule this great people of yours?"

The LORD was pleased that Solomon had asked for this, and so he said to him, "Because you have asked for the wisdom to rule justly, instead of long life for yourself or riches or the death of your enemies, I will do what you have asked. I will give you more wisdom and understanding than anyone has ever had before or will ever have again. I will also give you what you have not asked for: all your life you will have wealth and honour, more than that of any other king. And if you obey me and keep my laws and commands, as your father David did, I will give you a long life."

Solomon woke up and realized that God had spoken to him in the dream.

An example of Solomon's wise judgements
1 Kings 3.16–28

One day two prostitutes came and presented themselves before King Solomon. One of them said, "Your Majesty, this woman and I live in the same house, and I gave birth to a baby boy at home while she was there. Two days after my child was born she also gave birth to a baby boy. Only the two of us were in the house—no one else was present. Then one night she accidentally rolled over on her baby and smothered it. She got up during the night, took my son from my side while I was asleep, and carried him to her bed; then she put the dead child in my bed. The next morning, when I woke up and was going to feed my baby, I saw that it was dead. I looked at it more closely and saw that it was not my child."

But the other woman said, "No! The living child is mine, and the dead one is yours!"

The first woman answered, "No! The dead child is yours, and the living one is mine!"

And so they argued before the king.

Then King Solomon said, "Each of you claims that the living child is hers and that the dead child belongs to the other one." He sent for a sword, and when it was brought, he said, "Cut the living child in two and give each woman half of it."

The real mother, her heart full of love for her son, said to the king, "Please, Your Majesty, don't kill the child! Give it to her!"

But the other woman said, "Don't give it to either of us; go ahead and cut it in two."

Then Solomon said, "Don't kill the child! Give it to the first woman—she is its real mother."

When the people of Israel heard of Solomon's decision, they were all filled with deep respect for him, because they knew then that God had given him the wisdom to settle disputes fairly.

Respect for Solomon grows
1 Kings 4.20–21, 29–30, 32–34, 10.14–15

The country of Israel was more powerful during Solomon's reign than at any other time. Foreign kings seemed so keen to keep in his favour that he was often sent expensive presents from abroad.

The people of Judah and Israel were as numerous as the grains of sand on the seashore; they ate and drank, and were happy. Solomon's kingdom included all the nations from the River Euphrates to Philistia and the Egyptian border. They paid him taxes and were subject to him all his life...

God gave Solomon unusual wisdom and insight, and knowledge too great to be measured. Solomon was wiser than the wise men of the East or the wise men of Egypt...

He composed three thousand proverbs and more than a thousand songs.

He spoke of trees and plants, from the Lebanon cedars to the hyssop that grows on walls; he talked about animals, birds, reptiles, and fish. Kings all over the world heard of his wisdom and sent people to listen to him ...

Every year King Solomon received almost twenty-three thousand kilogrammes of gold in addition to the taxes paid by merchants, the profits from trade, and tribute paid by the Arabian kings and the governors of the Israelite districts.

The visit of the queen of Sheba   1 Kings 10.1–9

The queen of Sheba heard of Solomon's fame, and she travelled to Jerusalem to test him with difficult questions. She brought with her a large group of attendants, as well as camels loaded with spices, jewels, and a large amount of gold. When she and Solomon met, she asked him all the questions that she could think of. He answered them all; there was nothing too difficult for him to explain. The queen of Sheba heard Solomon's wisdom and saw the palace he had built. She saw the food that was served at his table, the living quarters for his officials, the organization of his palace staff and the uniforms they wore, the servants who waited on him at feasts, and the sacrifices he offered in the Temple. It left her breathless and amazed. She said to King Solomon, "What I heard in my own country about you and your wisdom is true! But I couldn't believe it until I had come and seen it all for myself. But I didn't hear even half of it; your wisdom and wealth are much greater than what I was told. How fortunate are your wives! And how fortunate your servants, who are always in your presence and are privileged to hear your wise sayings! Praise the LORD your God! He has shown how pleased he is with you by making you king of Israel. Because his love for Israel is eternal, he has made you their king so that you can maintain law and justice."

Solomon builds the Temple
1 Kings 5.1–5, 6.1, 7, 15, 19, 21, 22, 38

David had one great ambition which he was not able to fulfill. This was to build a permanent place for worship, a temple for God, in Jerusalem. The Covenant Box had been kept in a large tent known as the "Tent of the Lord's Presence". This was where the Israelites had worshipped God as they travelled through the desert on their way to Canaan. The tent was now at Shiloh, the place where Samuel had heard God speak, but David had taken the Covenant Box to Jerusalem.

David felt that God deserved more than a tent and had bought a piece of ground in a noticeable place in the capital city. He began to get the building materials together, but God told him not to build the Temple.

That was for Solomon to do, during the long period of peace and prosperity in his reign.

King Hiram of Tyre had always been a friend of David's, and when he heard that Solomon had succeeded his father David as king he sent ambassadors to him. Solomon sent back this message to Hiram: "You know that because of the constant wars my father David had to fight against the enemy countries all round him, he could not build a temple for the worship of the LORD his God until the LORD had given him victory over all his enemies. But now the LORD my God has given me peace on all my borders. I have no enemies, and there is no danger of attack. The LORD promised my father David, 'Your son, whom I will make king after you, will build a temple for me.' And I have now decided to build that temple for the worship of the LORD my God..."

Four hundred and eighty years after the people of Israel left Egypt, during the fourth year of Solomon's reign over Israel, in the second month, the month of Ziv, Solomon began work on the Temple...

The stones with which the Temple was built had been prepared at the quarry, so that there was no noise made by hammers, axes, or any other iron tools as the Temple was being built...

The inside walls were covered with cedar panels from the floor to the ceiling, and the floor was made of pine...

In the rear of the Temple an inner room was built, where the LORD's Covenant Box was to be placed...

The inside of the Temple was covered with gold, and gold chains were placed across the entrance of the inner room, which was also covered with gold. The whole interior of the Temple was covered with gold, as well as the altar in the Most Holy Place...

In the eighth month, the month of Bul, in the eleventh year of Solomon's reign, the Temple was completely finished exactly as it had been planned. It had taken Solomon seven years to build it.

The house of God   Psalm 84.1–2, 10–12

The Israelites who lived outside Jerusalem made regular journeys to the Temple to worship and make sacrifices. This Psalm was often sung by pilgrims on their way to Jerusalem. It tells of their love for the Temple — the house of God.

How I love your Temple, LORD Almighty!
    How I want to be there!
    I long to be in the LORD's Temple.

With my whole being I sing for joy
   to the living God ...

One day spent in your Temple
   is better than a thousand anywhere else;
I would rather stand at the gate of the house of my God
   than live in the homes of the wicked.
The LORD is our protector and glorious king,
   blessing us with kindness and honour.
He does not refuse any good thing
   to those who do what is right.
LORD Almighty, how happy are those who trust in you!

The prophets speak out for God

The kings had listened to the prophets carefully (and often asked their advice about important matters). They expected God to speak through his prophets, and although they sometimes ignored God's commands, they did know how important the covenant was. But things changed. As Solomon got older, he began to allow foreign "gods" to be worshipped in Israel. After his death this happened even more. A civil war split the country in two. The larger part in the north kept the name Israel. The smaller southern part was called Judah, after one of the main tribes. Some kings of Judah and Israel did not care about the covenant and actually encouraged the Israelites to worship idols. The prophets had a difficult time. More and more often they warned that disaster would come. Sometimes the king and people listened, but they often forgot very quickly.

Elijah and the prophets of Baal   1 Kings 18.20–39

Ahab was one of the kings of Israel (the northern kingdom). Things got very bad during his reign. He married a foreign wife, Jezebel, who became very powerful. She made trouble for the prophets, and actually killed some of them. For a time anyone who worshipped God was in great danger and people did not know what to do.

Jezebel worshipped a "baal" and she was determined that all her subjects should do the same. ("Baal" is a Hebrew word meaning "a master or husband", but it was often used to mean a pagan god.) Jezebel persuaded Ahab to build a temple for her god in his capital city, and she invited many prophets and priests of the baal to come to Israel.

The country was in trouble because of a drought—there had been no rain for two years. By now, there were very few prophets of the Lord, the God of Israel. One of them was a man called Elijah. He arranged a meeting with Ahab and threw down a public challenge.

So Ahab summoned all the Israelites and the prophets of Baal to meet at Mount Carmel. Elijah went up to the people and said, "How much longer will it take you to make up your minds? If the LORD is God, worship him; but if Baal is God, worship him!" But the people didn't say a word. Then Elijah said, "I am the only prophet of the LORD still left, but there are 450 prophets of Baal. Bring two bulls; let the prophets of Baal take one, kill it, cut it in pieces, and put it on the wood—but don't light the fire. I will do the same with the other bull. Then let the prophets of Baal pray to their god, and I will pray to the LORD, and the one who answers by sending fire—he is God."

The people shouted their approval.

Then Elijah said to the prophets of Baal, "Since there are so many of you, you take a bull and prepare it first. Pray to your god, but don't set fire to the wood."

They took the bull that was brought to them, prepared it, and prayed to Baal until noon. They shouted, "Answer us, Baal!" and kept dancing round the altar they had built. But no answer came.

At noon Elijah started making fun of them: "Pray louder! He is a god! Maybe he is day-dreaming or relieving himself, or perhaps he's gone on a journey! Or maybe he's sleeping, and you've got to wake him up!" So the prophets prayed louder and cut themselves with knives and daggers, according to their ritual, until blood flowed. They kept on ranting and raving until the middle of the afternoon; but no answer came, not a sound was heard.

Then Elijah said to the people, "Come closer to me," and they all gathered round him. He set about repairing the altar of the LORD which had been torn down. He took twelve stones, one for each of the twelve tribes named after the sons of Jacob, the man to whom the LORD had given the name Israel. With these stones he rebuilt the altar for the worship of the LORD. He dug a trench round it, large enough to hold almost fourteen litres of water. Then he placed the wood on the altar, cut the bull in pieces, and laid it on the wood. He said, "Fill four jars with water and pour it on the offering and the wood." They did so, and he said, "Do it again"—and they did. "Do it once more," he said—and they did. The water ran down round the altar and filled the trench.

At the hour of the afternoon sacrifice the prophet Elijah approached the altar and prayed, "O LORD, the God of Abraham, Isaac, and Jacob, prove now that you are the God of Israel and that I am your servant and have done all this at your command. Answer me, LORD, answer me, so that this people will know that you, the LORD, are God, and that you are bringing them back to yourself.''

The LORD sent fire down, and it burnt up the sacrifice, the wood, and the stones, scorched the earth and dried up the water in the trench. When the people saw this, they threw themselves on the ground and exclaimed, ''The LORD is God; the LORD alone is God!''

The earthquake, the fire, and the whisper
1 Kings 19.1–18

King Ahab told his wife Jezebel everything that Elijah had done and how he had put all the prophets of Baal to death. She sent a message to Elijah: ''May the gods strike me dead if by this time tomorrow I don't do the same thing to you that you did to the prophets.'' Elijah was afraid, and fled for his life; he took his servant and went to Beersheba in Judah.

Leaving the servant there, Elijah walked a whole day into the wilderness. He stopped and sat down in the shade of a tree and wished he would die. "It's too much, LORD," he prayed. "Take away my life; I might as well be dead!"

He lay down under the tree and fell asleep. Suddenly an angel touched him and said, "Wake up and eat." He looked round, and saw a loaf of bread and a jar of water near his head. He ate and drank, and lay down again. The LORD's angel returned and woke him up a second time, saying, "Get up and eat, or the journey will be too much for you." Elijah got up, ate and drank, and the food gave him enough strength to walk forty days to Sinai, the holy mountain. There he went into a cave to spend the night.

Suddenly the LORD spoke to him, "Elijah, what are you doing here?"

He answered, "LORD God Almighty, I have always served you—you alone. But the people of Israel have broken their covenant with you, torn down your altars, and killed all your prophets. I am the only one left—and they are trying to kill me!"

"Go out and stand before me on top of the mountain," the LORD said to him. Then the LORD passed by and sent a furious wind that split the hills and shattered the rocks—but the LORD was not in the wind. The wind stopped blowing, and then there was an earthquake—but the LORD was not in the earthquake. After the earthquake, there was a fire—but the LORD was not in the fire. And after the fire, there was the soft whisper of a voice.

When Elijah heard it, he covered his face with his cloak and went out and stood at the entrance of the cave. A voice said to him, "Elijah, what are you doing here?"

He answered, "LORD God Almighty, I have always served you—you alone. But the people of Israel have broken their covenant with you, torn down your altars, and killed all your prophets. I am the only one left—and they are trying to kill me."

The LORD said, "Return to the wilderness near Damascus, then enter the city and anoint Hazael as king of Syria; anoint Jehu son of Nimshi as king of Israel, and anoint Elisha son of Shaphat from Abel Meholah to succeed you as prophet. Anyone who escapes being put to death by Hazael will be killed by Jehu, and anyone who escapes Jehu will be killed by Elisha. Yet I will leave seven thousand people alive in Israel—all those who are loyal to me and have not bowed to Baal or kissed his idol."

A new prophet is called 1 Kings 19.19–21

Elijah left and found Elisha ploughing with a team of oxen; there were eleven teams ahead of him, and he was ploughing with the last one. Elijah took off his cloak and put it on Elisha. Elisha then left his oxen, ran after Elijah, and said, "Let me kiss my father and mother good-bye, and then I will go with you."

Elijah answered, "All right, go back. I'm not stopping you!"

Then Elisha went to his team of oxen, killed them, and cooked the meat, using the yoke as fuel for the fire. He gave the meat to the people, and they ate it. Then he went and followed Elijah as his helper.

Trouble over Naboth's vineyard 1 Kings 21.1–24, 27–29

Like David, Ahab had to learn that kings of Israel were expected to keep the Law. But God was merciful, even to Ahab, when he was truly sorry for what he had done.

Near King Ahab's palace in Jezreel there was a vineyard owned by a man named Naboth. One day Ahab said to Naboth, "Let me have your vineyard; it is close to my palace, and I want to use the land for a vegetable garden. I will give you a better vineyard for it, or, if you prefer, I will pay you a fair price."

"I inherited this vineyard from my ancestors," Naboth replied. "The LORD forbid that I should let you have it!"

Ahab went home, depressed and angry over what Naboth had said to him. He lay down on his bed, facing the wall, and would not eat. His wife Jezebel went to him and asked, "Why are you so depressed? Why won't you eat?"

He answered, "Because of what Naboth said to me. I offered to buy his vineyard, or, if he preferred, to give him another one for it, but he told me that I couldn't have it!"

"Well, are you the king or aren't you?" Jezebel replied. "Get out of bed, cheer up and eat. I will get you Naboth's vineyard!"

Then she wrote some letters, signed them with Ahab's name, sealed them with his seal, and sent them to the officials and leading citizens of Jezreel. The letters said: "Proclaim a day of fasting, call the people together, and give Naboth the place of honour. Get a couple of scoundrels to accuse him to his face of cursing God and the king. Then take him out of the city and stone him to death."

The officials and leading citizens of Jezreel did what Jezebel had commanded. They proclaimed a day of fasting, called the people together, and gave Naboth the place of honour. The two scoundrels publicly accused him of cursing God and the king, and so he was taken outside the city and stoned to death. The message was sent to Jezebel: "Naboth has been put to death."

As soon as Jezebel received the message, she said to Ahab, "Naboth is dead. Now go and take possession of the vineyard which he refused to sell to you." At once Ahab went to the vineyard to take possession of it.

Then the LORD said to Elijah, the prophet from Tishbe, "Go to King Ahab of Samaria. You will find him in Naboth's vineyard, about to take possession of it. Tell him that I, the LORD, say to him, 'After murdering the man, are you taking over his property as well?' Tell him that this is what I say: 'In the very place that the dogs licked up Naboth's blood they will lick up your blood!'"

When Ahab saw Elijah, he said, "Have you caught up with me, my enemy?"

"Yes, I have," Elijah answered. "You have devoted yourself completely to doing what is wrong in the LORD's sight. So the LORD says to you, 'I will bring disaster on you. I will do away with you and get rid of every male in your family, young and old alike. Your family will become like the family of King Jeroboam son of Nebat and like the family of King Baasha son of Ahijah, because you have stirred up my anger by leading Israel into sin.' And concerning Jezebel, the LORD says that dogs will eat her body in the city of Jezreel. Any of your relatives who die in the city will be eaten by dogs, and any who die in the open country will be eaten by vultures"...

When Elijah finished speaking, Ahab tore his clothes, took them off, and put on sackcloth. He refused food, slept in the sackcloth, and went about gloomy and depressed.

The LORD said to the prophet Elijah, "Have you noticed how Ahab has humbled himself before me? Since he has done this, I will not bring disaster on him during his lifetime; it will be during his son's lifetime that I will bring disaster on Ahab's family."

Elijah is taken up to heaven   2 Kings 2.1–13

Elisha asks to "receive the share of your power that will make me your successor". This means that he is asking Elijah to treat him as his eldest son. Elijah was the greatest of the prophets. In New Testament times many Jews believed that one day God would send Elijah back to earth.

The time came for the LORD to take Elijah up to heaven in a whirlwind. Elijah and Elisha set out from Gilgal, and on the way Elijah said to Elisha, "Now stay here; the LORD has ordered me to go to Bethel."

But Elisha answered, "I swear by my loyalty to the living LORD and to you that I will not leave you." So they went on to Bethel.

A group of prophets who lived there went to Elisha and asked him, "Do you know that the LORD is going to take your master away from you today?"

"Yes, I know," Elisha answered. "But let's not talk about it."

Then Elijah said to Elisha, "Now stay here; the LORD has ordered me to go to Jericho."

But Elisha answered, "I swear by my loyalty to the living LORD and to you that I will not leave you." So they went on to Jericho.

A group of prophets who lived there went to Elisha and asked him, "Do you know that the LORD is going to take your master away from you today?"

"Yes, I know," Elisha answered. "But let's not talk about it."

Then Elijah said to Elisha, "Now stay here; the LORD has ordered me to go to the River Jordan."

But Elisha answered, "I swear by my loyalty to the living LORD and to you that I will not leave you." So they went on, and fifty of the prophets followed them to the Jordan. Elijah and Elisha stopped by the river, and the fifty prophets stood a short distance away. Then Elijah took off his cloak, rolled it up, and struck the water with it; the water divided, and he and Elisha crossed to the other side on dry ground. There, Elijah said to Elisha, "Tell me what you want me to do for you before I am taken away."

"Let me receive the share of your power that will make me your successor," Elisha answered.

"That is a difficult request to grant," Elijah replied. "But you will receive it if you see me as I am being taken away from you; if you don't see me, you won't receive it."

They kept talking as they walked on; then suddenly a chariot of fire pulled by horses of fire came between them, and Elijah was taken up to heaven by a whirlwind. Elisha saw it and cried out to Elijah, "My father, my father! Mighty defender of Israel! You are gone!" And he never saw Elijah again.

In grief, Elisha tore his cloak in two. Then he picked up Elijah's cloak that had fallen from him, and went back and stood on the bank of the Jordan.

Naaman is cured   2 Kings 5.1–14

God cared about other people as well as the Israelites. His power showed them that he was the only true God.

Naaman, the commander of the Syrian army, was highly respected and esteemed by the king of Syria, because through Naaman the LORD had given victory to the Syrian forces. He was a great soldier, but he suffered from a dreaded skin-disease. In one of their raids against Israel, the Syrians had carried off a little Israelite girl, who became a servant of Naaman's wife. One day she said to her mistress, "I wish that my master could go to the prophet who lives in Samaria! He would cure him of his disease." When Naaman heard of this, he went to the king and told him what the girl had said. The king said, "Go to the king of Israel and take this letter to him."

So Naaman set out, taking thirty thousand pieces of silver, six thousand pieces of gold, and ten changes of fine clothes. The letter that he took read: "This letter will introduce my officer Naaman. I want you to cure him of his disease."

When the king of Israel read the letter, he tore his clothes in dismay and exclaimed, "How can the king of Syria expect me to cure this man? Does he think that I am God, with the power of life and death? It's plain that he is trying to start a quarrel with me!"

When the prophet Elisha heard what had happened, he sent word to the king: "Why are you so upset? Send the man to me, and I'll show him that there is a prophet in Israel!"

So Naaman went with his horses and chariot, and stopped at the entrance to Elisha's house. Elisha sent a servant out to tell him to go and wash himself seven times in the River Jordan, and he would be completely cured of his disease. But Naaman left in a rage, saying, "I thought that he would at least come out to me, pray to the LORD his God, wave his hand over the diseased spot, and cure me! Besides, aren't the rivers Abana and Pharpar, back in Damascus, better than any river in Israel? I could have washed in them and been cured!"

His servants went up to him and said, "Sir, if the prophet had told you to do something difficult, you would have done it. Now why can't you just wash yourself, as he said, and be cured?" So Naaman went down to the Jordan, dipped himself in it seven times, as Elisha had instructed, and he was completely cured. His flesh became firm and healthy, like that of a child.

The prophets speak out against wrongdoing

The work of prophets like Elijah and Elisha changed the Israelites for a while. But then they went on worshipping idols. When they did worship God they often thought that it was enough just to offer sacrifices. Some prophets spoke out strongly, saying that God wanted his people to live good lives and treat each other fairly. If they did not try to live this way, offering sacrifices was useless, and God was insulted by it.

"Do what is right"   Amos 5.10–15, 21–24

You people hate anyone who challenges injustice and speaks the whole truth in court. You have oppressed the poor and robbed them of their grain. And so you will not live in the fine stone houses you build or drink wine from the beautiful vineyards you plant. I know how terrible your sins are and how many crimes you have committed. You persecute good men, take bribes, and prevent the poor from getting justice in the courts. And so, keeping quiet in such evil times is the clever thing to do!

Make it your aim to do what is right, not what is evil, so that you may live. Then the LORD God Almighty really will be with you, as you claim he is. Hate what is evil, love what is right, and see that justice prevails in the courts. Perhaps the LORD will be merciful to the people of this nation who are still left alive...

The LORD says, "I hate your religious festivals; I cannot stand them! When you bring me burnt-offerings and grain-offerings, I will not accept them; I will not accept the animals you have fattened to bring me as offerings. Stop your noisy songs; I do not want to listen to your harps. Instead, let justice flow like a stream, and righteousness like a river that never goes dry."

The rich and the poor   Amos 8.4–10

The rich treated the poor badly. They were always cheating them and made them become slaves if they could not pay their debts. When rich people were taken to court, they bribed the judges, so that the poor could not get justice. But the prophet Amos said that riches would not help people escape from God's punishment.

Listen to this, you that trample on the needy and try to destroy the poor of the country. You say to yourselves, "We can hardly wait for the holy days to be over so that we can sell our corn. When will the Sabbath end, so that we can start selling again? Then we can overcharge, use false measures, and tamper with the scales to cheat our customers. We can sell worthless wheat at a high price. We'll find a poor man who can't pay his debts, not even the price of a pair of sandals, and we'll buy him as a slave."

The LORD, the God of Israel, has sworn, "I will never forget their evil deeds. And so the earth will quake, and everyone in the land will be in distress. The whole country will be shaken; it will rise and fall like the River Nile. The time is coming when I will make the sun go down at noon and the earth grow dark in daytime. I, the Sovereign LORD, have spoken. I will turn your festivals into funerals and change your glad songs into cries of grief. I will make you shave your heads and wear sackcloth, and you will be like parents mourning for their only son. That day will be bitter to the end."

What God wants   Micah 6.6–8

Micah told the people what God wanted of them. He lived in the southern kingdom (Judah) a little later than Amos. He, too, said how important it was that there should be justice and right living. Calves, sheep, and olive-oil were often offered as sacrifices. In some countries people still killed their first-born child as an offering to the gods.

What shall I bring to the LORD, the God of heaven, when I come to worship him? Shall I bring the best calves to burn as offerings to him? Will the LORD be pleased if I bring him thousands of sheep or endless streams of olive-oil? Shall I offer him my first-born child to pay for my sins? No, the LORD has told us what is good. What he requires of us is this: to do what is just, to show constant love, and to live in humble fellowship with our God.

Obeying God   Psalm 15

The Psalms are songs written by different people at different times during Israel's history. This one echoes the words of the prophets.

LORD, who may enter your Temple?
　　Who may worship on Zion, your sacred hill?

A person who obeys God in everything
　　and always does what is right,
whose words are true and sincere,
　　and who does not slander others.
He does no wrong to his friends
　　nor spreads rumours about his neighbours.

He despises those whom God rejects,
  but honours those who obey the LORD.
He always does what he promises,
  no matter how much it may cost.
He makes loans without charging interest
  and cannot be bribed to testify against the innocent.

Whoever does these things will always be secure.

God's love for his rebellious people   Hosea 11.1–4

Hosea was another prophet who attacked injustice (people being unfair)—but he also spoke of God's constant love.

The LORD says,
"When Israel was a child, I loved him
  and called him out of Egypt as my son.
But the more I called to him,
  the more he turned away from me.
My people sacrificed to Baal;
  they burnt incense to idols.
Yet I was the one who taught Israel to walk.
I took my people up in my arms,
  but they did not acknowledge that I took care of them.
I drew them to me with affection and love.
  I picked them up and held them to my cheek;
  I bent down to them and fed them."

The disobedient prophet

Jonah runs away   Jonah 1.1–6

The words spoken by Amos, Hosea, and Micah (their "prophecies") are recorded in books named after them. The Book of Jonah is rather different, because it is told as a story describing the prophet's adventures. Nineveh was the capital of Assyria, which was Israel's powerful and deadly enemy.

One day, the LORD spoke to Jonah son of Amittai. He said, "Go to Nineveh, that great city, and speak out against it; I am aware how wicked its people are." Jonah, however, set out in the opposite direction in order to get away from the LORD. He went to Joppa, where he found a ship about to go to Spain. He paid his fare and went aboard with the crew to sail to Spain, where he would be away from the LORD. But the LORD sent a strong wind on the sea, and the storm was so violent that the ship was in danger of breaking up. The sailors were terrified and cried out for help, each one to his own god. Then, in order to lessen the danger, they threw the cargo overboard. Meanwhile, Jonah had gone below and was lying in the ship's hold, sound asleep.

The captain found him there and said to him, "What are you doing asleep? Get up and pray to your god for help. Maybe he will feel sorry for us and spare our lives."

"Man overboard!"   Jonah 1.7–17; 2.10

Sailors have always been noted for their superstitions, and these were particularly strong in ancient times. If there was a bad storm they thought that the gods were angry or trying to punish someone.

The Israelites were afraid of the sea and tried to avoid it. Many of their enemies attacked from the sea, so they often pictured their enemies as sea monsters. In Jonah's story, though, the great fish does something very unusual.

The sailors said to one another, "Let's draw lots and find out who is to blame for getting us into this danger." They did so, and Jonah's name was drawn. So they said to him: "Now then, tell us! Who is to blame for this? What are you doing here? What country do you come from? What is your nationality?"

"I am a Hebrew," Jonah answered. "I worship the LORD, the God of heaven, who made land and sea." Jonah went on to tell them that he was running away from the LORD.

The sailors were terrified, and said to him, "That was an awful thing to do!" The storm was getting worse all the time, so the sailors asked him, "What should we do to you to stop the storm?"

Jonah answered, "Throw me into the sea, and it will calm down. I know it is my fault that you are caught in this violent storm."

Instead, the sailors tried to get the ship to shore, rowing with all their might. But the storm was getting worse and worse, and they got nowhere. So they cried out to the LORD, "O LORD, we pray, don't punish us with death for taking this man's life! You, O LORD, are responsible for all this; it is your doing." Then they picked Jonah up and threw him into the sea, and it calmed down at once. This made the sailors so afraid of the LORD that they offered a sacrifice and promised to serve him.

At the LORD's command a large fish swallowed Jonah, and he was inside the fish for three days and nights...

Then the LORD ordered the fish to spew Jonah up on the beach, and it did.

Jonah gets a second chance   Jonah 3.1–10

Once again the LORD spoke to Jonah. He said, "Go to Nineveh, that great city, and proclaim to the people the message I have given you." So Jonah obeyed the LORD and went to Nineveh, a city so large that it took three days to walk through it. Jonah started through the city, and after walking a whole day, he proclaimed, "In forty days Nineveh will be destroyed!"

The people of Nineveh believed God's message. So they decided that everyone should fast, and all the people, from the greatest to the least, put on sackcloth to show that they had repented.

When the king of Nineveh heard about it, he got up from his throne, took off his robe, put on sackcloth, and sat down in ashes. He sent out a proclamation to the people of Nineveh: "This is an order from the king and his officials: No one is to eat anything; all persons, cattle, and sheep are forbidden to eat or drink. All persons and animals must wear sackcloth. Everyone must pray earnestly to God and must give up his wicked behaviour and his evil actions. Perhaps God will change his mind; perhaps he will stop being angry, and we will not die!"

God saw what they did; he saw that they had given up their wicked behaviour. So he changed his mind and did not punish them as he had said he would.

The truth comes out   Jonah 4.1–11

At last we find out why Jonah did not want to go to Nineveh. He knew that God would forgive and protect the people if they turned to him.

The story had a lot to teach the Israelites about God's love for the people of other countries—even those they thought of as enemies.

Jonah was very unhappy about this and became angry. So he prayed, "LORD, didn't I say before I left home that this is just what you would do? That's why I did my best to run away to Spain! I knew that you are a loving and merciful God, always patient, always kind, and always ready to change your mind and not punish. Now, LORD, let me die. I am better off dead than alive."

The LORD answered, "What right have you to be angry?"

Jonah went out east of the city and sat down. He made a shelter for himself and sat in its shade, waiting to see what would happen to

Nineveh. Then the LORD God made a plant grow up over Jonah to give him some shade, so that he would be more comfortable. Jonah was extremely pleased with the plant. But at dawn the next day, at God's command, a worm attacked the plant, and it died. After the sun had risen, God sent a hot east wind, and Jonah was about to faint from the heat of the sun beating down on his head. So he wished he were dead. "I am better off dead than alive," he said.

But God said to him, "What right have you to be angry about the plant?"

Jonah replied, "I have every right to be angry—angry enough to die!"

The LORD said to him, "This plant grew up in one night and disappeared the next; you didn't do anything for it, and you didn't make it grow—yet you feel sorry for it! How much more, then, should I have pity on Nineveh, that great city. After all, it has more than 120,000 innocent children in it, as well as many animals!"

Hope and despair

The people of Nineveh had repented, but in Israel the people did not take any notice of the prophets' warnings. The punishment they had been warned about came. The Assyrians attacked Israel and took the people away to other countries. In their place they brought in foreigners. The Assyrians split people up into small groups, each speaking a different language, so that it would be difficult for anyone to rebel. Only the Israelites in Judah were left in charge of their own land. At first they took warning from what had happened to their neighbours.

God calls another prophet   Isaiah 6.1–8

Because Isaiah was an Israelite he was very conscious that no one was good enough to meet God or survive in his presence. One day when he was in the Temple in Jerusalem he had a vision of the Lord.

In the year that King Uzziah died, I saw the Lord. He was sitting on his throne, high and exalted, and his robe filled the whole Temple. Round him flaming creatures were standing, each of which had six wings. Each creature covered its face with two wings, and its body with two, and used the other two for flying. They were calling out to each other:

"Holy, holy, holy!
The LORD Almighty is holy!
His glory fills the world."

The sound of their voices made the foundation of the Temple shake, and the Temple itself was filled with smoke.

I said, "There is no hope for me! I am doomed because every word that passes my lips is sinful, and I live among a people whose every word is sinful. And yet, with my own eyes, I have seen the King, the LORD Almighty!"

Then one of the creatures flew down to me, carrying a burning coal that he had taken from the altar with a pair of tongs. He touched my lips with the burning coal and said, "This has touched your lips, and now your guilt is gone, and your sins are forgiven."

Then I heard the Lord say, "Whom shall I send? Who will be our messenger?"

I answered, "I will go! Send me!"

The Assyrians threaten Jerusalem
Isaiah 36.1–2, 13–21; 37.5–7, 9–11, 14–20

The Assyrians had already conquered the Israelites in the northern part of the country, and now they threatened to do the same to the south. King Ahaz paid the Assyrians with silver and gold taken from the Temple in order to stop them attacking. The country could not afford to do this, and when Hezekiah became king he stopped the payments. Sennacherib, the new Assyrian Emperor, was angry and led a large army to Jerusalem.

In the fourteenth year that Hezekiah was king of Judah, Sennacherib, the emperor of Assyria, attacked the fortified cities of Judah and captured them. Then he ordered his chief official to go from Lachish to Jerusalem with a large military force to demand that King Hezekiah should surrender...

Then the official stood up and shouted in Hebrew, "Listen to what the emperor of Assyria is telling you. He warns you not to let Hezekiah deceive you. Hezekiah can't save you. And don't let him persuade you to rely on the LORD. Don't think that the LORD will save you and that he will stop our Assyrian army from capturing your city. Don't listen to Hezekiah! The emperor of Assyria commands you to come out of the city and surrender. You will all be allowed to eat grapes from your own vines and figs from your own trees, and to drink water from your own wells— until the emperor resettles you in a country much like your own, where there are vineyards to give wine and there is corn for making bread. Don't let Hezekiah fool you into thinking that the LORD will rescue you. Did the gods of any other nations save their countries from the emperor of Assyria? Where are they now, the gods of Hamath and Arpad? Where are the gods of Sepharvaim? Did anyone save Samaria? When did any of the gods of all these countries ever save their country from our emperor? Then what makes you think the LORD can save Jerusalem?"

The people kept quiet, just as King Hezekiah had told them to; they did not say a word...

When Isaiah received King Hezekiah's message, he sent back this answer: "The LORD tells you not to let the Assyrians frighten you by their claims that he cannot save you. The LORD will cause the emperor to hear a rumour that will make him go back to his own country, and the LORD will have him killed there"...

Word reached the Assyrians that the Egyptian army, led by King Tirhakah of Sudan, was coming to attack them. When the emperor heard this, he sent a letter to King Hezekiah of Judah to say to him, "The god you are trusting in has told you that you will not fall into my hands, but don't let that deceive you. You have heard what an Assyrian emperor does to any country he decides to destroy. Do you think that you can escape?..."

King Hezekiah took the letter from the messengers and read it. Then he went to the Temple, placed the letter there in the presence of the LORD, and prayed, "Almighty LORD, God of Israel, enthroned above the winged creatures, you alone are God, ruling all the kingdoms of the world. You created the earth and the sky. Now, LORD, hear us and look at what is happening to us. Listen to all the things that Sennacherib is saying to insult you, the living God. We all know, LORD, that the emperors of Assyria have destroyed many nations, made their lands desolate, and burnt up their gods—which were no gods at all, only images of wood and stone made by human hands. Now, LORD our God, rescue us from the Assyrians, so that all the nations of the world will know that you alone are God."

Death in the camp   Isaiah 37.21–37

It is difficult to know exactly what the "angel of the LORD" was. The Israelites said this when they saw that God was at work. According to a Greek historian called Herodotus, hordes of mice went into the Assyrian camp and ate the soldiers' bow-strings. Some people think the mice may have been carriers of bubonic plague. Whatever happened, the people of Jerusalem were saved, and they believed that God himself had helped them.

Then Isaiah sent a message telling King Hezekiah that in answer to the king's prayer the LORD had said, "The city of Jerusalem laughs at you,

136

Sennacherib, and despises you. Whom do you think you have been insulting and ridiculing? You have been disrespectful to me, the holy God of Israel. You sent your servants to boast to me that with all your chariots you had conquered the highest mountains of Lebanon. You boasted that there you cut down the tallest cedars and the finest cypress-trees, and that you reached the deepest parts of the forests. You boasted that you dug wells and drank water in foreign lands, and that the feet of your soldiers tramped the River Nile dry.

"Have you never heard that I planned all this long ago? And now I have carried it out. I gave you the power to turn fortified cities into piles of rubble. The people who lived there were powerless; they were frightened and stunned. They were like grass in a field or weeds growing on a roof when the hot east wind blasts them.

"But I know everything about you, what you do and where you go. I know how you rage against me. I have received the report of that rage and that pride of yours, and now I will put a hook through your nose and a bit in your mouth and will take you back by the road on which you came."

Then Isaiah said to King Hezekiah, "This is a sign of what will happen. This year and next you will have only wild grain to eat, but the following year you will be able to sow your corn and harvest it, and plant vines and eat grapes. Those in Judah who survive will flourish like plants that send roots deep into the ground and produce fruit. There will be people in Jerusalem and on Mount Zion who will survive, because the LORD Almighty is determined to make this happen.

"This is what the LORD has said about the Assyrian emperor: 'He will not enter this city or shoot a single arrow against it. No soldiers with shields will come near the city, and no siege-mounds will be built round it. He will go back by the road on which he came, without entering this city. I, the LORD, have spoken. I will defend this city and protect it, for the sake of my own honour and because of the promise I made to my servant David.'"

An angel of the LORD went to the Assyrian camp and killed 185,000 soldiers. At dawn the next day there they lay, all dead! Then the Assyrian emperor Sennacherib withdrew and returned to Nineveh.

A hope for peace   Isaiah 11.1–9

In the middle of troubled times Isaiah looked forward to a time of real peace. Many people now see that Isaiah's reference to the royal line of David was important: King David was one of Jesus' ancestors.

The royal line of David is like a tree that has been cut down; but just as new branches sprout from a stump, so a new king will arise from among David's descendants.

The spirit of the LORD will give him wisdom,
and the knowledge and skill to rule his people.
He will know the LORD's will and have reverence for him,
and find pleasure in obeying him.
He will not judge by appearance or hearsay;
he will judge the poor fairly
and defend the rights of the helpless.
At his command the people will be punished,
and evil persons will die.
He will rule his people with justice and integrity.

Wolves and sheep will live together in peace,
and leopards will lie down with young goats.
Calves and lion cubs will feed together,
and little children will take care of them.
Cows and bears will eat together,
and their calves and cubs will lie down in peace.
Lions will eat straw as cattle do.
Even a baby will not be harmed
if it plays near a poisonous snake.
On Zion, God's sacred hill,
there will be nothing harmful or evil.
The land will be as full of knowledge of the LORD
as the seas are full of water.

A frightening discovery   2 Kings 22.1–13

The people of Jerusalem and Judah soon forgot Hezekiah's example. He had got rid of idol worship, but soon after his death things were almost the same as they had been before he started. In fact they went back to some of the things, like child sacrifice, which had hardly ever taken place since the Israelites took over Canaan. Although Hezekiah's son and grandson encouraged this, he would have been proud of his great grandson, Josiah.

Josiah was eight years old when he became king of Judah, and he ruled in Jerusalem for thirty-one years. His mother was Jedidah, the daughter of Adaiah, from the town of Bozkath. Josiah did what was pleasing to the LORD; he followed the example of his ancestor King David, strictly obeying all the laws of God.

In the eighteenth year of his reign, King Josiah sent the court secretary Shaphan, the son of Azaliah and grandson of Meshullam, to the Temple

138

with the order: "Go to the High Priest Hilkiah and get a report on the amount of money that the priests on duty at the entrance to the Temple have collected from the people. Tell him to give the money to the men who are in charge of the repairs in the Temple. They are to pay the carpenters, the builders, and the masons, and buy the timber and the stones used in the repairs. The men in charge of the work are thoroughly honest, so there is no need to require them to account for the funds."

Shaphan delivered the king's order to Hilkiah, and Hilkiah told him that he had found the book of the Law in the Temple. Hilkiah gave him the book, and Shaphan read it. Then he went back to the king and reported: "Your servants have taken the money that was in the Temple and have handed it over to the men in charge of the repairs." And then he said, "I have here a book that Hilkiah gave me." And he read it aloud to the king.

When the king heard the book being read, he tore his clothes in dismay, and gave the following order to Hilkiah the priest, to Ahikam son of Shaphan, to Achbor son of Micaiah, to Shaphan, the court secretary, and to Asaiah, the king's attendant: "Go and consult the LORD for me and for all the people of Judah about the teachings of this book. The LORD is angry with us because our ancestors have not done what this book says must be done."

What the book said   Deuteronomy 6.1–9, 12–15

This may well be part of what Shaphan would have read, and could have inspired Josiah's actions.

"These are all the laws that the LORD your God commanded me to teach you. Obey them in the land that you are about to enter and occupy. As long as you live, you and your descendants are to honour the LORD your God and obey all his laws that I am giving you, so that you may live in that land a long time. Listen to them, people of Israel, and obey them! Then all will go well with you, and you will become a mighty nation and live in that rich and fertile land, just as the LORD, the God of our ancestors, has promised.

"Israel, remember this! The LORD—and the LORD alone—is our God. Love the LORD your God with all your heart, with all your soul, and with all your strength. Never forget these commands that I am giving you today. Teach them to your children. Repeat them when you are at home and when you are away, when you are resting and when you are working. Tie them on your arms and wear them on your foreheads as a reminder. Write them on the door-posts of your houses and on your gates...

"Make certain that you do not forget the LORD who rescued you from Egypt, where you were slaves. Honour the LORD your God, worship only him, and make your promises in his name alone. Do not worship other gods, any of the gods of the peoples around you. If you do worship other gods, the LORD's anger will come against you like fire and will destroy you completely, because the LORD your God, who is present with you, tolerates no rivals."

Josiah attempts to renew the covenant   2 Kings 23.1–6

King Josiah summoned all the leaders of Judah and Jerusalem, and together they went to the Temple, accompanied by the priests and the prophets and all the rest of the people, rich and poor alike. Before them all, the king read aloud the whole book of the covenant which had been found in the Temple. He stood by the royal column and made a covenant with the LORD to obey him, to keep his laws and commands with all his heart and soul, and to put into practice the demands attached to the covenant, as written in the book. And all the people promised to keep the covenant.

Then Josiah ordered the High Priest Hilkiah, his assistant priests, and the guards on duty at the entrance to the Temple to bring out of the Temple all the objects used in the worship of Baal, of the goddess Asherah, and of the stars. The king burnt all these objects outside the city near the valley of the Kidron, and then had the ashes taken to Bethel. He removed from office the priests that the kings of Judah had ordained to offer sacrifices on the pagan altars in the cities of Judah and in places near Jerusalem—all the priests who offered sacrifices to Baal, to the sun, the moon, the planets, and the stars. He removed from the Temple the symbol of the goddess Asherah, took it out of the city to the valley of the Kidron, burnt it, pounded its ashes to dust, and scattered it over the public burial-ground.

All is still not well

Jeremiah's call to be a prophet   Jeremiah 1.4–10

Although Josiah was serious about renewing the covenant, Jeremiah's writings suggest that not everybody agreed with him. Jeremiah had a hard message to give the people and he did not really want to become a prophet.

The LORD said to me, "I chose you before I gave you life, and before you were born I selected you to be a prophet to the nations."

I answered, "Sovereign LORD, I don't know how to speak; I am too young."

But the LORD said to me, "Do not say that you are too young, but go to the people I send you to, and tell them everything I command you to say. Do not be afraid of them, for I will be with you to protect you. I, the LORD, have spoken!"

Then the LORD stretched out his hand, touched my lips, and said to me, "Listen, I am giving you the words you must speak. Today I give you authority over nations and kingdoms to uproot and to pull down, to destroy and to overthrow, to build and to plant."

A last desperate warning   Jeremiah 7.1–11

Many people believed that they were perfectly safe in Jerusalem. This was the home of the Temple and they were sure that, whatever they did, God would not allow it to fall into enemy hands. Jeremiah knew this was not true.

The LORD sent me to the gate of the Temple where the people of Judah went in to worship. He told me to stand there and announce what the LORD Almighty, the God of Israel, had to say to them: "Change the way you are living and the things you are doing, and I will let you go on living here. Stop believing those deceitful words, 'We are safe! This is the LORD's Temple, this is the LORD's Temple, this is the LORD's Temple!'

"Change the way you are living and stop doing the things you are doing. Be fair in your treatment of one another. Stop taking advantage of aliens, orphans, and widows. Stop killing innocent people in this land. Stop worshipping other gods, for that will destroy you. If you change, I will let you go on living here in the land which I gave your ancestors as a permanent possession.

"Look, you put your trust in deceitful words. You steal, murder, commit adultery, tell lies under oath, offer sacrifices to Baal, and worship gods that you had not known before. You do these things I hate, and then you come and stand in my presence, in my own Temple, and say, 'We are safe!' Do you think that my Temple is a hiding place for robbers?"

God's new covenant   Jeremiah 31.31–34

Jeremiah saw that the people of Israel were going to suffer because they had continually broken the old covenant. But he also foresaw a time when God would make a new covenant.

The LORD says, "The time is coming when I will make a new covenant with the people of Israel and with the people of Judah. It will not be like the old covenant that I made with their ancestors when I took them by the hand and led them out of Egypt. Although I was like a husband to them, they did not keep that covenant. The new covenant that I will make with the people of Israel will be this: I will put my law within them and write it on their hearts. I will be their God, and they will be my people. None of them will have to teach his fellow-countryman to know the LORD, because all will know me, from the least to the greatest. I will forgive their sins and I will no longer remember their wrongs. I, the LORD, have spoken."

Jerusalem is destroyed   Jeremiah 52.3–11

For many years different prophets had said that there would be a disaster unless the Israelites turned back to God. But people took little notice of these warnings. Meanwhile, under their Emperor Nebuchadnezzar the Babylonians became the most powerful nation. After a long siege in the year 587 BC, the Babylonians captured Jerusalem. Many Israelites were taken away to Babylon.

Zedekiah was the last king of Judah.

Zedekiah rebelled against King Nebuchadnezzar of Babylonia, and so Nebuchadnezzar came with all his army and attacked Jerusalem on the tenth day of the tenth month of the ninth year of Zedekiah's reign. They set up camp outside the city, built siege walls round it, and kept it under siege until Zedekiah's eleventh year. On the ninth day of the fourth month of that same year, when the famine was so bad that the people had nothing left to eat, the city walls were broken through. Although the Babylonians were surrounding the city, all the soldiers escaped during the night. They left by way of the royal garden, went through the gateway connecting the two walls, and fled in the direction of the Jordan Valley. But the Babylonian army pursued King Zedekiah, captured him in the plains near Jericho, and all his soldiers deserted him. Zedekiah was taken to King Nebuchadnezzar, who was in the city of Riblah in the territory of Hamath, and there Nebuchadnezzar passed sentence on him. At Riblah he put Zedekiah's sons to death while Zedekiah was looking on and he also had the officials of Judah executed. After that, he had Zedekiah's eyes put out and had him placed in chains and taken to Babylon. Zedekiah remained in prison in Babylon until the day he died.

6

The great promise

Hope in despair

The Babylonians were very civilized people and they were quite generous to their captives. The Israelites who were taken off to Babylon were allowed to build houses there and earn a living. For most of the time they were even allowed to keep their own customs and religion. But there was one important thing they could not do—they were not free to go home. They were exiled in a foreign country. It was not far from where Abraham was born, but it was a long way from the land God had promised to Abraham's descendants. The Temple was the symbol of God's presence, but it lay in ruins hundreds of miles away. Like most exiles they stayed together in a group and formed a community. It was here in exile that they began to think more deeply about some of the things they had ignored in their own country.

Ezekiel sees a vision of God   Ezekiel 1.1, 3–9, 22–28

Before Ezekiel was taken into exile he was training to be a priest at the Temple in Jerusalem. At that time priests could only serve God there in the Temple, so Ezekiel thought that all his hopes of serving God were gone. Then he discovered that God had a special purpose for him in Babylon. He found this out in a very dramatic way.

On the fifth day of the fourth month of the thirtieth year, I, Ezekiel the priest, son of Buzi, was living with the Jewish exiles by the River Chebar in Babylonia. The sky opened, and I saw a vision of God...There in Babylonia beside the River Chebar, I heard the LORD speak to me and I felt his power.

I looked up and saw a storm coming from the north. Lightning was flashing from a huge cloud, and the sky round it was glowing. Where the lightning was flashing, something shone like bronze. At the centre of the storm, I saw what looked like four living creatures in human form, but each of them had four faces and four wings. Their legs were straight, and they had hoofs like those of a bull. They shone like polished bronze. In addition to their four faces and four wings, they each had four human hands, one under each wing. Two wings of each creature were spread out so that the creatures formed a square with their wing tips touching. When they moved, they moved as a group without turning their bodies...

Above the heads of the creatures there was something that looked like a dome made of dazzling crystal. There under the dome stood the creatures, each stretching out two wings towards the ones next to it and covering its body with the other two wings. I heard the noise their wings made in flight; it sounded like the roar of the sea, like the noise of a huge army, like the voice of Almighty God. When they stopped flying, they folded their wings, but there was still a sound coming from above the dome over their heads.

Above the dome there was something that looked like a throne made of sapphire, and sitting on the throne was a figure that looked like a man. The figure seemed to be shining like bronze in the middle of a fire. It shone all over with a bright light that had in it all the colours of the rainbow. This was the dazzling light that shows the presence of the LORD.

God calls Ezekiel to be a prophet Ezekiel 1.28 — 2.5

When I saw this, I fell face downwards on the ground. Then I heard a voice saying, "Mortal man, stand up. I want to talk to you." While the voice was speaking, God's spirit entered me and raised me to my feet, and I heard the voice continue, "Mortal man, I am sending you to the people of Israel. They have rebelled and turned against me and are still rebels, just as their ancestors were. They are stubborn and do not respect me, so I am sending you to tell them what I, the Sovereign LORD, am saying to them. Whether those rebels listen to you or not, they will know that a prophet has been among them."

Sheep in need of a shepherd Ezekiel 34.11–15

So Ezekiel spoke to the people. All his listeners would know about sheep farming. They knew how often wild animals attacked and scattered the flock. It took a brave shepherd to protect his sheep. Ezekiel compared the people with scattered sheep and the rulers of Israel with bad shepherds. But God himself would be the good shepherd.

"I, the Sovereign LORD, tell you that I myself will look for my sheep and take care of them in the same way as a shepherd takes care of his sheep that were scattered and are brought together again. I will bring them back from all the places where they were scattered on that dark, disastrous day. I will take them out of foreign countries, gather them together, and bring them back to their own land. I will lead them back to the mountains and the streams of Israel and will feed them in pleasant pastures. I will let them graze in safety in the mountain meadows and the valleys and in all the green pastures of the land of Israel. I myself will be the shepherd of my sheep, and I will find them a place to rest. I, the Sovereign LORD, have spoken."

The valley of dry bones   Ezekiel 37.1–14

Ezekiel spoke about many visions from God. In this one, being in exile is compared with death. The people had as much chance of going home as dry bones had of coming alive. But God brings hope to even the most hopeless situation.

I felt the powerful presence of the LORD, and his spirit took me and set me down in a valley where the ground was covered with bones. He led me all round the valley, and I could see that there were very many bones and that they were very dry. He said to me, "Mortal man, can these bones come back to life?"

I replied, "Sovereign LORD, only you can answer that!"

He said, "Prophesy to the bones. Tell these dry bones to listen to the word of the LORD. Tell them that I, the Sovereign LORD, am saying to them: I am going to put breath into you and bring you back to life. I will give you sinews and muscles, and cover you with skin. I will put breath into you and bring you back to life. Then you will know that I am the LORD."

So I prophesied as I had been told. While I was speaking, I heard a rattling noise, and the bones began to join together. While I watched, the bones were covered with sinews and muscles, and then with skin. But there was no breath in the bodies.

God said to me, "Mortal man, prophesy to the wind. Tell the wind that the Sovereign LORD commands it to come from every direction, to breathe into these dead bodies, and to bring them back to life."

So I prophesied as I had been told. Breath entered the bodies, and they came to life and stood up. There were enough of them to form an army.

God said to me, "Mortal man, the people of Israel are like these bones. They say that they are dried up, without any hope and with no future. So

prophesy to my people Israel and tell them that I, the Sovereign LORD, am going to open their graves. I am going to take them out and bring them back to the land of Israel. When I open the graves where my people are buried and bring them out, they will know that I am the LORD. I will put my breath in them, bring them back to life, and let them live in their own land. Then they will know that I am the LORD. I have promised that I would do this—and I will. I, the LORD, have spoken."

149

Victory out of suffering

Words of hope   Isaiah 40. 1–8

Here a prophet compares the difficulties of the Israelites returning home to a traveller crossing the wilderness. Again, the power of God brings hope even when things look impossible.

"Comfort my people," says our God. "Comfort them!
Encourage the people of Jerusalem.
Tell them they have suffered long enough
   and their sins are now forgiven.
I have punished them in full for all their sins."

A voice cries out,
"Prepare in the wilderness a road for the LORD!
   Clear the way in the desert for our God!
Fill every valley;
   level every mountain.
The hills will become a plain,
   and the rough country will be made smooth.
Then the glory of the LORD will be revealed,
   and all mankind will see it.
The LORD himself has promised this."

A voice cries out, "Proclaim a message!"
"What message shall I proclaim?" I ask.
"Proclaim that all mankind are like grass;
   they last no longer than wild flowers.
Grass withers and flowers fade,
   when the LORD sends the wind blowing over them.
   People are no more enduring than grass.
Yes, grass withers and flowers fade,
   but the word of our God endures for ever."

God's suffering servant   Isaiah 53.7–12

Many people think that the servant in this passage referred to the people of Israel. The prophet compares the servant to a criminal about to die. But this criminal is God's servant and his suffering will achieve something of great importance. In the New Testament people saw the servant as Jesus.

"He was treated harshly, but endured it humbly;
   he never said a word.
Like a lamb about to be slaughtered,

like a sheep about to be sheared,
    he never said a word.
He was arrested and sentenced and led off to die,
    and no one cared about his fate.
He was put to death for the sins of our people.
He was placed in a grave with evil men,
    he was buried with the rich,
even though he had never committed a crime
    or ever told a lie."

The LORD says,
"It was my will that he should suffer;
    his death was a sacrifice to bring forgiveness.
And so he will see his descendants;
    he will live a long life,
    and through him my purpose will succeed.
After a life of suffering, he will again have joy;
    he will know that he did not suffer in vain.
My devoted servant, with whom I am pleased,
    will bear the punishment of many
    and for his sake I will forgive them.
And so I will give him a place of honour,
    a place among great and powerful men.
He willingly gave his life
    and shared the fate of evil men.
He took the place of many sinners
    and prayed that they might be forgiven."

Daniel's visions   Daniel 7.1, 9–10, 13–14

Daniel was a young Israelite who had been taken into exile shortly before Ezekiel. He was a very clever young man and had an important job, working for the Babylonian government. Like Ezekiel, he had a number of visions. These are recorded in the book named after him.

Much later, the first Christians believed that the reference to the one who "looked like a human being" was a prophecy about Jesus. The Book of Daniel was particularly encouraging to the Jewish people when they were treated badly by foreigners.

In the first year that Belshazzar was king of Babylonia, I had a dream and saw a vision in the night. I wrote the dream down, and this is the record of what I saw that night...

While I was looking, thrones were put in place. One who had been living for ever sat down on one of the thrones. His clothes were white as snow, and his hair was like pure wool. His throne, mounted on fiery wheels, was blazing with fire, and a stream of fire was pouring out from it. There were many thousands of people there to serve him, and millions of people stood before him. The court began its session, and the books were opened...

During this vision in the night, I saw what looked like a human being. He was approaching me, surrounded by clouds, and he went to the one who had been living for ever and was presented to him. He was given authority, honour, and royal power, so that the people of all nations, races, and languages would serve him. His authority would last for ever, and his kingdom would never end.

The fiery furnace   Daniel 3.1–2, 5–6, 8, 12, 19–25

Furnaces are used to purify metals. The things that are not wanted are burnt out, but pure metal is left behind, unharmed.

This story helped people to believe that those who were faithful to God had nothing to fear.

King Nebuchadnezzar had a gold statue made, twenty-seven metres high and nearly three metres wide, and he had it set up in the plain of Dura in the province of Babylon. Then the king gave orders for all his officials to come together—the princes, governors, lieutenant-governors, commissioners, treasurers, judges, magistrates, and all the other officials of the provinces...

"As soon as the music starts, you are to bow down and worship the gold statue that King Nebuchadnezzar has set up. Anyone who does not bow down and worship will immediately be thrown into a blazing furnace"...

It was then that some Babylonians took the opportunity to denounce the Jews...

"There are some Jews whom you put in charge of the province of Babylon—Shadrach, Meshack and Abednego—who are disobeying Your Majesty's orders. They do not worship your god or bow down to the statue you set up"...

Then Nebuchadnezzar lost his temper, and his face turned red with anger at Shadrach, Meshach, and Abednego. So he ordered his men to heat the furnace seven times hotter than usual. And he commanded the strongest men in his army to tie the three men up and throw them into the blazing furnace. So they tied them up, fully dressed—shirts, robes, caps, and all—and threw them into the blazing furnace. Now because the king had given strict orders for the furnace to be made extremely hot, the flames burnt up the guards who took the men to the furnace. Then

Shadrach, Meshach, and Abednego, still tied up, fell into the heart of the blazing fire.

Suddenly Nebuchadnezzar leapt to his feet in amazement. He asked his officials, "Didn't we tie up three men and throw them into the blazing furnace?"

They answered, "Yes, we did, Your Majesty."

"Then why do I see four men walking about in the fire?" he asked. "They are not tied up, and they show no sign of being hurt—and the fourth one looks like an angel."

The writing on the wall   Daniel 5.1–12

Later on, Nebuchadnezzar suffered from a mental illness which made him behave like an animal. His son, Belshazzar, became the next king.

One night King Belshazzar invited a thousand noblemen to a great banquet, and they drank wine together. While they were drinking, Belshazzar gave orders to bring in the gold and silver cups and bowls which his father Nebuchadnezzar had carried off from the Temple in Jerusalem. The king sent for them so that he, his noblemen, his wives, and his concubines could drink out of them. At once the gold cups and bowls were brought in, and they all drank wine out of them and praised gods made of gold, silver, bronze, iron, wood, and stone.

Suddenly a human hand appeared and began writing on the plaster wall of the palace, where the light from the lamps was shining most brightly. And the king saw the hand as it was writing. He turned pale and was so frightened that his knees began to shake. He shouted for someone to bring in the magicians, wizards, and astrologers. When they came in, the king said to them, "Anyone who can read this writing and tell me what it means will be dressed in robes of royal purple, wear a gold chain of honour round his neck, and be the third in power in the kingdom." The royal advisers came forward, but none of them could read the writing or tell the king what it meant. In his distress King Belshazzar grew even paler, and his noblemen had no idea what to do.

The queen mother heard the noise made by the king and his noblemen and entered the banqueting-hall. She said, "May Your Majesty live for ever! Please do not be so disturbed and look so pale. There is a man in your kingdom who has the spirit of the holy gods in him. When your father was king, this man showed good sense, knowledge, and wisdom like the wisdom of the gods. And King Nebuchadnezzar, your father, made him chief of the fortune-tellers, magicians, wizards, and astrologers. He has unusual ability and is wise and skilful in interpreting dreams, solving riddles, and explaining mysteries; so send for this man Daniel, whom the king named Belteshazzar, and he will tell you what all this means."

Daniel explains the writing   Daniel 5.13–31

Daniel was brought at once into the king's presence, and the king said to him, "Are you Daniel, that Jewish exile whom my father the king brought here from Judah? I have heard that the spirit of the holy gods is in you and that you are skilful and have knowledge and wisdom. The advisers and magicians were brought in to read this writing and tell me what it means, but they could not discover the meaning. Now I have heard that you can find hidden meanings and explain mysteries. If you can read this writing and tell me what it means, you will be dressed in robes of royal purple, wear a gold chain of honour round your neck, and be the third in power in the kingdom."

Daniel replied, "Keep your gifts for yourself or give them to someone else. I will read for Your Majesty what has been written and tell you what it means.

"The Supreme God made your father Nebuchadnezzar a great king and gave him dignity and majesty. He was so great that people of all nations, races, and languages were afraid of him and trembled. If he wanted to kill someone, he did; if he wanted to keep someone alive, he did. He honoured or disgraced anyone he wanted to. But because he became proud, stubborn, and cruel, he was removed from his royal throne and lost his place of honour. He was driven away from human society, and his mind became like that of an animal. He lived with wild donkeys, ate grass like an ox, and slept in the open air with nothing to protect him from the dew. Finally he admitted that the Supreme God controls all human kingdoms and can give them to anyone he chooses.

"But you, his son, have not humbled yourself, even though you knew all this. You acted against the Lord of heaven and brought in the cups and bowls taken from his Temple. You, your noblemen, your wives, and your concubines drank wine out of them and praised gods made of gold, silver, bronze, iron, wood, and stone—gods that cannot see or hear and that do not know anything. But you did not honour the God who determines whether you live or die and who controls everything you do. That is why God has sent the hand to write these words.

"This is what was written: 'Number, number, weight, divisions.' And this is what it means: *number*, God has numbered the days of your kingdom and brought it to an end; *weight*, you have been weighed on the scales and found to be too light; *divisions*, your kingdom is divided up and given to the Medes and Persians."

Immediately Belshazzar ordered his servants to dress Daniel in a robe of royal purple and to hang a gold chain of honour round his neck. And he made him the third in power in the kingdom. That same night Belshazzar, the king of Babylonia, was killed; and Darius the Mede, who was then sixty-two years old, seized the royal power.

Daniel in the pit of lions   Daniel 6.1–22

Darius decided to appoint a hundred and twenty governors to hold office throughout his empire. In addition, he chose Daniel and two others to supervise the governors and to look after the king's interests. Daniel soon showed that he could do better work than the other supervisors or the governors. Because he was so outstanding, the king considered putting him in charge of the whole empire. Then the other supervisors and the governors tried to find something wrong with the way Daniel administered the empire, but they couldn't, because Daniel was reliable and did not do anything wrong or dishonest. They said to one another, "We are not going to find anything of which to accuse Daniel unless it is something in connection with his religion."

So they went to see the king and said, "King Darius, may Your Majesty live for ever! All of us who administer your empire—the supervisors, the governors, the lieutenant-governors, and the other officials—have agreed that Your Majesty should issue an order and enforce it strictly. Give orders that for thirty days no one be permitted to request anything from any god or from any man except from Your Majesty. Anyone who violates this order is to be thrown into a pit filled with lions. So let Your Majesty issue this order and sign it, and it will be in force, a law of the Medes and Persians, which cannot be changed." And so King Darius signed the order. When Daniel learnt that the order had been signed, he went home. In an upstairs room of his house there were windows that faced towards Jerusalem. There, just as he had always done, he knelt down at the open windows and prayed to God three times a day.

When Daniel's enemies observed him praying to God, all of them went together to the king to accuse Daniel. They said, "Your Majesty, you signed an order that for the next thirty days anyone who requested anything from any god or from any man except you, would be thrown into a pit filled with lions."

The king replied, "Yes, a strict order, a law of the Medes and Persians, which cannot be changed."

Then they said to the king, "Daniel, one of the exiles from Judah, does not respect Your Majesty or obey the order you issued. He prays regularly three times a day."

When the king heard this, he was upset and did his best to find some way

to rescue Daniel. He kept trying until sunset. Then the men came back to the king and said to him, "Your Majesty knows that according to the laws of the Medes and Persians no order which the king issues can be changed."

So the king gave orders for Daniel to be arrested and he was thrown into the pit filled with lions. He said to Daniel, "May your God, whom you serve so loyally, rescue you." A stone was put over the mouth of the pit, and the king placed his own royal seal and the seal of his noblemen on the stone, so that no one could rescue Daniel. Then the king returned to the palace and spent a sleepless night, without food or any form of entertainment.

At dawn the king got up and hurried to the pit. When he got there, he called out anxiously, "Daniel, servant of the living God! Was the God you serve so loyally able to save you from the lions?"

Daniel answered, "May Your Majesty live for ever! God sent his angel to shut the mouths of the lions so that they would not hurt me. He did this because he knew that I was innocent and because I have not wronged you, Your Majesty."

Freedom out of exile

Almost at the same time the Persians were secretly making their way into the city of Babylon. This turned out to be the best news the Israelite exiles had heard for years. The new Persian king was happy for the exiles to go home and rebuild the Temple.

Incredible news   Ezra 1.1–4

The prophets had often spoken of God using powerful nations to fulfil his purposes.

In the first year that Cyrus of Persia was emperor, the LORD made what he had said through the prophet Jeremiah come true. He prompted Cyrus to issue the following command and send it out in writing to be read aloud everywhere in his empire:

"This is the command of Cyrus, Emperor of Persia. The LORD, the God of Heaven, has made me ruler over the whole world and has given me the responsibility of building a temple for him in Jerusalem in Judah. May God be with all of you who are his people. You are to go to Jerusalem and rebuild the Temple of the LORD, the God of Israel, the God who is worshipped in Jerusalem. If any of his people in exile need help to return, their neighbours are to give them this help. They are to provide them with silver and gold, supplies and pack animals, as well as offerings to present in the Temple of God in Jerusalem."

A dream come true   Psalm 126.1–3

So the Israelites went home to Jerusalem.

When the LORD brought us back to Jerusalem,
    it was like a dream!
How we laughed, how we sang for joy!
    Then the other nations said about us,
    "The LORD did great things for them."
Indeed he did great things for us;
    how happy we were!

The flame burns again on the altar   Ezra 3.1–7

By the seventh month the people of Israel were all settled in their towns. Then they all assembled in Jerusalem, and Joshua son of Jehozadak, his fellow-priests, and Zerubbabel son of Shealtiel, together with his relatives, rebuilt the altar of the God of Israel, so that they could burn sacrifices on it according to the instructions written in the Law of Moses, the man of God. Even though the returning exiles were afraid of the people who were living in the land, they rebuilt the altar where it had stood before. Then they began once again to burn on it the regular morning and evening sacrifices. They celebrated the Festival of Shelters according to the regulations; each day they offered the sacrifices required for that day; and in addition they offered the regular sacrifices to be burnt whole and those to be offered at the New Moon Festival and at all the other regular assemblies at which the LORD is worshipped, as well as all the offerings that were given to the LORD voluntarily. Although the people had not yet started to rebuild the Temple, they began on the first day of the seventh month to burn sacrifices to the LORD.

The people gave money to pay the stonemasons and the carpenters and gave food, drink, and olive-oil to be sent to the cities of Tyre and Sidon in exchange for cedar-trees from Lebanon, which were to be brought by sea to Joppa. All this was done with the permission of Cyrus, emperor of Persia.

Opposition   Ezra 4.4–5

When the Assyrians had invaded the northern part of Israel they had taken foreigners, who worshipped other gods, to live there. When

Jerusalem was conquered these people and their descendants spread southwards. They did not wish to see the Temple rebuilt.

Then the people who had been living in the land tried to discourage and frighten the Jews and keep them from building. They also bribed Persian government officials to work against them. They kept on doing this throughout the reign of Cyrus and into the reign of Darius.

Rebuild the Temple!   Haggai 1.2–9

The people had settled in Jerusalem but were finding it hard to live. They had not yet started to rebuild the Temple.

The LORD Almighty said to Haggai, "These people say that this is not the right time to rebuild the Temple." The LORD then gave this message to the people through the prophet Haggai: "My people, why should you be living in well-built houses while my Temple lies in ruins? Don't you see what is happening to you? You have sown much corn, but have harvested very little. You have food to eat, but not enough to make you full. You have wine to drink, but not enough to get drunk on! You have clothing, but not enough to keep you warm. And the working man cannot earn enough to live on. Can't you see why this has happened? Now go up into the hills, get timber, and rebuild the Temple; then I will be pleased and will be worshipped as I should be.

"You hoped for large harvests, but they turned out to be small. And when you brought the harvest home, I blew it away. Why did I do that? Because my Temple lies in ruins while every one of you is busy working on his own house."

Nehemiah goes to Jerusalem   Nehemiah 2.1–8

Artaxerxes ruled the empire after Darius. Nehemiah asked if he could return to Jerusalem to rebuild the Temple.

One day four months later, when Emperor Artaxerxes was dining, I took the wine to him. He had never seen me look sad before, so he asked, "Why are you looking so sad? You aren't ill, so it must be that you're unhappy."

I was startled and answered, "May Your Majesty live for ever! How can I help looking sad when the city where my ancestors are buried is in ruins and its gates have been destroyed by fire?"

The emperor asked, "What is it that you want?"

I prayed to the God of Heaven, and then I said to the emperor, "If Your

Majesty is pleased with me and is willing to grant my request, let me go to the land of Judah, to the city where my ancestors are buried, so that I can rebuild the city."

The emperor, with the empress sitting at his side, approved my request. He asked me how long I would be gone and when I would return, and I told him.

Then I asked him to grant me the favour of giving me letters to the governors of West Euphrates Province, instructing them to let me travel to Judah. I asked also for a letter to Asaph, keeper of the royal forests, instructing him to supply me with timber for the gates of the fort that guards the Temple, for the city walls, and for the house I was to live in. The emperor gave me all I asked for, because God was with me.

A night ride through the ruins   Nehemiah 2.11–20

I went on to Jerusalem, and for three days I did not tell anyone what God had inspired me to do for Jerusalem. Then in the middle of the night I got up and went out, taking a few of my companions with me. The only animal we took was the donkey that I rode on. It was still night as I left the city through the Valley Gate on the west and went south past Dragon's Fountain to the Rubbish Gate. As I went, I inspected the broken walls of the city and the gates that had been destroyed by fire. Then on the east side of the city I went north to the Fountain Gate and the King's Pool. The donkey I was riding could not find any path through the rubble, so I went down into the valley of the Kidron and rode along, looking at the wall. Then I returned the way I had come and went back into the city through the Valley Gate.

None of the local officials knew where I had been or what I had been doing. So far I had not said anything to any of my fellow-Jews—the priests, the leaders, the officials, or anyone else who would be taking part in the work. But now I said to them, "See what trouble we are in because Jerusalem is in ruins and its gates are destroyed! Let's rebuild the city walls and put an end to our disgrace." And I told them how God had been with me and helped me, and what the emperor had said to me.

They responded, "Let's start rebuilding!" And they got ready to start the work.

When Sanballat, Tobiah, and an Arab named Geshem heard what we were planning to do, they laughed at us and said, "What do you think you're doing? Are you going to rebel against the emperor?"

I answered, "The God of Heaven will give us success. We are his servants, and we are going to start building. But you have no right to any property in Jerusalem, and you have no share in its traditions."

A sword in one hand and a trowel in the other
Nehemiah 4.1–23

When Sanballat heard that we Jews had begun rebuilding the wall, he was furious and began to ridicule us. In front of his companions and the Samaritan troops he said, "What do these miserable Jews think they're doing? Do they intend to rebuild the city? Do they think that by offering sacrifices they can finish the work in one day? Can they make building stones out of heaps of burnt rubble?"

Tobiah was standing there beside him, and he added, "What kind of wall could they ever build? Even a fox could knock it down!"

I prayed, "Listen to them mocking us, O God! Let their ridicule fall on their own heads. Let them be robbed of everything they have, and let them be taken as prisoners to a foreign land. Don't forgive the evil they do and don't forget their sins, for they have insulted us who are building."

So we went on rebuilding the wall, and soon it was half its full height, because the people were eager to work.

Sanballat, Tobiah, and the people of Arabia, Ammon, and Ashdod heard that we were making progress in rebuilding the wall of Jerusalem and that the gaps in the wall were being closed, and they were very angry. So they all plotted together to come and attack Jerusalem and create confusion, but we prayed to our God and kept men on guard against them day and night.

The people of Judah had a song they sang:
   "We grow weak carrying burdens;
   There's so much rubble to take away.
   How can we build the wall today?"

Our enemies thought we would not see them or know what was happening until they were already upon us, killing us and putting an end to our work. But time after time Jews who were living among our enemies came to warn us of the plans our enemies were making against us. So I armed the people with swords, spears, and bows, and stationed them by clans behind the wall, wherever it was still unfinished.

I saw that the people were worried, so I said to them and to their leaders and officials, "Don't be afraid of our enemies. Remember how great and terrifying the Lord is, and fight for your fellow-countrymen, your children, your wives, and your homes." Our enemies heard that we had found out what they were plotting, and they realized that God had defeated their plans. Then all of us went back to rebuilding the wall.

From then on half my men worked and half stood guard, wearing coats of armour and armed with spears, shields, and bows. And our leaders gave

their full support to the people who were rebuilding the wall. Even those who carried building materials worked with one hand and kept a weapon in the other, and everyone who was building kept a sword strapped to his waist. The man who was to sound the alarm on the bugle stayed with me. I told the people and their officials and leaders, "The work is spread out over such a distance that we are widely separated from one another on the wall. If you hear the bugle, gather round me. Our God will fight for us." So every day, from dawn until the stars came out at night, half of us worked on the wall, while the other half stood guard with spears.

During this time I told the men in charge that they and all their helpers had to stay in Jerusalem at night, so that we could guard the city at night as well as work in the daytime. I didn't take off my clothes even at night, neither did any of my companions nor my servants nor my bodyguard. And we all kept our weapons to hand.

Plots against Nehemiah   Nehemiah 6.1–14

Sanballat, Tobiah, Geshem, and the rest of our enemies heard that we had finished building the wall and that there were no gaps left in it, although we still had not set up the gates in the gateways. So Sanballat and Geshem sent me a message, suggesting that I meet with them in one of the villages in the Plain of Ono. This was a trick of theirs to try to harm me. I sent messengers to say to them, "I am doing important work and can't go down there. I am not going to let the work stop just to go and see you."

They sent me the same message four times, and each time I sent them the same reply.

Then Sanballat sent one of his servants to me with a fifth message, this one in the form of an unsealed letter. It read:

"Geshem tells me that a rumour is going round among the neighbouring peoples that you and the Jewish people intend to revolt and that this is why you are rebuilding the wall. He also says you plan to make yourself king and that you have arranged for some prophets to proclaim in Jerusalem that you are the king of Judah. His Majesty is certain to hear about this, so I suggest that you and I meet to talk the situation over."

I sent a reply to him: "Nothing of what you are saying is true. You have made it all up yourself."

They were trying to frighten us into stopping work. I prayed, "But now, God, make me strong!"

About this time I went to visit Shemaiah, the son of Delaiah and grandson of Mehetabel, who was unable to leave his house. He said to me, "You and I must go and hide together in the Holy Place of the Temple and lock the doors, because they are coming to kill you. Any night now they will come to kill you."

I answered, "I'm not the kind of man that runs and hides. Do you think I would try to save my life by hiding in the Temple? I won't do it."

When I thought it over, I realized that God had not spoken to Shemaiah, but that Tobiah and Sanballat had bribed him to give me this warning. They hired him to frighten me into sinning, so that they could ruin my reputation and humiliate me.

I prayed, "God, remember what Tobiah and Sanballat have done and punish them. Remember that woman Nodiah and all the other prophets who tried to frighten me."

The wall is finished!   Nehemiah 6.15–16

After fifty-two days of work the entire wall was finished on the twenty-fifth day of the month of Elul. When our enemies in the surrounding nations heard this, they realized that they had lost face, since everyone knew that the work had been done with God's help.

The covenant is renewed
Nehemiah 8.1–3, 5–8; 9.1, 38; 10.28–29

By the seventh month the people of Israel were all settled in their towns. On the first day of that month they all assembled in Jerusalem, in the square just inside the Water Gate. They asked Ezra, the priest and scholar of the Law which the LORD had given Israel through Moses, to get the book of the Law. So Ezra brought it to the place where the people had gathered—men, women, and the children who were old enough to understand. There in the square by the gate he read the Law to them from dawn until noon, and they all listened attentively...

As Ezra stood there on the platform high above the people, they all kept their eyes fixed on him. As soon as he opened the book, they all stood up. Ezra said, "Praise the LORD, the great God!"

All the people raised their arms in the air and answered, "Amen! Amen!" They knelt in worship, with their faces to the ground.

Then they rose and stood in their places, and the Levites explained the Law to them. They gave an oral translation of God's Law and explained it so that the people could understand it.

On the twenty-fourth day of the same month the people of Israel assembled to fast in order to show sorrow for their sins...

Because of all that has happened, we, the people of Israel, hereby make a solemn written agreement, and our leaders, our Levites, and our priests put their seals to it...

We, the people of Israel, the priests, the Levites, the temple guards, the temple musicians, the temple workmen, and all others who in obedience to God's Law have separated themselves from the foreigners living in our land, we, together with our wives and all our children old enough to understand, do hereby join with our leaders in an oath, under penalty of a curse if we break it, that we will live according to God's Law, which God gave through his servant Moses; that we will obey all that the LORD, our Lord, commands us; and that we will keep all his laws and requirements.

The New Testament

Introduction to New Testament

For hundreds of years the Jews had been ruled by one foreign power after the other. This was because the main roads joining Europe, Asia, and Africa all passed through Palestine (where the Jews lived) making it an important piece of land to control.

At one stage the Jews rebelled and achieved a surprise victory against the Greeks and Syrians, who were forced to leave the country. But freedom did not last long before the Romans arrived. Rome was in control of the North and much of its food came from Egypt in the South. They were determined to keep control of Palestine and did so with great skill. Sometimes, in order to keep control, they were very brutal.

No nation likes to be ruled by foreigners but it was particularly bad for the Jews. They remembered God's promise to Abraham about giving his descendants a land and this made the land itself special to them. They did not like foreign interference, especially in their religious practices. They believed there was only one God, but the Greeks and Syrians had tried to force them to worship foreign gods. The Romans treated their emperor as a god and expected the Jews to make sacrifices to him. The Jews were always reminded of this when they saw the emperor's head on the coins they used and his standard (or emblem) displayed in their towns.

The Jewish prophets had forecast times of suffering and hardship but many had also said that God would one day visit his people in a special way. Some thought this would happen by a miracle and others thought that it would happen through the events of history. A number of prophets had spoken of God working through a descendant of King David. Over the centuries the Jews had come to believe that God would send a "Messiah". The word means "God's chosen one" or "anointed one", and the Jews expected the Messiah to rescue their nation and show the power of the God of Israel to the world.

The Jewish people expected a period of suffering to prepare them for the Messiah's coming. They had suffered a great deal in recent years. So everything seemed ready for the Messiah to come. But the Jews had many different ideas of what he would be like and what he would do. The writers of the stories that follow show that many of the ideas the Jews had were wrong. When he came, the Messiah was not what most people expected.

I

When Jesus
was young

The prophet is born

The Israelites (the people of the Jewish nation) thought that God would send a special prophet to introduce the Messiah. Many thought that the prophet Elijah would be sent back to earth for this purpose.

One day a priest called Zechariah was doing his work at the Temple in Jerusalem. As he was burning incense at the altar he had a vision in which he was told that he and his wife would have a son. He would be a prophet "like Elijah". But Zechariah and his wife Elizabeth thought they were too old to have children, so Zechariah did not believe the message. Zechariah asked for a sign to prove that the message was true. The angel said that as a sign Zechariah would be unable to speak until the day that God's promise to Zechariah came true.

His name is to be John   Luke 1.57–66

It was the custom to name children after well-respected members of the family. Zechariah had been told in his vision that his son should be called John. For the Jews a person's name was important, because it told you a lot about them. "John" means "God is loving"

The time came for Elizabeth to have her baby, and she gave birth to a son. Her neighbours and relatives heard how wonderfully good the Lord had been to her, and they all rejoiced with her.

When the baby was a week old, they came to circumcise him, and they were going to name him Zechariah, after his father. But his mother said, "No! His name is to be John."

They said to her, "But you have no relatives with that name!" Then they made signs to his father, asking him what name he would like the boy to have.

Zechariah asked for a writing tablet and wrote, "His name is John." How surprised they all were! At that moment Zechariah was able to speak again, and he started praising God. The neighbours were all filled with fear, and the news about these things spread through all the hill-country of Judaea. Everyone who heard of it thought about it and asked, "What is this child going to be?" For it was plain that the Lord's power was upon him.

Zechariah's prophecy   Luke 1.67–80

What Zechariah had to say about his son must have surprised everyone.

John's father Zechariah was filled with the Holy Spirit, and he spoke God's message:

"Let us praise the Lord, the God of Israel!
    He has come to the help of his people and has set them free.
He has provided for us a mighty Saviour,
    a descendant of his servant David.
He promised through his holy prophets long ago
    that he would save us from our enemies,
    from the power of all those who hate us.
He said he would show mercy to our ancestors
    and remember his sacred covenant.
With a solemn oath to our ancestor Abraham
    he promised to rescue us from our enemies
    and allow us to serve him without fear,
so that we might be holy and righteous before him
    all the days of our life.

"You, my child, will be called a prophet of the Most High God.
You will go ahead of the Lord
    to prepare his road for him,
to tell his people that they will be saved
    by having their sins forgiven.
Our God is merciful and tender.
He will cause the bright dawn of salvation to rise on us
    and to shine from heaven on all those who live in the dark shadow of
        death,
    to guide our steps into the path of peace."

The child grew and developed in body and spirit. He lived in the desert until the day when he appeared publicly to the people of Israel.

The first Christmas

Mary receives amazing news   Luke 1.26–38

God speaks to people in many different ways. The early history of Israel shows God speaking to his people mainly through the prophets. But there had been no prophets or messages from God for many years. Now, he chose to speak through a special messenger (the word "angel" simply means "a messenger").

In the sixth month of Elizabeth's pregnancy God sent the angel Gabriel to a town in Galilee named Nazareth. He had a message for a girl promised in marriage to a man named Joseph, who was a descendant of King David. The girl's name was Mary. The angel came to her and said, "Peace be with you! The Lord is with you and has greatly blessed you!"

Mary was deeply troubled by the angel's message, and she wondered what his words meant. The angel said to her, "Don't be afraid, Mary; God has been gracious to you. You will become pregnant and give birth to a son, and you will name him Jesus. He will be great and will be called the Son of the Most High God. The Lord God will make him a king, as his ancestor David was, and he will be the king of the descendants of Jacob for ever; his kingdom will never end!"

Mary said to the angel, "I am a virgin. How, then, can this be?"

The angel answered, "The Holy Spirit will come on you, and God's power will rest upon you. For this reason the holy child will be called the Son of God. Remember your relative Elizabeth. It is said that she cannot have children, but she herself is now six months pregnant, even though she is very old. For there is nothing that God cannot do."

"I am the Lord's servant," said Mary; "may it happen to me as you have said." And the angel left her.

Mary visits Elizabeth   Luke 1.39–45

Nazareth, where Mary and Joseph lived, was in the northern part of Palestine. Elizabeth and Zechariah lived in Judaea, which was an area in the south. Mary decided to go and visit Elizabeth.

Soon afterwards Mary got ready and hurried off to a town in the hill-country of Judaea. She went into Zechariah's house and greeted Elizabeth. When Elizabeth heard Mary's greeting, the baby moved within her. Elizabeth was filled with the Holy Spirit and said in a loud voice, "You are the most blessed of all women, and blessed is the child you will bear! Why should this great thing happen to me, that my Lord's

mother comes to visit me? For as soon as I heard your greeting, the baby within me jumped with gladness. How happy you are to believe that the Lord's message to you will come true!''

Mary's song of praise   Luke 1.46 – 56

Mary's words of praise have been set to music in many different ways and are often sung in churches today. These songs are often called the "Magnificat" which is the first word of the Latin translation of Mary's song.

Mary said,

"My heart praises the Lord;
　my soul is glad because of God my Saviour,
　for he has remembered me, his lowly servant!
From now on all people will call me happy,
　because of the great things the Mighty God has done for me.
His name is holy;
　from one generation to another
　he shows mercy to those who honour him.
He has stretched out his mighty arm
　and scattered the proud with all their plans.
He has brought down mighty kings from their thrones,
　and lifted up the lowly.
He has filled the hungry with good things,
　and sent the rich away with empty hands.
He has kept the promise he made to our ancestors,
　and has come to the help of his servant Israel.
He has remembered to show mercy to Abraham
　and to all his descendants for ever!''

Mary stayed about three months with Elizabeth and then went back home.

Jesus is born   Luke 2.1–7

The Romans wanted to make sure that people did not avoid paying their taxes. Because it was easy to move from place to place, everyone had to return to where their family had come from when the Romans wanted to hold a census—that is, to count the number of people that were living in the land. In Joseph's case this was Bethlehem, which was famous as the birthplace of King David. Since the Jews believed that the Messiah would be a descendant of King David's, Luke (who wrote this account) takes the trouble to show that Jesus came from David's family.

At that time the Emperor Augustus ordered a census to be taken throughout the Roman Empire. When this first census took place, Quirinius was the governor of Syria. Everyone, then, went to register himself, each to his own town.

Joseph went from the town of Nazareth in Galilee to the town of Bethlehem in Judaea, the birthplace of King David. Joseph went there because he was a descendant of David. He went to register with Mary, who was promised in marriage to him. She was pregnant, and while they were in Bethlehem, the time came for her to have her baby. She gave birth to her first son, wrapped him in strips of cloth and laid him in a manger—there was no room for them to stay in the inn.

The news is given to the shepherds   Luke 2.8–20

There were some shepherds in that part of the country who were spending the night in the fields, taking care of their flocks. An angel of the Lord appeared to them, and the glory of the Lord shone over them. They were terribly afraid, but the angel said to them, "Don't be afraid! I am here with good news for you, which will bring great joy to all the people. This very day in David's town your Saviour was born—Christ the Lord! And this is what will prove it to you: you will find a baby wrapped in strips of cloth and lying in a manger."

Suddenly a great army of heaven's angels appeared with the angel, singing praises to God:
   "Glory to God in the highest heaven,
      and peace on earth to those with whom he is pleased!"

When the angels went away from them back into heaven, the shepherds said to one another, "Let's go to Bethlehem and see this thing that has happened, which the Lord has told us."

So they hurried off and found Mary and Joseph and saw the baby lying in the manger. When the shepherds saw him, they told them what the angel had said about the child. All who heard it were amazed at what the shepherds said. Mary remembered all these things and thought deeply about them. The shepherds went back, singing praises to God for all they had heard and seen; it had been just as the angel had told them.

Gold, frankincense, and myrrh

Today we are much more aware of the importance of gold than of the other two gifts.

Frankincense was burnt by the priests in the Temple, just as in some churches today incense is still burnt as part of the worship. Myrrh was a kind of spice used in cosmetics. It was also used to preserve bodies. Some people think that there may be special significance in the fact that Jesus was offered things associated with royalty, worshipping God, and death.

Visitors from the East   Matthew 2.1–12

Herod was what we call a "puppet king". He was put in power by the Romans and allowed to rule as long as he kept law and order, encouraged the Jews to pay their taxes, and obeyed all commands from Rome. What Herod feared most was someone else taking power and stirring up trouble. If this happened Herod would lose the trust of the Romans and his kingdom.

Jesus was born in the town of Bethlehem in Judaea, during the time when Herod was king. Soon afterwards, some men who studied the stars came from the east to Jerusalem and asked, "Where is the baby born to be the king of the Jews? We saw his star when it came up in the east, and we have come to worship him."

When King Herod heard about this, he was very upset, and so was everyone else in Jerusalem. He called together all the chief priests and the teachers of the Law and asked them, "Where will the Messiah be born?"

"In the town of Bethlehem in Judaea," they answered. "For this is what the prophet wrote:
    'Bethlehem in the land of Judah,
        you are by no means the least of the leading cities of Judah;
    for from you will come a leader
        who will guide my people Israel.'"

So Herod called the visitors from the east to a secret meeting and found out from them the exact time the star had appeared. Then he sent them to Bethlehem with these instructions: "Go and make a careful search for the child, and when you find him, let me know, so that I too may go and worship him."

And so they left, and on their way they saw the same star they had seen in the east. When they saw it, how happy they were, what joy was theirs! It went ahead of them until it stopped over the place where the child was. They went into the house, and when they saw the child with his mother Mary, they knelt down and worshipped him. They brought out their gifts of gold, frankincense, and myrrh, and presented them to him.

Then they returned to their country by another road, since God had warned them in a dream not to go back to Herod.

The escape to Egypt   Matthew 2.13–15

After they had left, an angel of the Lord appeared in a dream to Joseph and said, "Herod will be looking for the child in order to kill him. So get up, take the child and his mother and escape to Egypt, and stay there until I tell you to leave."

Joseph got up, took the child and his mother, and left during the night for Egypt, where he stayed until Herod died. This was done to make what the Lord had said through the prophet come true, "I called my Son out of Egypt."

The children are killed   Matthew 2.16

When Herod realized that the visitors from the east had tricked him, he was furious. He gave orders to kill all the boys in Bethlehem and its neighbourhood who were two years old and younger—this was done in accordance with what he had learned from the visitors about the time when the star had appeared.

It is safe to return   Matthew 2.19–23

After Herod died, an angel of the Lord appeared in a dream to Joseph in Egypt and said, "Get up, take the child and his mother, and go back to the land of Israel, because those who tried to kill the child are dead." So Joseph got up, took the child and his mother, and went back to Israel.

But when Joseph heard that Archelaus had succeeded his father Herod as king of Judaea, he was afraid to go there. He was given more instructions in a dream, so he went to the province of Galilee and made his home in a town named Nazareth. And so what the prophets had said came true: "He will be called a Nazarene."

Jesus is given his name   Luke 2.21

It was, and still is, the custom for every Jewish male child to go through a ceremony called "circumcision". This ceremony is seen as a sign of God's promises to his people. It takes place when a boy is eight days old. On this day the boys are given names. The name "Jesus" is the same as the Hebrew name "Joshua" and means "Saviour".

A week later, when the time came for the baby to be circumcised, he was named Jesus, the name which the angel had given him before he had been conceived.

Jesus is presented in the Temple Luke 2.22–38

Simeon lived in Jerusalem. God had promised him that he would see the Saviour before he died. Simeon surprised many people when he spoke about Jesus. His words suggest that the Messiah had come for everyone: not just the Jews but also the Gentiles (non-Jews).

The time came for Joseph and Mary to perform the ceremony of purification, as the Law of Moses commanded. So they took the child to Jerusalem to present him to the Lord, as it is written in the law of the Lord: "Every first-born male is to be dedicated to the Lord." They also went to offer a sacrifice of a pair of doves or two young pigeons, as required by the law of the Lord.

At that time there was a man named Simeon living in Jerusalem. He was a good, God-fearing man and was waiting for Israel to be saved. The Holy Spirit was with him and had assured him that he would not die before he had seen the Lord's promised Messiah. Led by the Spirit, Simeon went into the Temple. When the parents brought the child Jesus into the Temple to do for him what the Law required, Simeon took the child in his arms and gave thanks to God:

> "Now, Lord, you have kept your promise,
> and you may let your servant go in peace.
> With my own eyes I have seen your salvation,
> which you have prepared in the presence of all peoples:
> A light to reveal your will to the Gentiles
> and bring glory to your people Israel."

The child's father and mother were amazed at the things Simeon said about him. Simeon blessed them and said to Mary, his mother, "This child is chosen by God for the destruction and the salvation of many in Israel. He will be a sign from God which many people will speak against and so reveal their secret thoughts. And sorrow, like a sharp sword, will break your own heart."

There was a very old prophetess, a widow named Anna, daughter of Phanuel of the tribe of Asher. She had been married for only seven years and was now eighty-four years old. She never left the Temple; day and night she worshipped God, fasting and praying. That very same hour she arrived and gave thanks to God and spoke about the child to all who were waiting for God to set Jerusalem free.

Jesus, aged twelve, in the Temple   Luke 2.41–52

When a Jewish boy was twelve years old he was regarded as a man and could join in the religious ceremonies.

It was the custom, during religious festivals, for the priests and religious leaders to talk and answer questions in the Temple courtyard. Sometimes they would themselves put questions to those around them. Now he was twelve, Jesus could take part in the discussions.

Every year the parents of Jesus went to Jerusalem for the Passover Festival. When Jesus was twelve years old, they went to the festival as

usual. When the festival was over, they started back home, but the boy Jesus stayed in Jerusalem. His parents did not know this; they thought that he was with the group, so they travelled a whole day and then started looking for him among their relatives and friends. They did not find him, so they went back to Jerusalem looking for him. On the third day they found him in the Temple, sitting with the Jewish teachers, listening to them and asking questions. All who heard him were amazed at his intelligent answers. His parents were astonished when they saw him, and his mother said to him, "My son, why have you done this to us? Your father and I have been terribly worried trying to find you."

He answered them, "Why did you have to look for me? Didn't you know that I had to be in my Father's house?" But they did not understand his answer.

So Jesus went back with them to Nazareth, where he was obedient to them. His mother treasured all these things in her heart. Jesus grew both in body and in wisdom, gaining favour with God and men.

2
How Jesus lived

About eighteen years have passed since Jesus visited the Temple as a boy. We know very little about his life during this period. But he probably worked as a carpenter in Nazareth, as his father Joseph did.

What we do know is that when Jesus was about thirty he left Nazareth and travelled around Palestine, preaching and doing things that amazed people throughout the land. He probably did this for about three years. There are four accounts of it in the Bible and they are placed at the beginning of the New Testament. They are called "Gospels", or "Good News", according to Matthew, Mark, Luke, and John (this is another John and not John the Baptist).

John prepares the way

This was before the days of radio and television, telephones, or even a postal service. So it was the custom, if a king or important official was going anywhere, for a herald or forerunner to go on in advance, to tell people to make the necessary preparations. Zechariah had prophesied that his son, John, would do this for the Messiah.

The preaching of John the Baptist   Luke 3.2–7

John did not look like the sort of person who would announce the coming of the Messiah. He did not preach in the cities where everybody lived, but miles away in the desert. His message was unusual and hard-hitting. He surprised the Jews by telling them that God would be angry with them as well as other nations. Although they were Abraham's descendants they should not expect special treatment unless they took God seriously.

At that time the word of God came to John son of Zechariah in the desert. So John went throughout the whole territory of the River Jordan, preaching, "Turn away from your sins and be baptized, and God will forgive your sins." As it is written in the book of the prophet Isaiah:
> "Someone is shouting in the desert:
>> 'Get the road ready for the Lord;
>> make a straight path for him to travel!
> Every valley must be filled up,
>> every hill and mountain levelled off.
> The winding roads must be made straight,
>> and the rough paths made smooth.
> All mankind will see God's salvation!'"

Crowds of people came out to John to be baptized by him. "You snakes!" he said to them. "Who told you that you could escape from the punishment God is about to send?"

Jesus comes to be baptized Matthew 3.4–6, 13–17

John's clothes were made of camel's hair; he wore a leather belt round his waist, and his food was locusts and wild honey. People came to him from Jerusalem, from the whole province of Judaea, and from all the country near the River Jordan. They confessed their sins, and he baptized them in the Jordan...

At that time Jesus arrived from Galilee and came to John at the Jordan to be baptized by him. But John tried to make him change his mind. "I ought to be baptized by you," John said, "and yet you have come to me!"

But Jesus answered him, "Let it be so for now. For in this way we shall do all that God requires." So John agreed.

As soon as Jesus was baptized, he came up out of the water. Then heaven was opened to him, and he saw the Spirit of God coming down like a dove and alighting on him. Then a voice said from heaven, "This is my own dear Son, with whom I am pleased."

Jesus begins his work

Jesus is tempted Matthew 4.1–11

Jesus had remarkable powers. Before he began his ministry he was tempted to use his powers in a way that he believed God did not want. This is what happened:

Then the Spirit led Jesus into the desert to be tempted by the Devil. After spending forty days and nights without food, Jesus was hungry. Then the Devil came to him and said, "If you are God's Son, order these stones to turn into bread."

But Jesus answered, "The scripture says, 'Man cannot live on bread alone, but needs every word that God speaks.'"

Then the Devil took Jesus to Jerusalem, the Holy City, set him on the highest point of the Temple, and said to him, "If you are God's Son, throw yourself down, for the scripture says,

'God will give orders to his angels about you;
they will hold you up with their hands,
so that not even your feet will be hurt on the stones.'"

Jesus answered, "But the scripture also says, 'Do not put the Lord your God to the test.'"

Then the Devil took Jesus to a very high mountain and showed him all the kingdoms of the world in all their greatness. "All this I will give you," the Devil said, "if you kneel down and worship me."

Then Jesus answered, "Go away, Satan! The scripture says, 'Worship the Lord your God and serve only him!'"

Then the Devil left Jesus; and angels came and helped him.

Jesus calls four fishermen   Mark 1.14–20

In New Testament times there were many religious teachers, some of whom went from place to place sharing their ideas. If they were Jews they were called "Rabbis". Each Rabbi would have a group of disciples, or followers, who would be expected to leave home, follow the teacher wherever he went, memorize his teachings, and pass them on to others. Before Jesus asked his disciples to follow him, they had been brought up among very ordinary people and had done very ordinary jobs.

After John had been put in prison, Jesus went to Galilee and preached the Good News from God. "The right time has come," he said, "and the Kingdom of God is near! Turn away from your sins and believe the Good News!"

As Jesus walked along the shore of Lake Galilee, he saw two fishermen, Simon and his brother Andrew, catching fish with a net. Jesus said to them, "Come with me, and I will teach you to catch men." At once they left their nets and went with him.

He went a little farther on and saw two other brothers, James and John, the sons of Zebedee. They were in their boat getting their nets ready. As soon as Jesus saw them, he called them; they left their father Zebedee in the boat with the hired men and went with Jesus.

The wedding in Cana   John 2.1–12

John's Gospel follows a rather different line from the other three. After describing how Jesus called a number of disciples, John reports this incident.

Two days later there was a wedding in the town of Cana in Galilee. Jesus' mother was there, and Jesus and his disciples had also been invited to the wedding. When the wine had given out, Jesus' mother said to him, "They have no wine left."

"You must not tell me what to do," Jesus replied. "My time has not yet come."

Jesus' mother then told the servants, "Do whatever he tells you."

The Jews have rules about ritual washing, and for this purpose six stone water jars were there, each one large enough to hold about a hundred litres. Jesus said to the servants, "Fill these jars with water." They filled them to the brim, and then he told them, "Now draw some water out and take it to the man in charge of the feast." They took him the water, which now had turned into wine, and he tasted it. He did not know where this wine had come from (but, of course, the servants who had drawn out the water knew); so he called the bridegroom and said to him, "Everyone else serves the best wine first, and after the guests have had plenty to drink, he serves the ordinary wine. But you have kept the best wine until now!"

Jesus performed this first miracle in Cana in Galilee; there he revealed his glory, and his disciples believed in him.

After this, Jesus and his mother, brothers, and disciples went to Capernaum and stayed there a few days.

Jesus demonstrates God's power to the people

A man with an evil spirit   Mark 1.21–28

As it is today, a synagogue used to be the place where Jews went to learn about God. Sacrifices were not made there, but in the Temple. Each Sabbath day (our Saturday) the Jewish Law was taught and the people would gather for a service. A Rabbi or religious teacher would read from the scriptures, comment upon them, and often answer questions raised by those listening to him. It was sometimes the custom to ask a visiting Rabbi to do this.

The subject of evil spirits is still a difficult one to understand. We know that many people believed that evil spirits caused illness and that God's power was needed to cure the illness. Whatever it was that made the man behave as he did, Jesus had power over it. Jesus emphasized what he said by what he did. In both, he seemed to do things with God's authority.

Jesus and his disciples came to the town of Capernaum, and on the next Sabbath Jesus went to the synagogue and began to teach. The people who heard him were amazed at the way he taught, for he wasn't like the teachers of the Law; instead, he taught with authority.

Just then a man with an evil spirit in him came into the synagogue and screamed, "What do you want with us, Jesus of Nazareth? Are you here to destroy us? I know who you are—you are God's holy messenger!"

Jesus ordered the spirit, "Be quiet, and come out of the man!"

The evil spirit shook the man hard, gave a loud scream, and came out of him. The people were all so amazed that they started saying to one another, "What is this? Is it some kind of new teaching? This man has authority to give orders to the evil spirits, and they obey him!"

And so the news about Jesus spread quickly everywhere in the province of Galilee.

Many diseases cured   Mark 1.29–34

Jesus and his disciples, including James and John, left the synagogue and went straight to the home of Simon and Andrew. Simon's mother-in-law was sick in bed with a fever, and as soon as Jesus arrived, he was told about her. He went to her, took her by the hand, and helped her up. The fever left her, and she began to wait on them.

After the sun had set and evening had come, people brought to Jesus all the sick and those who had demons. All the people of the town gathered in front of the house. Jesus healed many who were sick with all kinds of diseases and drove out many demons. He would not let the demons say anything, because they knew who he was.

Everyone is looking for Jesus   Mark 1.35–39

When Jesus went out to pray in the morning people wondered where he was.

Very early the next morning, long before daylight, Jesus got up and left the house. He went out of the town to a lonely place, where he prayed. But Simon and his companions went out searching for him, and when they found him, they said, "Everyone is looking for you."

But Jesus answered, "We must go on to the other villages round here. I have to preach in them also, because that is why I came."

So he travelled all over Galilee, preaching in the synagogues and driving out demons.

Jesus heals a dreaded skin-disease   Mark 1.40–45

Many people believed that any kind of skin-disease was a mark of God's punishment. Anyone suffering from such a disease was isolated from everyone else in case contact with the disease would make other people unacceptable to God. As the disease was thought of as a punishment from God, it was thought that only God could cure it. If a person thought that God had cured his disease, the priest had to examine the person and decide whether or not the disease had gone. Only then could the sufferer mix with the rest of society again.

In curing the man Jesus showed that God was working through him.

A man suffering from a dreaded skin-disease came to Jesus, knelt down, and begged him for help. "If you want to," he said, "you can make me clean."

Jesus was filled with pity, and stretched out his hand and touched him. "I do want to," he answered. "Be clean!" At once the disease left the man, and he was clean. Then Jesus spoke sternly to him and sent him away at once, after saying to him, "Listen, don't tell anyone about this. But go straight to the priest and let him examine you; then in order to prove to everyone that you are cured, offer the sacrifice that Moses ordered."

But the man went away and began to spread the news everywhere. Indeed, he talked so much that Jesus could not go into a town publicly. Instead, he stayed out in lonely places, and people came to him from everywhere.

Jesus heals a paralysed man   Mark 2.1–12

The people of Capernaum had seen Jesus act with God's power, but here Jesus claims to forgive sins, something which only God could do. Some experts in the Jewish religion thought this was going much too far and accused him of blasphemy. This means insulting God and was viewed very seriously. By healing the man Jesus showed that, rather than insulting God, he was working directly for him.

A few days later Jesus went back to Capernaum, and the news spread that he was at home. So many people came together that there was no room left, not even out in front of the door. Jesus was preaching the message to them when four men arrived, carrying a paralysed man to Jesus. Because of the crowd, however, they could not get the man to him. So they made a hole in the roof right above the place where Jesus was. When they had made an opening, they let the man down, lying on his mat. Seeing how much faith they had, Jesus said to the paralysed man, "My son, your sins are forgiven."

Some teachers of the Law who were sitting there thought to themselves, "How does he dare to talk like this? This is blasphemy! God is the only one who can forgive sins!"

At once Jesus knew what they were thinking, so he said to them, "Why do you think such things? Is it easier to say to this paralysed man, 'Your sins are forgiven', or to say, 'Get up, pick up your mat, and walk'? I will prove to you, then, that the Son of Man has authority on earth to forgive sins." So he said to the paralysed man, "I tell you, get up, pick up your mat, and go home!"

195

While they all watched, the man got up, picked up his mat, and hurried away. They were all completely amazed and praised God, saying, "We have never seen anything like this!"

Jesus heals a blind beggar   Luke 18.35 – 43

As Jesus was coming near Jericho, there was a blind man sitting by the road, begging. When he heard the crowd passing by, he asked, "What is this?"

"Jesus of Nazareth is passing by," they told him.

He cried out, "Jesus! Son of David! Take pity on me!"

The people in front scolded him and told him to be quiet. But he shouted even more loudly, "Son of David! Take pity on me!"

So Jesus stopped and ordered the blind man to be brought to him. When he came near, Jesus asked him, "What do you want me to do for you?"

"Sir," he answered, "I want to see again."

Jesus said to him, "Then see! Your faith has made you well."

At once he was able to see, and he followed Jesus, giving thanks to God. When the crowd saw it, they all praised God.

Jesus is concerned for people

Jesus calls Matthew   Matthew 9.9–13

As a tax collector Matthew would have been hated by the Jewish people, because he took money from them and worked for the Romans. He would not have been allowed into the synagogue and most people would have been ashamed to know him. The Pharisees (important religious leaders) would have refused even to sit at the same table with him. They could not understand why Jesus had anything to do with such people.

Jesus left that place, and as he walked along, he saw a tax collector, named Matthew, sitting in his office. He said to him, "Follow me."

Matthew got up and followed him.

While Jesus was having a meal in Matthew's house, many tax collectors and other outcasts came and joined Jesus and his disciples at the table. Some Pharisees saw this and asked his disciples, "Why does your teacher eat with such people?"

Jesus heard them and answered, "People who are well do not need a doctor, but only those who are sick. Go and find out what is meant by the scripture that says: 'It is kindness that I want, not animal sacrifices.' I have not come to call respectable people, but outcasts."

Jesus has pity for the people   Matthew 9.35–38

Jesus went round visiting all the towns and villages. He taught in the synagogues, preached the Good News about the Kingdom, and healed people with every kind of disease and sickness. As he saw the crowds, his heart was filled with pity for them, because they were worried and helpless, like sheep without a shepherd. So he said to his disciples, "The harvest is large, but there are few workers to gather it in. Pray to the owner of the harvest that he will send out workers to gather in his harvest."

The question about fasting   Mark 2.18–20

"Fasting" means going without food. The Pharisees did this twice a week. However, if they were invited to a wedding they were allowed to eat, so that everyone could be happy and celebrate. Jesus uses this example to answer a question. The time when the Messiah would be on earth had often been described as being like a wedding feast.

On one occasion the followers of John the Baptist and the Pharisees were fasting. Some people came to Jesus and asked him, "Why is it that the disciples of John the Baptist and the disciples of the Pharisees fast, but yours do not?"

Jesus answered, "Do you expect the guests at a wedding party to go without food? Of course not! As long as the bridegroom is with them, they will not do that. But the day will come when the bridegroom will be taken away from them, and then they will fast."

Crowds of people struggle to get to Jesus   Mark 3.7–12

Jesus and his disciples went away to Lake Galilee, and a large crowd followed him. They had come from Galilee, from Judaea, from Jerusalem, from the territory of Idumea, from the territory on the east side of the Jordan, and from the region round the cities of Tyre and Sidon. All these people came to Jesus because they had heard of the things he was doing. The crowd was so large that Jesus told his disciples to get a boat ready for him, so that the people would not crush him. He had healed many people, and all those who were ill kept pushing their way to him in order to touch him. And whenever the people who had evil spirits in them saw him, they would fall down before him and scream, "You are the Son of God!"

Jesus sternly ordered the evil spirits not to tell anyone who he was.

A new family chosen by Jesus

Jesus chooses the twelve apostles   Mark 3.13–19

The word "apostle" means someone who is sent out to do a special job for God, and Jesus chose twelve men to do just that. Jesus was to spend a lot of time with these men and when he left them they spread his message to the world.

Then Jesus went up a hill and called to himself the men he wanted. They came to him, and he chose twelve, whom he named apostles. "I have chosen you to be with me," he told them. "I will also send you out to preach, and you will have authority to drive out demons."

These are the twelve he chose: Simon (Jesus gave him the name Peter); James and his brother John, the sons of Zebedee (Jesus gave them the name Boanerges, which means "Men of Thunder"); Andrew, Philip, Bartholomew, Matthew, Thomas, James son of Alphaeus, Thaddaeus, Simon the Patriot, and Judas Iscariot, who betrayed Jesus.

Jesus' mother and brothers   Mark 3.31–35

Then Jesus' mother and brothers arrived. They stood outside the house and sent in a message, asking for him. A crowd was sitting round Jesus, and they said to him, "Look, your mother and your brothers and sisters are outside, and they want you."

Jesus answered, "Who is my mother? Who are my brothers?" He looked at the people sitting round him and said, "Look! Here are my mother and my brothers! Whoever does what God wants him to do is my brother, my sister, my mother."

Who is this man?   Mark 4.35–41

The lake mentioned in this story is Lake Galilee. It is about 21 kilometres long and 13 kilometres across at its widest point. It is common for sudden violent storms to blow up there.

On the evening of that same day Jesus said to his disciples, "Let us go across to the other side of the lake." So they left the crowd; the disciples got into the boat in which Jesus was already sitting, and they took him with them. Other boats were there too. Suddenly a strong wind blew up, and the waves began to spill over into the boat, so that it was about to fill with water. Jesus was in the back of the boat, sleeping with his head on a pillow. The disciples woke him up and said, "Teacher, don't you care that we are about to die?"

Jesus stood up and commanded the wind, "Be quiet!" and he said to the waves, "Be still!" The wind died down, and there was a great calm. Then Jesus said to his disciples, "Why are you frightened? Have you still no faith?"

But they were terribly afraid and said to one another, "Who is this man? Even the wind and the waves obey him!"

Jesus is unwelcome at Nazareth   Mark 6.1–6

The Gospels tell us all sorts of amazing things that Jesus did. In this story we read of something that he could not do. Can you see why?

Jesus went back to his home town, followed by his disciples. On the Sabbath he began to teach in the synagogue. Many people were there; and when they heard him, they were all amazed. "Where did he get all this?" they asked. "What wisdom is this that has been given him? How does he perform miracles? Isn't he the carpenter, the son of Mary, and the brother of James, Joseph, Judas, and Simon? Aren't his sisters living here?" And so they rejected him.

Jesus said to them, "A prophet is respected everywhere except in his own home town and by his relatives and his family."

He was not able to perform any miracles there, except that he placed his hands on a few sick people and healed them. He was greatly surprised, because the people did not have faith.

Then Jesus went to the villages round there, teaching the people.

Women who followed Jesus   Luke 8.1–3

Women were not thought to be very important by most people at this time. Rabbis did not allow women to be their followers. In this, as in most things, Jesus was unusual. He had women followers from many different backgrounds.

Some time later Jesus travelled through towns and villages, preaching the Good News about the Kingdom of God. The twelve disciples went with him, and so did some women who had been healed of evil spirits and diseases: Mary (who was called Magdalene), from whom seven demons had been driven out; Joanna, whose husband Chuza was an officer in Herod's court; and Susanna, and many other women who used their own resources to help Jesus and his disciples.

The would-be followers of Jesus   Luke 9.57–58

Many people said they would follow Jesus, but he made it clear that this would often be difficult. When they heard this, many of them changed their minds.

As they went on their way, a man said to Jesus, "I will follow you wherever you go."

Jesus said to him, "Foxes have holes, and birds have nests, but the Son of Man has nowhere to lie down and rest."

The good news spreads

Jairus' daughter   Mark 5.21–43

Jesus went back across to the other side of the lake. There at the lakeside a large crowd gathered round him. Jairus, an official of the local synagogue, arrived, and when he saw Jesus, he threw himself down at his feet and begged him earnestly, "My little daughter is very ill. Please come and place your hands on her, so that she will get well and live!"

Then Jesus started off with him. So many people were going along with Jesus that they were crowding him from every side.

There was a woman who had suffered terribly from severe bleeding for twelve years, even though she had been treated by many doctors. She had spent all her money, but instead of getting better she got worse all the time. She had heard about Jesus, so she came in the crowd behind him, saying to herself, "If I just touch his clothes, I will get well."

She touched his cloak, and her bleeding stopped at once; and she had the feeling inside herself that she was healed of her trouble. At once Jesus knew that power had gone out of him, so he turned round in the crowd and asked, "Who touched my clothes?"

His disciples answered, "You see how the people are crowding you; why do you ask who touched you?"

But Jesus kept looking round to see who had done it. The woman realized what had happened to her, so she came, trembling with fear, knelt at his feet, and told him the whole truth. Jesus said to her, "My daughter, your faith has made you well. Go in peace, and be healed of your trouble."

While Jesus was saying this, some messengers came from Jairus' house and told him, "Your daughter has died. Why bother the Teacher any longer?"

Jesus paid no attention to what they said, but told him, "Don't be afraid, only believe." Then he did not let anyone else go on with him except Peter and James and his brother John. They arrived at Jairus' house, where Jesus saw the confusion and heard all the loud crying and wailing. He went in and said to them, "Why all this confusion? Why are you crying? The child is not dead—she is only sleeping!"

They laughed at him, so he put them all out, took the child's father and mother and his three disciples, and went into the room where the child was lying. He took her by the hand and said to her, *"Talitha, koum,"* which means, "Little girl, I tell you to get up!"

She got up at once and started walking around. (She was twelve years old.) When his happened, they were completely amazed. But Jesus gave them strict orders not to tell anyone, and he said, "Give her something to eat."

Jesus sends out the twelve apostles   Mark 6.6–11

The word "apostle" means someone who is sent out to do a special job for God.

Then Jesus went to the villages round there, teaching the people. He called the twelve disciples together and sent them out two by two. He gave them authority over the evil spirits and ordered them, "Don't take anything with you on your journey except a stick—no bread, no beggar's bag, no money in your pockets. Wear sandals, but don't carry an extra

shirt." He also said, "Wherever you are welcomed, stay in the same house until you leave that place. If you come to a town where people do not welcome you or will not listen to you, leave it and shake the dust off your feet. That will be a warning to them!"

Jesus feeds five thousand men   Mark 6.30–44

The apostles returned and met with Jesus, and told him all they had done and taught. There were so many people coming and going that Jesus and his disciples didn't even have time to eat. So he said to them, "Let us go off by ourselves to some place where we will be alone and you can rest for a while." So they started out in a boat by themselves for a lonely place.

Many people, however, saw them leave and knew at once who they were; so they went from all the towns and ran ahead by land and arrived at the place ahead of Jesus and his disciples. When Jesus got out of the boat, he saw this large crowd, and his heart was filled with pity for them, because they were like sheep without a shepherd. So he began to teach them many things. When it was getting late, his disciples came to him and said, "It is already very late, and this is a lonely place. Send the people away, and let them go to the nearby farms and villages in order to buy themselves something to eat."

"You yourselves give them something to eat," Jesus answered.

They asked, "Do you want us to go and spend two hundred silver coins on bread in order to feed them?"

So Jesus asked them, "How much bread have you got? Go and see."

When they found out, they told him, "Five loaves and also two fish."

Jesus then told his disciples to make all the people divide into groups and sit down on the green grass. So the people sat down in rows, in groups of a hundred and groups of fifty. Then Jesus took the five loaves and the two fish, looked up to heaven, and gave thanks to God. He broke the loaves and gave them to his disciples to distribute to the people. He also divided the two fish among them all. Everyone ate and had enough. Then the disciples took up twelve baskets full of what was left of the bread and the fish. The number of men who were fed was five thousand.

Jesus walks on water   Mark 6.45–52

At once Jesus made his disciples get into the boat and go ahead of him to Bethsaida, on the other side of the lake, while he sent the crowd away. After saying good-bye to the people he went away to a hill to pray. When evening came, the boat was in the middle of the lake, while Jesus was alone on land. He saw that his disciples were straining at the oars, because they were rowing against the wind; so some time between three and six o'clock in the morning he came to them, walking on the water. He was going to pass them by, but they saw him walking on the water. "It's a ghost!" they thought, and screamed. They were all terrified when they saw him.

Jesus spoke to them at once, "Courage!" he said. "It is I. Don't be afraid!" Then he got into the boat with them, and the wind died down.

The disciples were completely amazed, because they had not understood the real meaning of the feeding of the five thousand; their minds could not grasp it.

Jesus in Gennesaret   Mark 6.53–56

They crossed the lake and came to land at Gennesaret, where they tied up the boat. As they left the boat, people recognized Jesus at once. So they ran throughout the whole region; and wherever they heard he was, they brought to him sick people lying on their mats. And everywhere Jesus went, to villages, towns, or farms, people would take those who were ill to the market-places and beg him to let them at least touch the edge of his cloak; and all who touched it were made well.

A woman's faith   Mark 7.24–30

The Jews were proud to be Abraham's descendants. They sometimes referred to non-Jews as "dogs". As happens today, leftover food was often given to the dog to eat. Jesus came first to his own people, the Jews, but they did not always listen to him. So Jesus sometimes left the Jewish areas and stayed in a Gentile (non-Jewish) part of Palestine. The woman in this story was not Jewish.

Then Jesus left and went away to the territory near the city of Tyre. He went into a house and did not want anyone to know he was there, but he could not stay hidden. A woman, whose daughter had an evil spirit in her, heard about Jesus and came to him at once and fell at his feet. The woman was a Gentile, born in the region of Phoenicia in Syria. She begged Jesus to drive the demon out of her daughter. But Jesus answered, "Let us first feed the children. It isn't right to take the children's food and throw it to the dogs."

"Sir," she answered, "even the dogs under the table eat the children's leftovers!"

So Jesus said to her, "Because of that answer, go back home, where you will find that the demon has gone out of your daughter!"

She went home and found her child lying on the bed; the demon had indeed gone out of her.

The Roman officer's servant   Luke 7.1–10

Jesus was concerned with everybody, Gentiles as well as Jews. The Roman officer was a Gentile but also a remarkable man. He cared for his servant and believed that Jesus would help him.

Jesus went to Capernaum. A Roman officer there had a servant who was very dear to him; the man was sick and about to die. When the officer heard about Jesus, he sent some Jewish elders to ask him to come and heal his servant. They came to Jesus and begged him earnestly, "This man really deserves your help. He loves our people and he himself built a synagogue for us."

So Jesus went with them. He was not far from the house when the officer sent friends to tell him, "Sir, don't trouble yourself. I do not deserve to have you come into my house, neither do I consider myself worthy to come to you in person. Just give the order, and my servant will get well. I, too, am a man placed under the authority of superior officers, and I have soldiers under me. I order this one, 'Go!' and he goes; I order that one, 'Come!' and he comes; and I order my slave, 'Do this!' and he does it."

Jesus was surprised when he heard this; he turned round and said to the crowd following him, "I tell you, I have never found faith like this, not even in Israel!"

The messengers went back to the officer's house and found his servant well.

The widow's son   Luke 7.11–17

The funeral was for a young man. His mother was a widow and he would have been the only person to look after her. Now he was dead—her only hope had gone.

Soon afterwards Jesus went to a town called Nain, accompanied by his disciples and a large crowd. Just as he arrived at the gate of the town, a funeral procession was coming out. The dead man was the only son of a woman who was a widow, and a large crowd from the town was with her. When the Lord saw her, his heart was filled with pity for her, and he said to her, "Don't cry." Then he walked over and touched the coffin, and the men carrying it stopped. Jesus said, "Young man! Get up, I tell you!" The dead man sat up and began to talk, and Jesus gave him back to his mother.

They all were filled with fear and praised God. "A great prophet has appeared among us!" they said; "God has come to save his people!"

This news about Jesus went out through all the country and the surrounding territory.

Jesus receives a message from prison
Luke 7.18–28, 31–35

King Herod had put John in prison for criticising him in public. Once there, John had a great deal of time to think about what had happened and what it meant. John was allowed visitors and he sent two of them to ask Jesus an important question.

When John's disciples told him about all these things, he called two of them and sent them to the Lord to ask him, "Are you the one John said was going to come, or should we expect someone else?"

When they came to Jesus, they said, "John the Baptist sent us to ask if you are the one he said was going to come, or if we should expect someone else."

At that very time Jesus cured many people of their sicknesses, diseases, and evil spirits, and gave sight to many blind people. He answered John's messengers, "Go back and tell John what you have seen and heard: the blind can see, the lame can walk, those who suffer from dreaded skin-diseases are made clean, the deaf can hear, the dead are raised to life, and the Good News is preached to the poor. How happy are those who have no doubts about me!"

After John's messengers had left, Jesus began to speak about him to the crowds: "When you went out to John in the desert, what did you expect to see? A blade of grass bending in the wind? What did you go out to see? A man dressed up in fancy clothes? People who dress like that and live in luxury are found in palaces! Tell me, what did you go out to see? A prophet? Yes indeed, but you saw much more than a prophet. For John is the one of whom the scripture says: 'God said, I will send my messenger ahead of you to open the way for you.' I tell you," Jesus added, "John is greater than any man who has ever lived. But he who is least in the Kingdom of God is greater than John" ...

Jesus continued, "Now to what can I compare the people of this day? What are they like? They are like children sitting in the market-place. One group shouts to the other, 'We played wedding music for you, but you wouldn't dance! We sang funeral songs, but you wouldn't cry!' John the Baptist came, and he fasted and drank no wine, and you said, 'He has a demon in him!' The Son of Man came, and he ate and drank, and you said, 'Look at this man! He is a glutton and a drinker, a friend of tax collectors and other outcasts!' God's wisdom, however, is shown to be true by all who accept it."

Jesus at the home of Simon the Pharisee   Luke 7.36–50

When guests arrived at someone's house the host was expected to get a servant to pour water over their feet and put a drop of cooling scented oil on their forehead to refresh them. They would then be led to a couch to eat. A kiss on the cheek was an accepted sign of welcome and respect.

The woman who poured oil on Jesus was thought to be a real sinner. Because of this she would have been looked down upon by everyone and regarded as evil.

A Pharisee invited Jesus to have dinner with him, and Jesus went to his house and sat down to eat. In that town was a woman who lived a sinful life. She heard that Jesus was eating in the Pharisee's house, so she brought an alabaster jar full of perfume and stood behind Jesus, by his feet, crying and wetting his feet with her tears. Then she dried his feet with her hair, kissed them, and poured the perfume on them. When the Pharisee saw this, he said to himself, "If this man really were a prophet, he would know who this woman is who is touching him; he would know what kind of sinful life she lives!"

Jesus spoke up and said to him, "Simon, I have something to tell you."

"Yes, Teacher," he said, "tell me."

"There were two men who owed money to a money-lender," Jesus began. "One owed him five hundred silver coins, and the other owed him fifty. Neither of them could pay him back, so he cancelled the debts of both. Which one, then, will love him more?"

"I suppose," answered Simon, "that it would be the one who was forgiven more."

"You are right," said Jesus. Then he turned to the woman and said to Simon, "Do you see this woman? I came into your home, and you gave me no water for my feet, but she has washed my feet with her tears and dried them with her hair. You did not welcome me with a kiss, but she has not stopped kissing my feet since I came. You provided no olive-oil for my head, but she has covered my feet with perfume. I tell you, then, the great love she has shown proves that her many sins have been forgiven. But whoever has been forgiven little shows only a little love."

Then Jesus said to the woman, "Your sins are forgiven."

The others sitting at the table began to say to themselves, "Who is this, who even forgives sins?"

But Jesus said to the woman, "Your faith has saved you; go in peace."

Humility and hospitality   Luke 14.7–14

At a wedding feast in Palestine the places were not marked with names, but it was understood that the most important guests would sit nearest the bride and groom. Sometimes people would arrive early to make sure they sat in a place that made them look important. This could sometimes have the opposite effect.

A "parable" is a story used to teach people about God.

Jesus noticed how some of the guests were choosing the best places, so he told this parable to all of them: "When someone invites you to a wedding feast, do not sit down in the best place. It could happen that someone more important than you has been invited, and your host, who invited both of you, would have to come and say to you, 'Let him have this place.' Then you would be embarrassed and have to sit in the lowest place. Instead, when you are invited, go and sit in the lowest place, so that your host will come to you and say, 'Come on up, my friend, to a better place.' This will bring you honour in the presence of all the other guests. For everyone who makes himself great will be humbled, and everyone who humbles himself will be made great."

Then Jesus said to his host, "When you give a lunch or a dinner, do not invite your friends or your brothers or your relatives or your rich neighbours—for they will invite you back, and in this way you will be paid for what you did. When you give a feast, invite the poor, the crippled, the lame, and the blind; and you will be blessed, because they are not able to pay you back. God will repay you on the day the good people rise from death."

Jesus and Zacchaeus   Luke 19.1–10

Collecting the taxes for the hated Romans was the most unpopular job any Jew could do. In order to find people who would take it on, the Romans allowed them to cheat by collecting more than was due and keeping what was left over.

Jesus went on into Jericho and was passing through. There was a chief tax collector there named Zacchaeus, who was rich. He was trying to see who Jesus was, but he was a little man and could not see Jesus because of the crowd. So he ran ahead of the crowd and climbed a sycamore tree to see Jesus, who was going to pass that way. When Jesus came to that place, he looked up and said to Zacchaeus, "Hurry down, Zacchaeus, because I must stay in your house today."

Zacchaeus hurried down and welcomed him with great joy. All the people who saw it started grumbling, "This man has gone as a guest to the home of a sinner!"

Zacchaeus stood up and said to the Lord, "Listen, sir! I will give half my belongings to the poor, and if I have cheated anyone, I will pay him back four times as much."

Jesus said to him, "Salvation has come to this house today, for this man, also, is a descendant of Abraham. The Son of Man came to seek and to save the lost."

Jesus heals a man born blind   John 9.1–11

If someone was born with a handicap then many people thought it must be the parents' sin that was being punished. Only God's power could heal such a person.

As Jesus was walking along, he saw a man who had been born blind. His disciples asked him, "Teacher, whose sin caused him to be born blind? Was it his own or his parents' sin?"

Jesus answered, "His blindness has nothing to do with his sins or his parents' sins. He is blind so that God's power might be seen at work in him. As long as it is day, we must keep on doing the work of him who sent me; night is coming when no one can work. While I am in the world, I am the light for the world."

After he said this, Jesus spat on the ground and made some mud with the spittle; he rubbed the mud on the man's eyes and said, "Go and wash your face in the Pool of Siloam." (This name means "Sent.") So the man went, washed his face, and came back seeing.

His neighbours, then, and the people who had seen him begging before this, asked, "Isn't this the man who used to sit and beg?"

Some said, "He is the one," but others said, "No he isn't; he just looks like him."

So the man himself said, "I am the man."

"How is it that you can now see?" they asked him.

He answered, "The man called Jesus made some mud, rubbed it on my eyes, and told me to go to Siloam and wash my face. So I went, and as soon as I washed, I could see."

3
Stories told
by Jesus

People often use stories to help us understand the answer to a difficult question. They sometimes set puzzles or riddles to make us think more carefully. The Jewish Rabbis were well known for this kind of teaching and were very good at it. The gospels describe many times when Jesus told a story, either in answer to a question, or to make people think.

Sometimes he would make the stories up. Sometimes they would be based on things that had happened and sometimes he would gather a crowd by beginning a story everyone knew and shock them by changing the ending. Wherever the stories came from they all had a meaning. They are called "parables", which means "putting things side by side".

Now, if someone tells you a story to teach you something, it is usually about things that are familiar to you. Jesus' parables were all about things the people knew about.

Often their experiences were the same as ours. People grew crops, worked farms, had family rows, worried about money, and went to parties. Sometimes, though, it helps us to have a better understanding of the meaning of a story if we know a little about the customs of the time. Where this is important, we have tried to make it clear before you come to read the story.

Stories about God's rule

There were some people who thought God hated everyone who disobeyed his laws. They could not imagine God ever being interested in such people. These parables show that this idea was wrong.

The parable of the lost sheep   Luke 15.1–7

As you can imagine from looking at the picture there were plenty of places to lose sheep in Palestine. Shepherds were personally responsible for the sheep and were experts in tracking animals over the hills. The sheep would often belong to groups of people in the village, who would all be keen to celebrate when a shepherd rescued a missing animal.

One day when many tax collectors and other outcasts came to listen to Jesus, the Pharisees and the teachers of the Law started grumbling, "This man welcomes outcasts and even eats with them!" So Jesus told them this parable:

"Suppose one of you has a hundred sheep and loses one of them—what does he do? He leaves the other ninety-nine sheep in the pasture and goes looking for the one that got lost until he finds it. When he finds it, he is so happy that he puts it on his shoulders and carries it back home. Then he calls his friends and neighbours together and says to them, 'I am so happy I found my lost sheep. Let us celebrate!' In the same way, I tell you, there will be more joy in heaven over one sinner who repents than over ninety-nine respectable people who do not need to repent."

The parable of the lost coin   Luke 15.8–10

It was the custom for married women to have a head-dress made up of ten silver coins. It had the same sort of meaning as a wedding ring has today and was just as important. People were very upset if one of the coins got lost and the head-dress was spoilt. They would be especially upset as the coin would be very hard to look for in a dark house with a floor covered in dried reeds, with only an oil lamp as a light. Remember that Jesus is speaking to people who ask why he welcomes outcasts.

"Or suppose a woman who has ten silver coins loses one of them—what does she do? She lights a lamp, sweeps her house, and looks carefully everywhere until she finds it. When she finds it, she calls her friends and neighbours together, and says to them, 'I am so happy I found the coin I lost. Let us celebrate!' In the same way, I tell you, the angels of God rejoice over one sinner who repents."

The parable of the lost son   Luke 15.11–32

In Palestine it was usual that if a man died leaving two sons, two thirds of his property would go to his elder son and one third to the younger. If a father wished he could hand over his property before he died. All who listened to this story would have thought of God as the father. But for the son to feed pigs would have been seen as a disgrace by the Jews (who thought of them as "unclean" animals) and he would have become an outcast, with no rights at all. He would not expect his father to treat him as a son. However, Jesus' story is full of surprises. It helps us to see that God accepts people as his children whoever they are and whatever they have done. A ring was the sign of the father's authority, and slaves, or hired workers, did not wear shoes. Jesus uses the story to make a new point.

Jesus went on to say, "There was once a man who had two sons. The younger one said to him, 'Father, give me my share of the property now.' So the man divided his property between his two sons. After a few days the younger son sold his part of the property and left home with the money. He went to a country far away, where he wasted his money in reckless living. He spent everything he had. Then a severe famine spread over that country, and he was left without a thing. So he went to work for one of the citizens of that country, who sent him out to his farm to take care of the pigs. He wished he could fill himself with the bean pods the pigs ate, but no one gave him anything to eat. At last he came to his senses and said, 'All my father's hired workers have more than they can eat, and here I am about to starve! I will get up and go to my father and say, Father, I have sinned against God and against you. I am no longer fit to be called your son; treat me as one of your hired workers.' So he got up and started back to his father.

"He was still a long way from home when his father saw him; his heart was filled with pity, and he ran, threw his arms round his son, and kissed him. 'Father,' the son said, 'I have sinned against God and against you. I am no longer fit to be called your son.' But the father called his servants. 'Hurry!' he said. 'Bring the best robe and put it on him. Put a ring on his finger and shoes on his feet. Then go and get the prize calf and kill it, and let us celebrate with a feast! For this son of mine was dead, but now he is alive; he was lost, but now he has been found.' And so the feasting began.

"In the meantime the elder son was out in the field. On his way back, when he came close to the house, he heard the music and dancing. So he

called one of the servants and asked him, 'What's going on?' 'Your brother has come back home,' the servant answered, 'and your father has killed the prize calf, because he got him back safe and sound.'

"The elder brother was so angry that he would not go into the house; so his father came out and begged him to come in. But he answered his father, 'Look, all these years I have worked for you like a slave, and I have never disobeyed your orders. What have you given me? Not even a goat for me to have a feast with my friends! But this son of yours wasted all your property on prostitutes, and when he comes back home, you kill the prize calf for him!' 'My son,' the father answered, 'you are always here with me, and everything I have is yours. But we had to celebrate and be happy, because your brother was dead, but now he is alive; he was lost, but now he has been found.'"

Stories about God's Kingdom

People were used to countries being ruled by a king. He had full control in his country. In its simplest sense the "Kingdom of God" means "where God rules". For many years the Jews had looked for a time when God would rule on earth. Because the Jews did not like to use the name of God, Matthew calls it the "Kingdom of Heaven". A number of parables are introduced with the words "The Kingdom of Heaven is like this".

The parable of the weeds   Matthew 13.24–30

Jesus told them another parable: "The Kingdom of heaven is like this. A man sowed good seed in his field. One night, when everyone was asleep, an enemy came and sowed weeds among the wheat and went away. When the plants grew and the ears of corn began to form, then the weeds showed up. The man's servants came to him and said, 'Sir, it was good seed you sowed in your field; where did the weeds come from?' 'It was some enemy who did this ,' he answered. 'Do you want us to go and pull up the weeds?' they asked him. 'No,' he answered, 'because as you gather the weeds you might pull up some of the wheat along with them. Let the wheat and the weeds both grow together until harvest. Then I will tell the harvest workers to pull up the weeds first, tie them in bundles and burn them, and then to gather in the wheat and put it in my barn.'"

The parable of the mustard seed   Matthew 13.31–32

Jesus told them another parable: "The Kingdom of heaven is like this. A man takes a mustard seed and sows it in his field. It is the smallest of all seeds, but when it grows up, it is the biggest of all plants. It becomes a tree, so that birds come and make their nests in its branches."

The parable of the yeast   Matthew 13.33

Jesus told them still another parable: "The Kingdom of heaven is like this. A woman takes some yeast and mixes it with forty litres of flour until the whole batch of dough rises."

The parable of the hidden treasure   Matthew 13.44

"The Kingdom of heaven is like this. A man happens to find a treasure hidden in a field. He covers it up again, and is so happy that he goes and sells everything he has, and then goes back and buys that field."

The parable of the fine pearl   Matthew 13.45–46

"Also, the Kingdom of heaven is like this. A man is looking for fine pearls, and when he finds one that is unusually fine, he goes and sells everything he has, and buys that pearl."

The parable of the net   Matthew 13.47–50

This parable refers to a kind of fishing common in Palestine. The fishermen worked from the shore with a very fine mesh net. It was thrown into the water a bit like a lasso and caught whatever kind of fish was there.

"Also, the Kingdom of heaven is like this. Some fishermen throw their net out in the lake and catch all kinds of fish. When the net is full, they pull it to shore and sit down to divide the fish: the good ones go into their buckets, the worthless ones are thrown away. It will be like this at the end of the age: the angels will go out and gather up the evil people from among the good and will throw them into the fiery furnace, where they will cry and grind their teeth."

The parable of the growing seed   Mark 4.26–29

Jesus went on to say, "The Kingdom of God is like this. A man scatters seed in his field. He sleeps at night, is up and about during the day, and all the while the seeds are sprouting and growing. Yet he does not know how it happens. The soil itself makes the plants grow and bear fruit; first the tender stalk appears, then the ear, and finally the ear full of corn. When the corn is ripe, the man starts cutting it with his sickle, because harvest time has come."

The parable of the fig-tree which did not grow fruit
Luke 13.6–9

This parable teaches us that if we love God we must also serve him.

Then Jesus told them this parable: "There was once a man who had a fig-tree growing in his vineyard. He went looking for figs on it but found none. So he said to his gardener, 'Look, for three years I have been coming here looking for figs on this fig-tree, and I haven't found any. Cut it down! Why should it go on using up the soil?' But the gardener answered, 'Leave it alone, sir, just one more year; I will dig round it and put in some manure. Then if the tree bears figs next year, so much the better; if not, then you can have it cut down.'"

The parable of the great feast   Luke 14.15–24

One of the ideas many Jews had about what it would be like when the Messiah came was of a great party with lots to eat and drink.

Parties in Palestine were a little different from our own. Everybody knew who else had been invited and if they did not like the people on the guest list they would not come. When everything was ready the servants would go out and tell the guests to come. To decide not to come at this stage would be a great insult to all the other guests and to the host himself.

When one of the men sitting at table heard this, he said to Jesus, "How happy are those who will sit down at the feast in the Kingdom of God!"

Jesus said to him, "There was once a man who was giving a great feast to which he invited many people. When it was time for the feast, he sent his servant to tell his guests, 'Come, everything is ready! But they all began, one after another, to make excuses. The first one told the servant, 'I have bought a field and must go and look at it; please accept my apologies.' Another one said, 'I have bought five pairs of oxen and am on my way to try them out; please accept my apologies.' Another one said, 'I have just got married, and for that reason I cannot come.'

"The servant went back and told all this to his master. The master was furious and said to his servant, 'Hurry out to the streets and alleys of the town, and bring back the poor, the crippled, the blind, and the lame.' Soon the servant said, 'Your order has been carried out, sir, but there is room for more.' So the master said to the servant, 'Go out to the country roads and lanes and make people come in, so that my house will be full. I tell you all that none of those men who were invited will taste my dinner!'"

The parable of the sower   Luke 8.4–8

To appreciate what Jesus is describing we should understand something about the way farmers worked at the time. They worked in a different order to the way we do today. They ploughed the field after they had scattered the seed. So they did not know where the rocky ground was.

People kept coming to Jesus from one town after another; and when a great crowd gathered, Jesus told this parable:

"Once there was a man who went out to sow corn. As he scattered the seed in the field, some of it fell along the path, where it was stepped on, and the birds ate it up. Some of it fell on rocky ground, and when the plants sprouted, they dried up because the soil had no moisture. Some of the seed fell among thorn bushes, which grew up with the plants and choked them. And some seeds fell in good soil; the plants grew and produced corn, a hundred grains each."

And Jesus concluded, "Listen, then, if you have ears!"

Jesus explains the parable   Luke 8.11–15

This is one of the few parables which is explained in the gospels.

"This is what the parable means: the seed is the word of God. The seeds that fell along the path stand for those who hear; but the Devil comes and takes the message away from their hearts in order to keep them from believing and being saved. The seeds that fell on rocky ground stand for those who hear the message and receive it gladly. But it does not sink deep into them; they believe only for a while but when the time of testing comes, they fall away. The seeds that fell among thorn bushes stand for those who hear; but the worries and riches and pleasures of this life crowd in and choke them, and their fruit never ripens. The seeds that fell in good soil stand for those who hear the message and retain it in a good and obedient heart, and they persist until they bear fruit."

Stories about keeping alert

By this time Jesus had told his disciples that he would come back to them after he had died; they must watch and wait for him. These stories show the sort of watchfulness that he is asking for.

The parable of the ten girls   Matthew 25.1–13

As part of the celebrations of a Jewish wedding the bridegroom would head a torchlight procession to the bride's house. Sometimes the wedding feast would be held there and sometimes they would go back to the bridegroom's house or to their new home. In any case it was the custom to shut the door and not let anyone in, so that nothing could interrupt the joyful celebration. As no one knew what time the bridegroom would be ready to start the procession, those waiting to join it needed to be alert and well prepared. Jesus calls on his disciples to be alert in the same way.

"At that time the Kingdom of heaven will be like this. Once there were ten girls who took their oil lamps and went out to meet the bridegroom. Five of them were foolish, and the other five were wise. The foolish ones took their lamps but did not take any extra oil with them, while the wise ones took containers full of oil for their lamps. The bridegroom was late in coming, so the girls began to nod and fall asleep.

"It was already midnight when the cry rang out, 'Here is the bridegroom! Come and meet him!' The ten girls woke up and trimmed their lamps. Then the foolish ones said to the wise ones, 'Let us have some of your oil, because our lamps are going out.' 'No, indeed,' the wise ones answered, 'there is not enough for you and for us. Go to the shop and buy some for yourselves.' So the foolish girls went off to buy some oil; and while they were gone, the bridegroom arrived. The five girls who were ready went in with him to the wedding feast, and the door was closed.

"Later the other girls arrived. 'Sir, sir! Let us in!' they cried out. 'Certainly not! I don't know you,' the bridegroom answered."

And Jesus concluded, "Be on your guard, then, because you do not know the day or the hour."

The parable of the three servants   Matthew 25.14–30

It was quite usual for the owner of a business to leave parts of it in the hands of servants for a time while he was out of the country.

"At that time the Kingdom of heaven will be like this. Once there was a man who was about to go on a journey; he called his servants and put them in charge of his property. He gave to each one according to his ability: to one he gave five thousand gold coins, to another he gave two thousand, and to another he gave one thousand. Then he left on his journey. The servant who had received five thousand coins went at once and invested his money and earned another five thousand. In the same way the servant who received two thousand coins earned another two thousand. But the servant who had received one thousand coins went off, dug a hole in the ground, and hid his master's money.

"After a long time the master of those servants came back and settled accounts with them. The servant who had received five thousand coins came in and handed over the other five thousand. 'You gave me five thousand coins, sir,' he said. 'Look! Here are another five thousand that I have earned.' 'Well done, you good and faithful servant!' said his master. 'You have been faithful in managing small amounts, so I will put you in charge of large amounts. Come on in and share my happiness!'

"Then the servant who had been given two thousand coins came in and said, 'You gave me two thousand coins, sir. Look! Here are another two thousand that I have earned.' 'Well done, you good and faithful servant!' said his master. 'You have been faithful in managing small amounts, so I will put you in charge of large amounts. Come on in and share my happiness!'

"Then the servant who had received one thousand coins came in and said, 'Sir, I know you are a hard man; you reap harvests where you did not sow, and you gather crops where you did not scatter seed. I was afraid, so I went off and hid your money in the ground. Look! Here is what belongs to you.'

"'You bad and lazy servant!' his master said. 'You knew, did you, that I reap harvests where I did not sow, and gather crops where I did not scatter seed? Well, then, you should have deposited my money in the bank, and I would have received it all back with interest when I returned. Now, take the money away from him and give it to the one who has ten thousand coins. For to every person who has something, even more will be given, and he will have more than enough; but the person who has nothing, even the little that he has will be taken away from him. As for this useless servant—throw him outside in the darkness; there he will cry and grind his teeth.'"

Watchful servants   Luke 12.35–40

When the master of a house went out he would not always be able to let his servants know when he was returning, but he would expect them to be prepared to welcome him home whenever it was.

"Be ready for whatever comes, dressed for action and with your lamps lit, like servants who are waiting for their master to come back from a wedding feast. When he comes and knocks, they will open the door for him at once. How happy are those servants whose master finds them awake and ready when he returns! I tell you, he will take off his coat, ask them to sit down, and will wait on them. How happy they are if he finds them ready, even if he should come at midnight or even later! And you can be sure that if the owner of a house knew the time when the thief would come, he would not let the thief break into his house. And you, too, must be ready, because the Son of Man will come at an hour when you are not expecting him."

The parable of the tenants in the vineyard   Luke 20.9–15

In Palestine when land was taken on by tenants (people who farmed but did not own the land) it was usually agreed that a part of the harvest would be paid as the year's rent. This would either be taken to the owner or he would send his servant to collect it.

Then Jesus told the people this parable: "There was once a man who planted a vineyard, let it out to tenants, and then left home for a long time. When the time came to gather the grapes, he sent a slave to the tenants to receive from them his share of the harvest. But the tenants beat the slave and sent him back without a thing. So he sent another slave; but the tenants beat him also, treated him shamefully, and sent him back without a thing. Then he sent a third slave; the tenants wounded him, too, and threw him out. Then the owner of the vineyard said, 'What shall I do? I will send my own dear son; surely they will respect him!' But when the tenants saw him, they said to one another, 'This is the owner's son. Let's kill him, and his property will be ours!' So they threw him out of the vineyard and killed him.

"What, then, will the owner of the vineyard do to the tenants?" Jesus asked.

Stories about prayer

The gospel writers were keen to show that, while we wait for Jesus, we can still be in touch with him and hear him through prayer. These three stories illustrate different aspects of prayer.

The parable of the friend at midnight   Luke 11.5–8

And Jesus said to his disciples, "Suppose one of you should go to a friend's house at midnight and say to him, 'Friend, let me borrow three loaves of bread. A friend of mine who is on a journey has just come to my house, and I haven't got any food for him!' And suppose your friend should answer from inside, 'Don't bother me! The door is already locked, and my children and I are in bed. I can't get up and give you anything.' Well, what then? I tell you that even if he will not get up and give you the bread because you are his friend, yet he will get up and give you everything you need because you are not ashamed to keep on asking."

The parable of the widow and the judge   Luke 18.1–8

Then Jesus told his disciples a parable to teach them that they should always pray and never become discouraged. "In a certain town there was a judge who neither feared God nor respected man. And there was a widow in that same town who kept coming to him and pleading for her rights, saying, 'Help me against my opponent!' For a long time the judge refused to act, but at last he said to himself, 'Even though I don't fear God or respect man, yet because of all the trouble this widow is giving me, I will see to it that she gets her rights. If I don't, she will keep on coming and finally wear me out!'"

And the Lord continued, "Listen to what that corrupt judge said. Now, will God not judge in favour of his own people who cry to him day and night for help? Will he be slow to help them? I tell you, he will judge in their favour and do it quickly. But will the Son of Man find faith on earth when he comes?"

The parable of the Pharisee and the tax collector
Luke 18.9–14

Jesus also told this parable to people who were sure of their own goodness and despised everybody else. "Once there were two men who went up to the Temple to pray: one was a Pharisee, the other a tax collector.

"The Pharisee stood apart by himself and prayed, 'I thank you, God, that I am not greedy, dishonest, or an adulterer, like everybody else. I thank you that I am not like that tax collector over there. I fast two days a week, and I give you a tenth of all my income.'

"But the tax collector stood at a distance and would not even raise his face to heaven, but beat on his breast and said, 'God, have pity on me, a sinner!' I tell you," said Jesus, "the tax collector, and not the Pharisee, was in the right with God when he went home. For everyone who makes himself great will be humbled, and everyone who humbles himself will be made great."

Stories about what really matters

These stories ask the question, "Is money more important than God?"

The parable of the unforgiving servant
Matthew 18.21–35

Then Peter came to Jesus and asked, "Lord, if my brother keeps on sinning against me, how many times do I have to forgive him? Seven times?"

"No, not seven times," answered Jesus, "but seventy times seven, because the Kingdom of heaven is like this. Once there was a king who decided to check on his servants' accounts. He had just begun to do so when one of them was brought in who owed him millions of pounds. The servant did not have enough to pay his debt, so the king ordered him to be sold as a slave, with his wife and his children and all that he had, in order to pay the debt. The servant fell on his knees before the king. 'Be patient with me,' he begged, 'and I will pay you everything!' The king felt sorry for him, so he forgave him the debt and let him go.

"Then the man went out and met one of his fellow-servants who owed him a few pounds. He grabbed him and started choking him. 'Pay back what you owe me!' he said. His fellow-servant fell down and begged him, 'Be patient with me, and I will pay you back!' But he refused; instead, he had him thrown into jail until he should pay the debt. When the other servants saw what had happened, they were very upset and went to the king and told him everything. So he called the servant in. 'You worthless slave!' he said. 'I forgave you the whole amount you owed me, just because you asked me to. You should have had mercy on your fellow-servant, just as I had mercy on you.' The king was very angry, and he sent the servant to jail to be punished until he should pay back the whole amount."

And Jesus concluded, "That is how my Father in heaven will treat every one of you unless you forgive your brother from your heart."

The parable of the rich fool Luke 12.13–21

It was the custom for people to come to Rabbis and ask them to settle disputes. This man does not get the answer he wants.

A man in the crowd said to Jesus, "Teacher, tell my brother to divide with me the property our father left us."

Jesus answered him, "My friend, who gave me the right to judge or to divide the property between you two?" And he went on to say to them all, "Watch out and guard yourselves from every kind of greed; because a person's true life is not made up of the things he owns, no matter how rich he may be."

Then Jesus told them this parable: "There was once a rich man who had land which bore good crops. He began to think to himself, 'I haven't anywhere to keep all my crops. What can I do? This is what I will do,' he told himself; 'I will tear down my barns and build bigger ones, where I will store my corn and all my other goods. Then I will say to myself, Lucky man! You have all the good things you need for many years. Take life easy, eat, drink, and enjoy yourself!' But God said to him, 'You fool!

This very night you will have to give up your life; then who will get all these things you have kept for yourself?' "

And Jesus concluded, "This is how it is with those who pile up riches for themselves but are not rich in God's sight."

The rich man and Lazarus   Luke 16.19–31

Parties are always given by somebody. The Jews thought of heaven almost as if it were a party to be given by Abraham. He was their founder and they expected him to be very important in heaven. "Hades" was a place where the dead suffered. Today it would be described as "Hell".

"There was once a rich man who dressed in the most expensive clothes and lived in great luxury every day. There was also a poor man named Lazarus, covered with sores, who used to be brought to the rich man's door, hoping to eat the bits of food that fell from the rich man's table. Even the dogs would come and lick his sores.

"The poor man died and was carried by the angels to sit beside Abraham at the feast in heaven. The rich man died and was buried, and in Hades, where he was in great pain, he looked up and saw Abraham, far away, with Lazarus at his side. So he called out, 'Father Abraham! Take pity on me, and send Lazarus to dip his finger in some water and cool my tongue, because I am in great pain in this fire!'

"But Abraham said, 'Remember, my son, that in your lifetime you were given all the good things, while Lazarus got all the bad things. But now he is enjoying himself here, while you are in pain. Besides all that, there is a deep pit lying between us, so that those who want to cross over from here to you cannot do so, nor can anyone cross over to us from where you are.' The rich man said, 'Then I beg you, father Abraham, send Lazarus to my father's house, where I have five brothers. Let him go and warn them so that they, at least, will not come to this place of pain.'

"Abraham said, 'Your brothers have Moses and the prophets to warn them; your brothers should listen to what they say.' The rich man answered, 'That is not enough, father Abraham! But if someone were to rise from death and go to them, then they would turn from their sins.' But Abraham said, 'If they will not listen to Moses and the prophets, they will not be convinced even if someone were to rise from death.' ' "

Things are not always what they seem

The parable of the two sons   Matthew 21.28–32

"Now, what do you think? There was once a man who had two sons. He went to the elder one and said, 'Son, go and work in the vineyard today.' 'I don't want to,' he answered, but later he changed his mind and went. Then the father went to the other son and said the same thing. 'Yes, sir,' he answered, but he did not go. Which one of the two did what his father wanted?"

"The elder one," they answered.

So Jesus said to them, "I tell you: the tax collectors and the prostitutes are going into the Kingdom of God ahead of you. For John the Baptist came to you showing you the right path to take, and you would not believe him; but the tax collectors and the prostitutes believed him. Even when you saw this, you did not later change your minds and believe him."

The parable of the good Samaritan   Luke 10.25–37

The Samaritans lived between Judaea and Galilee, the two parts of Palestine where most of the Jews lived. They were a mixed race, descended from the Assyrians who had married Jews. Because of differences in customs, religion, and politics, there was much bad feeling between the Jews and the Samaritans.

A teacher of the Law came up and tried to trap Jesus. "Teacher," he asked, "what must I do to receive eternal life?"

Jesus answered him, "What do the Scriptures say? How do you interpret them?"

The man answered, "Love the Lord your God with all your heart, with all your soul, with all your strength, and with all your mind'; and 'Love your neighbour as you love yourself.'"

"You are right," Jesus replied; "do this and you will live."

But the teacher of the Law wanted to justify himself, so he asked Jesus, "Who is my neighbour?"

Jesus answered, "There was once a man who was going down from Jerusalem to Jericho when robbers attacked him, stripped him, and beat him up, leaving him half dead. It so happened that a priest was going down that road; but when he saw the man, he walked on by, on the other side. In the same way a Levite also came along, went over and looked at the man, and then walked on by, on the other side. But a Samaritan who was travelling that way came upon the man, and when he saw him, his heart was filled with pity. He went over to him, poured oil and wine on his wounds and bandaged them; then he put the man on his own animal and took him to an inn, where he took care of him. The next day he took out two silver coins and gave them to the innkeeper. 'Take care of him,' he told the innkeeper, 'and when I come back this way, I will pay you whatever else you spend on him.'"

And Jesus concluded, "In your opinion, which one of these three acted like a neighbour towards the man attacked by the robbers?"

The teacher of the Law answered, "The one who was kind to him."

Jesus replied, "You go, then, and do the same."

The story of the final judgement   Matthew 25.31–46

We are not judged by what we pretend to be.

In some countries some kinds of sheep and goats look very much alike. One of the jobs the shepherd in Palestine had to do regularly was to separate his sheep from wild goats who joined themselves to the flock as they roamed around. The sheep were taken into the sheepfold and the goats were sent away. Jesus used this event to illustrate another kind of separation.

"When the Son of Man comes as King and all the angels with him, he will sit on his royal throne, and the people of all the nations will be gathered before him. Then he will divide them into two groups, just as a shepherd separates the sheep from the goats. He will put the righteous people on his right and the others on his left. Then the King will say to the people on his right, 'Come, you that are blessed by my Father! Come and possess the kingdom which has been prepared for you ever since the creation of the world. I was hungry and you fed me, thirsty and you gave me a drink; I was a stranger and you received me in your homes, naked and you clothed me; I was sick and you took care of me, in prison and you visited me.'

"The righteous will then answer him, 'When, Lord, did we ever see you hungry and feed you, or thirsty and give you a drink? When did we ever see you a stranger and welcome you in our homes, or naked and clothe you? When did we ever see you sick or in prison, and visit you?' The King will reply, 'I tell you, whenever you did this for one of the least important of these brothers of mine, you did it for me!'

229

"Then he will say to those on his left, 'Away from me, you that are under God's curse! Away to the eternal fire which has been prepared for the Devil and his angels! I was hungry but you would not feed me, thirsty but you would not give me a drink; I was a stranger but you would not welcome me in your homes, naked but you would not clothe me; I was sick and in prison but you would not take care of me.'

"Then they will answer him, 'When, Lord, did we ever see you hungry or thirsty or a stranger or naked or sick or in prison, and would not help you?' The King will reply, 'I tell you, whenever you refused to help one of these least important ones, you refused to help me.' These, then, will be sent off to eternal punishment, but the righteous will go to eternal life."

4
Jesus teaches

Parables were just one way Jesus used to teach his followers. He also gave his followers many sayings to think about and remember. He discussed issues with people and debated with groups. It was the duty of a disciple to remember his master's teaching accurately and pass it on to others. Here are some examples of Jesus' teaching.

The Sermon on the Mount

This is one of the most famous examples of Jesus' teaching. It is a collection of sayings about how Jesus wanted his followers to behave. Much of what he said was quite different from anything his hearers had heard before.

Providing the salt   Matthew 5.13

Although salt is now mainly used for flavouring, before the days of fridges and freezers it was used to stop food going bad.

"You are like salt for all mankind. But if salt loses its saltiness, there is no way to make it salty again. It has become worthless, so it is thrown out and people trample on it."

Letting your light shine   Matthew 5.14–16

"You are like light for the whole world. A city built on a hill cannot be hidden. No one lights a lamp and puts it under a bowl; instead he puts it on the lampstand, where it gives light for everyone in the house. In the same way your light must shine before people, so that they will see the good things you do and praise your Father in heaven."

Teaching about anger   Matthew 5.21–26

"You have heard that people were told in the past, 'Do not commit murder; anyone who does will be brought to trial.' But now I tell you: whoever is angry with his brother will be brought to trial, whoever calls his brother 'You good-for-nothing!' will be brought before the Council, and whoever calls his brother a worthless fool will be in danger of going to the fire of hell. So if you are about to offer your gift to God at the altar and there you remember that your brother has something against you, leave your gift there in front of the altar, go at once and make peace with your brother, and then come back and offer your gift to God.

"If someone brings a lawsuit against you and takes you to court, settle the dispute with him while there is time, before you get to court. Once you are there, he will hand you over to the judge, who will hand you over to the police, and you will be put in jail. There you will stay, I tell you, until you pay the last penny of your fine."

Teaching about revenge   Matthew 5.38–42

"An eye for an eye and a tooth for a tooth" was a well-known saying on which many old laws were based. If a man was found guilty of attacking another and causing injury, the punishment should not have been greater than the injury caused.

A much more recent Roman law said that a Roman soldier could force a Jew to carry his pack for about one kilometre. The Jews greatly resented this.

"You have heard that it was said, 'An eye for an eye, and a tooth for a tooth.' But now I tell you: do not take revenge on someone who wrongs you. If anyone slaps you on the right cheek, let him slap your left cheek too. And if someone takes you to court to sue you for your shirt, let him have your coat as well. And if one of the occupation troops forces you to carry his pack one kilometre, carry it two kilometres. When someone asks you for something, give it to him; when someone wants to borrow something, lend it to him."

Love your enemies   Matthew 5.43–48

In this passage Jesus mentions two groups of people. The words "tax collector" would immediately make his audience think of someone who was greedy, dishonest, and despised. "Pagans" were people who did not worship the true God.

"You have heard that it was said, 'Love your friends, hate your enemies.' But now I tell you: love your enemies and pray for those who persecute you, so that you may become the sons of your Father in heaven. For he makes his sun to shine on bad and good people alike, and gives rain to those who do good and to those who do evil. Why should God reward you if you love only the people who love you? Even the tax collectors do that! And if you speak only to your friends, have you done anything out of the ordinary? Even the pagans do that! You must be perfect—just as your Father in heaven is perfect!"

Teaching about giving   Matthew 6.1–4

"Hypocrite" is the Greek word for an actor. It means someone who pretends to be what they are not.

"Make certain you do not perform your religious duties in public so that people will see what you do. If you do these things publicly, you will not have any reward from your Father in heaven.

"So when you give something to a needy person, do not make a big show of it, as the hypocrites do in the houses of worship and on the streets. They do it so that people will praise them. I assure you, they have already been paid in full. But when you help a needy person, do it in such a way that even your closest friend will not know about it. Then it will be a private matter. And your Father, who sees what you do in private, will reward you."

Teaching about prayer   Matthew 6.5–15

You may know this prayer but in slightly different words. The "Lord's prayer", as it is called, is a translation of what Jesus actually said.

It is the thoughts and ideas that are important, rather than the words used to express them.

"When you pray, do not be like the hypocrites! They love to stand up and pray in the houses of worship and on the street corners, so that everyone will see them. I assure you, they have already been paid in full. But when you pray, go to your room, close the door, and pray to your Father, who is unseen. And your Father, who sees what you do in private, will reward you.

"When you pray, do not use a lot of meaningless words, as the pagans do, who think that their gods will hear them because their prayers are long. Do not be like them. Your Father already knows what you need before you ask him. This, then, is how you should pray:

'Our Father in heaven:
  May your holy name be honoured;
  may your Kingdom come;
  may your will be done on earth as it is in heaven.
  Give us today the food we need.
  Forgive us the wrongs we have done,
  as we forgive the wrongs that others have done to us.
  Do not bring us to hard testing,
  but keep us safe from the Evil One.'

"If you forgive others the wrongs they have done to you, your Father in heaven will also forgive you. But if you do not forgive others, then your Father will not forgive the wrongs you have done."

Riches in heaven   Matthew 6.19–21

"Do not store up riches for yourselves here on earth, where moths and rust destroy, and robbers break in and steal. Instead, store up riches for yourselves in heaven, where moths and rust cannot destroy, and robbers cannot break in and steal. For your heart will always be where your riches are."

God and possessions   Matthew 6.24–34

"No one can be a slave of two masters; he will hate one and love the other; he will be loyal to one and despise the other. You cannot serve both God and money.

"This is why I tell you not to be worried about the food and drink you need in order to stay alive, or about clothes for your body. After all, isn't life worth more than food? And isn't the body worth more than clothes? Look at the birds: they do not sow seeds, gather a harvest and put it in barns; yet your Father in heaven takes care of them! Aren't you worth much more than birds? Can any of you live a bit longer by worrying about it?

"And why worry about clothes? Look how the wild flowers grow: they do not work or make clothes for themselves. But I tell you that not even King Solomon with all his wealth had clothes as beautiful as one of these flowers. It is God who clothes the wild grass—grass that is here today and gone tomorrow, burnt up in the oven. Won't he be all the more sure to clothe you? How little faith you have!

"So do not start worrying: 'Where will my food come from? or my drink? or my clothes?' (These are the things the pagans are always concerned about.) Your Father in heaven knows that you need all these things. Instead, be concerned above everything else with the Kingdom of God and with what he requires of you, and he will provide you with all these other things. So do not worry about tomorrow; it will have enough worries of its own. There is no need to add to the troubles each day brings."

Judging others   Matthew 7.1–6

"Do not judge others, so that God will not judge you, for God will judge you in the same way as you judge others, and he will apply to you the same rules you apply to others. Why, then, do you look at the speck in your brother's eye, and pay no attention to the log in your own eye? How dare you say to your brother, 'Please, let me take that speck out of your eye,' when you have a log in your own eye? You hypocrite! First take the log out of your own eye, and then you will be able to see clearly to take the speck out of your brother's eye.

"Do not give what is holy to dogs—they will only turn and attack you. Do not throw your pearls in front of pigs—they will only trample them underfoot."

Ask, seek, knock   Matthew 7.7–12

"Ask, and you will receive; seek, and you will find; knock, and the door will be opened to you. For everyone who asks will receive, and anyone who seeks will find, and the door will be opened to him who knocks. Would any of you who are fathers give your son a stone when he asks for bread? Or would you give him a snake when he asks for a fish? Bad as you are, you know how to give good things to your children. How much more, then, will your Father in heaven give good things to those who ask him!

"Do for others what you want them to do for you: this is the meaning of the Law of Moses and of the teachings of the prophets."

The narrow gate   Matthew 7.13–14

"Go in through the narrow gate, because the gate to hell is wide and the road that leads to it is easy, and there are many who travel it. But the gate to life is narrow and the way that leads to it is hard, and there are few people who find it."

A tree and its fruit   Matthew 7.15–20

"Be on your guard against false prophets; they come to you looking like sheep on the outside, but on the inside they are really like wild wolves. You will know them by what they do. Thorn bushes do not bear grapes, and briars do not bear figs. A healthy tree bears good fruit, but a poor tree bears bad fruit. A healthy tree cannot bear bad fruit, and a poor tree cannot bear good fruit. And any tree that does not bear good fruit is cut down and thrown in the fire. So then, you will know the false prophets by what they do."

I never knew you   Matthew 7.21–23

"Not everyone who calls me 'Lord, Lord' will enter the Kingdom of heaven, but only those who do what my Father in heaven wants them to do. When Judgement Day comes, many will say to me, 'Lord, Lord! In your name we spoke God's message, by your name we drove out many demons and performed many miracles!' Then I will say to them, 'I never knew you. Get away from me, you wicked people!'"

The two house builders   Matthew 7.24–27

"So then, anyone who hears these words of mine and obeys them is like a wise man who built his house on rock. The rain poured down, the rivers overflowed, and the wind blew hard against that house. But it did not fall, because it was built on rock.

"But anyone who hears these words of mine and does not obey them is like a foolish man who built his house on sand. The rain poured down, the rivers overflowed, the wind blew hard against that house, and it fell. And what a terrible fall that was!"

Crowd reaction   Matthew 7.28–29

When Jesus finished saying these things, the crowd was amazed at the way he taught. He wasn't like the teachers of the Law; instead, he taught with authority.

Jesus and the people who kept the Law

Some people believed that Jesus' teachings were important and should be followed. Others thought they were very dangerous because they ignored the rules they had always been taught to keep. So they tried to trap Jesus.

The Sadducees   Matthew 22.23–33

The Sadducees were a small Jewish religious party who based their beliefs mainly on the first five books of the Old Testament. They had several beliefs and practices which were different from those of the larger party of the Pharisees. The most important difference was that the Sadducees did not believe that people would come back to life after they had died.

That same day some Sadducees came to Jesus and claimed that people will not rise from death. "Teacher," they said, "Moses said that if a man who has no children dies, his brother must marry the widow so that they can have children who will be considered the dead man's children. Now, there were seven brothers who used to live here. The eldest got married and died without having children, so he left his widow to his brother. The same thing happened to the second brother, to the third, and finally to all seven. Last of all, the woman died. Now, on the day when the dead rise to life, whose wife will she be? All of them had married her."

Jesus answered them, "How wrong you are! It is because you don't know the Scriptures or God's power. For when the dead rise to life, they will be like the angels in heaven and will not marry. Now, as for the dead rising to life: haven't you ever read what God has told you? He said, 'I am the God of Abraham, the God of Isaac, and the God of Jacob.' He is the God of the living, not of the dead."

When the crowds heard this, they were amazed at his teaching.

The Pharisees   Matthew 23.1–7

This religious group were very strict in obeying the Law and the other rules which had been added to it during the centuries. But Jesus had many criticisms about their attitude towards the Law.

If a man was holding a feast he would reserve seats close to his own for special guests. To sit in these seats regularly would give others the impression that the person was of great importance. People were also impressed by long tassels on cloaks and verses of Scripture strapped to the body. The tassels were a sign of devotion to God and the straps were supposed to show respect for his Law.

Then Jesus spoke to the crowds and to his disciples. "The teachers of the Law and the Pharisees are the authorized interpreters of Moses' Law. So you must obey and follow everything they tell you to do; do not, however, imitate their actions, because they don't practise what they preach. They tie on to people's backs loads that are heavy and hard to carry, yet they aren't willing even to lift a finger to help them carry those loads. They do

240

everything so that people will see them. Look at the straps with scripture verses on them which they wear on their foreheads and arms, and notice how large they are! Notice also how long are the tassels on their cloaks! They love the best places at feasts and the reserved seats in the synagogues; they love to be greeted with respect in the market-places and to be called 'Teacher.'"

Blind guides!   Matthew 23.23–26

Jesus warned those people who obeyed the Law in little things but who ignored the really important teachings.

"How terrible for you, teachers of the Law and Pharisees! You hypocrites! You give to God a tenth even of the seasoning herbs, such as mint, dill, and cumin, but you neglect to obey the really important teachings of the Law, such as justice and mercy and honesty. These you should practise, without neglecting the others. Blind guides! You strain a fly out of your drink, but swallow a camel!

"How terrible for you, teachers of the Law and Pharisees! You hypocrites! You clean the outside of your cup and plate, while the inside is full of what you have obtained by violence and selfishness. Blind Pharisee! Clean what is inside the cup first, and then the outside will be clean too!"

Nicodemus   John 3.1–17

People seldom visited each other at night in Palestine. When this did happen it was often done to keep the visit a secret.

There was a Jewish leader named Nicodemus, who belonged to the party of the Pharisees. One night he went to Jesus and said to him, "Rabbi, we know that you are a teacher sent by God. No one could perform the miracles you are doing unless God were with him."

Jesus answered, "I am telling you the truth: no one can see the Kingdom of God unless he is born again."

"How can a grown man be born again?" Nicodemus asked. "He certainly cannot enter his mother's womb and be born a second time!"

"I am telling you the truth," replied Jesus. "No one can enter the Kingdom of God unless he is born of water and the Spirit. A person is born physically of human parents, but he is born spiritually of the Spirit. Do not be surprised because I tell you that you must all be born again. The wind blows wherever it wishes; you hear the sound it makes, but you do not know where it comes from or where it is going. It is like that with everyone who is born of the Spirit."

241

"How can this be?" asked Nicodemus.

Jesus answered, "You are a great teacher in Israel, and you don't know this? I am telling you the truth: we speak of what we know and report what we have seen, yet none of you is willing to accept our message. You do not believe me when I tell you about the things of this world; how will you ever believe me, then, when I tell you about the things of heaven? And no one has ever gone up to heaven except the Son of Man, who came down from heaven."

As Moses lifted up the bronze snake on a pole in the desert, in the same way the Son of Man must be lifted up, so that everyone who believes in him may have eternal life. For God loved the world so much that he gave his only Son, so that everyone who believes in him may not die but have eternal life. For God did not send his Son into the world to be its judge, but to be its saviour.

Jesus and people who broke the Law

The Samaritan woman   John 4.1–26

Most of the Jews despised the Samaritans. In fact those who lived in the North of Palestine would sometimes take a long detour around Samaria rather than go through it on their way to the South. Men of all races looked down on women and it would be most unusual for a man to be seen holding a conversation with a woman in public. Jesus seemed different in both respects.

The Pharisees heard that Jesus was winning and baptizing more disciples than John. (Actually, Jesus himself did not baptize anyone; only his disciples did.) So when Jesus heard what was being said, he left Judaea and went back to Galilee; on his way there he had to go through Samaria.

In Samaria he came to a town named Sychar, which was not far from the field that Jacob had given to his son Joseph. Jacob's well was there, and Jesus, tired out by the journey, sat down by the well. It was about noon.

A Samaritan woman came to draw some water, and Jesus said to her, "Give me a drink of water." (His disciples had gone into town to buy food.)

The woman answered, "You are a Jew, and I am a Samaritan—so how can you ask me for a drink?" (Jews will not use the same cups and bowls that Samaritans use.)

Jesus answered, "If only you knew what God gives and who it is that is asking you for a drink, you would ask him, and he would give you life-giving water."

"Sir," the woman said, "you haven't got a bucket, and the well is deep. Where would you get that life-giving water? It was our ancestor Jacob who gave us this well; he and his sons and his flocks all drank from it. You don't claim to be greater than Jacob, do you?"

Jesus answered, "Whoever drinks this water will be thirsty again, but whoever drinks the water that I will give him will never be thirsty again. The water that I will give him will become in him a spring which will provide him with life-giving water and give him eternal life."

"Sir," the woman said, "give me that water! Then I will never be thirsty again, nor will I have to come here to draw water."

"Go and call your husband," Jesus told her, "and come back."

"I haven't got a husband," she answered.

Jesus replied, "You are right when you say you haven't got a husband. You have been married to five men, and the man you live with now is not really your husband. You have told me the truth."

"I see you are a prophet, sir," the woman said. "My Samaritan ancestors worshipped God on this mountain, but you Jews say that Jerusalem is the place where we should worship God."

Jesus said to her, "Believe me, woman, the time will come when people will not worship the Father either on this mountain or in Jerusalem. You Samaritans do not really know whom you worship; but we Jews know whom we worship, because it is from the Jews that salvation comes. But the time is coming and is already here, when by the power of God's Spirit people will worship the Father as he really is, offering him the true worship that he wants. God is Spirit, and only by the power of his Spirit can people worship him as he really is."

The woman said to him, "I know that the Messiah will come, and when he comes, he will tell us everything."

Jesus answered, "I am he, I who am talking with you."

The woman caught in adultery   John 8.2–11

When a Rabbi was in the Temple it was the custom amongst the Jews to bring people who had broken the Law to be judged. Jesus sensed that in this case those who came were simply trying to put him in a difficult position. If he ordered the punishment they suggested, he would appear to be acting very harshly. If he did not do this, they were ready to accuse him of avoiding his responsibility and going against the Law of Moses.

243

Early the next morning he went back to the Temple. All the people gathered round him, and he sat down and began to teach them. The teachers of the Law and the Pharisees brought in a woman who had been caught committing adultery, and they made her stand before them all. "Teacher," they said to Jesus, "this woman was caught in the very act of committing adultery. In our Law Moses commanded that such a woman must be stoned to death. Now, what do you say?" They said this to trap Jesus, so that they could accuse him. But he bent over and wrote on the ground with his finger.

As they stood there asking him questions, he straightened himself up and said to them, "Whichever one of you has committed no sin may throw the first stone at her." Then he bent over again and wrote on the ground. When they heard this, they all left, one by one, the older ones first. Jesus was left alone, with the woman still standing there. He straightened himself up and said to her, "Where are they? Is there no one left to condemn you?"

"No one, sir," she answered.

"Well, then," Jesus said, "I do not condemn you either. Go, but do not sin again."

What sort of laws should we keep?

Things that make a person unclean   Matthew 15.10–20

One of the Pharisees' customs was that before they ate they had to go through a very complicated hand-washing ceremony. This was not for greater hygiene, but was meant to remove anything that would make them unclean or unacceptable to God.

Then Jesus called the crowd to him and said to them, "Listen and understand! It is not what goes into a person's mouth that makes him ritually unclean; rather, what comes out of it makes him unclean."

Then the disciples came to him and said, "Do you know that the Pharisees had their feelings hurt by what you said?"

"Every plant which my Father in heaven did not plant will be pulled up," answered Jesus. "Don't worry about them! They are blind leaders of the blind; and when one blind man leads another, both fall into a ditch."

Peter spoke up, "Explain this saying to us."

Jesus said to them, "You are still no more intelligent than the others. Don't you understand? Anything that goes into a person's mouth goes into his stomach and then on out of his body. But the things that come out of the mouth come from the heart, and these are the things that make a person ritually unclean. For from his heart come the evil ideas which lead him to kill, commit adultery, and do other immoral things; to rob, lie, and slander others. These are the things that make a person unclean. But to eat without washing your hands as they say you should—this doesn't make a person unclean."

The question about paying taxes   Matthew 22.15–22

The Jews believed that their land, Israel, belonged to God. So they did not think that they should have to pay taxes to a foreign power. They would not have expected the Messiah to encourage them to do so.

But to discourage the payment of taxes would lead to being severely punished by the Romans. The Pharisees thought they were being extremely clever in asking Jesus about this problem.

The Pharisees went off and made a plan to trap Jesus with questions. Then they sent to him some of their disciples and some members of Herod's party. "Teacher," they said, "we know that you tell the truth. You teach the truth about God's will for man, without worrying about what people think, because you pay no attention to a man's status. Tell us, then, what do you think? Is it against our Law to pay taxes to the Roman Emperor, or not?"

Jesus, however, was aware of their evil plan, and so he said, "You hypocrites! Why are you trying to trap me? Show me the coin for paying the tax!"

They brought him the coin, and he asked them, "Whose face and name are these?"

"The Emperor's," they answered.

So Jesus said to them, "Well, then, pay the Emperor what belongs to the Emperor, and pay God what belongs to God."

When they heard this, they were amazed; and they left him and went away.

The great commandment   Matthew 22.34–40

When the Pharisees heard that Jesus had silenced the Sadducees, they came together, and one of them, a teacher of the Law, tried to trap him with a question. "Teacher," he asked, "which is the greatest commandment in the Law?"

Jesus answered, "'Love the Lord your God with all your heart, with all your soul, and with all your mind.' This is the greatest and the most important commandment. The second most important commandment is like it: 'Love your neighbour as you love yourself.' The whole Law of Moses and the teachings of the prophets depend on these two commandments."

Jesus heals on the Sabbath   Luke 13.10–17

People at the time of Jesus linked illness with evil. The Jewish Law was also very strict about what was allowed on the Sabbath day (the day of rest).

One Sabbath Jesus was teaching in a synagogue. A woman there had an evil spirit that had made her ill for eighteen years; she was bent over and could not straighten up at all. When Jesus saw her, he called out to her, "Woman, you are free from your illness!" He placed his hands on her, and at once she straightened herself up and praised God.

The official of the synagogue was angry that Jesus had healed on the Sabbath, so he spoke up and said to the people, "There are six days in which we should work; so come during those days and be healed, but not on the Sabbath!"

The Lord answered him, "You hypocrites! Any one of you would untie his ox or his donkey from the stall and take it out to give it water on the Sabbath. Now here is this descendant of Abraham whom Satan has kept bound up for eighteen years; should she not be released on the Sabbath?" His answer made his enemies ashamed of themselves, while the people rejoiced over all the wonderful things that he did.

5
The road
to the cross

Jesus was popular with many people but opposition was growing. He had openly criticized the Pharisees and upset the Sadducees. These were very powerful groups. Together they formed much of the council which, with the Romans' permission, was in charge of anything to do with religion. The time of Jesus' death on the cross was drawing closer.

The great discovery

Peter realizes who Jesus is   Matthew 16.13–20

Lots of people wondered who Jesus was. Jesus seemed to be most concerned about who his disciples thought he was.

Jesus went to the territory near the town of Caesarea Philippi, where he asked his disciples, "Who do people say the Son of Man is?"

"Some say John the Baptist," they answered. "Others say Elijah, while others say Jeremiah or some other prophet."

"What about you?" he asked them. "Who do you say I am?"

Simon Peter answered, "You are the Messiah, the Son of the living God."

"Good for you, Simon son of John!" answered Jesus. "For this truth did not come to you from any human being, but it was given to you directly by my Father in heaven. And so I tell you, Peter: you are a rock, and on this rock foundation I will build my church, and not even death will ever be able to overcome it. I will give you the keys of the Kingdom of heaven;

248

what you prohibit on earth will be prohibited in heaven, and what you permit on earth will be permitted in heaven."

Then Jesus ordered his disciples not to tell anyone that he was the Messiah.

Jesus speaks about his suffering and death
Matthew 16.21–28

Up until now everyone had thought of the Messiah reigning as King of the Jews. Nobody had thought of him suffering.

From that time on Jesus began to say plainly to his disciples, "I must go to Jerusalem and suffer much from the elders, the chief priests, and the teachers of the Law. I will be put to death, but three days later I will be raised to life."

Peter took him aside and began to rebuke him. "God forbid it, Lord!" he said. "That must never happen to you!"

Jesus turned around and said to Peter, "Get away from me, Satan! You are an obstacle in my way, because these thoughts of yours don't come from God, but from man."

Then Jesus said to his disciples, "If anyone wants to come with me, he must forget self, carry his cross, and follow me. For whoever wants to save his own life will lose it; but whoever loses his life for my sake will find it. Will a person gain anything if he wins the whole world but loses his life? Of course not! There is nothing he can give to regain his life. For the Son of Man is about to come in the glory of his Father with his angels, and then he will reward each one according to his deeds. I assure you that there are some here who will not die until they have seen the Son of Man come as King."

The transfiguration   Mark 9.2–13

Six days later Jesus took with him Peter, James, and John, and led them up a high mountain, where they were alone. As they looked on, a change came over Jesus, and his clothes became shining white—whiter than anyone in the world could wash them. Then the three disciples saw Elijah and Moses talking with Jesus. Peter spoke up and said to Jesus, "Teacher, how good it is that we are here! We will make three tents, one for you, one for Moses, and one for Elijah." He and the others were so frightened that he did not know what to say.

Then a cloud appeared and covered them with its shadow, and a voice came from the cloud, "This is my own dear Son—listen to him!" They

took a quick look round but did not see anyone else; only Jesus was with them.

As they came down the mountain, Jesus ordered them, "Don't tell anyone what you have seen, until the Son of Man has risen from death."

They obeyed his order, but among themselves they started discussing the matter, "What does this 'rising from death' mean?" And they asked Jesus, "Why do the teachers of the Law say that Elijah has to come first?"

His answer was, "Elijah is indeed coming first in order to get everything ready. Yet why do the Scriptures say that the Son of Man will suffer much and be rejected? I tell you, however, that Elijah has already come and that people treated him just as they pleased, as the Scriptures say about him."

Humility goes with greatness

Jesus goes to great lengths to emphasize to his followers the importance of humility and service. To be a follower of Jesus, people had to put the needs of others before their own and to serve others, not themselves.

Who is the greatest?   Mark 9.33–37

They came to Capernaum, and after going indoors Jesus asked his disciples, "What were you arguing about on the road?"

But they would not answer him, because on the road they had been arguing among themselves about who was the greatest. Jesus sat down, called the twelve disciples, and said to them, "Whoever wants to be first must place himself last of all and be the servant of all." Then he took a child and made him stand in front of them. He put his arms round him and said to them, "Whoever welcomes in my name one of these children, welcomes me; and whoever welcomes me, welcomes not only me but also the one who sent me."

Whoever is not against us is for us   Mark 9.38–41

John said to him, "Teacher, we saw a man who was driving out demons in your name, and we told him to stop, because he doesn't belong to our group."

"Do not try to stop him," Jesus told them, "because no one who performs a miracle in my name will be able soon afterwards to say evil things about me. For whoever is not against us is for us. I assure you that anyone who gives you a drink of water because you belong to me will certainly receive his reward.''

Jesus blesses little children   Mark 10.13–16

Some people brought children to Jesus for him to place his hands on them, but the disciples scolded the people. When Jesus noticed this, he was angry and said to his disciples, "Let the children come to me, and do not stop them, because the Kingdom of God belongs to such as these. I assure you that whoever does not receive the Kingdom of God like a child will never enter it." Then he took the children in his arms, placed his hands on each of them, and blessed them.

The rich man   Mark 10.17–31

As Jesus was starting on his way again, a man ran up, knelt before him, and asked him, "Good Teacher, what must I do to receive eternal life?"

"Why do you call me good?" Jesus asked him. "No one is good except God alone. You know the commandments: 'Do not commit murder; do not commit adultery; do not steal; do not accuse anyone falsely; do not cheat; respect your father and your mother.'"

"Teacher," the man said, "ever since I was young, I have obeyed all these commandments."

Jesus looked straight at him with love and said, "You need only one thing. Go and sell all you have and give the money to the poor, and you will have riches in heaven; then come and follow me." When the man heard this, gloom spread over his face, and he went away sad, because he was very rich.

Jesus looked round at his disciples and said to them, "How hard it will be for rich people to enter the Kingdom of God!"

The disciples were shocked at these words, but Jesus went on to say, "My children, how hard it is to enter the Kingdom of God! It is much harder for a rich person to enter the Kingdom of God than for a camel to go through the eye of a needle."

At this the disciples were completely amazed and asked one another, "Who, then, can be saved?"

Jesus looked straight at them and answered, "This is impossible for man, but not for God; everything is possible for God."

Then Peter spoke up, "Look, we have left everything and followed you."

"Yes," Jesus said to them, "and I tell you that anyone who leaves home or brothers or sisters or mother or father or children or fields for me and for the gospel, will receive much more in this present age. He will receive a hundred times more houses, brothers, sisters, mothers, children and fields—and persecutions as well; and in the age to come he will receive eternal life. But many who now are first will be last, and many who now are last will be first."

The request of James and John   Mark 10.35–45

In royal courts the seats next to a king's throne would be occupied by his most important ministers.

Then James and John, the sons of Zebedee, came to Jesus. "Teacher," they said, "there is something we want you to do for us."

"What is it?" Jesus asked them.

They answered, "When you sit on your throne in your glorious Kingdom, we want you to let us sit with you, one at your right and one at your left."

Jesus said to them, "You don't know what you are asking for. Can you drink the cup of suffering that I must drink? Can you be baptized in the way I must be baptized?"

"We can," they answered.

Jesus said to them, "You will indeed drink the cup I must drink and be baptized in the way I must be baptized. But I do not have the right to choose who will sit at my right and my left. It is God who will give these places to those for whom he has prepared them."

When the other ten disciples heard about it, they became angry with James and John. So Jesus called them all together to him and said, "You know that the men who are considered rulers of the heathen have power over them, and the leaders have complete authority. This, however, is not the way it is among you. If one of you wants to be great, he must be the servant of the rest; and if one of you wants to be first, he must be the slave of all. For even the Son of Man did not come to be served; he came to serve and to give his life to redeem many people."

Jesus' love for Jerusalem   Luke 13.31–35

At that same time some Pharisees came to Jesus and said to him, "You must get out of here and go somewhere else, because Herod wants to kill you."

Jesus answered them, "Go and tell that fox: 'I am driving out demons and performing cures today and tomorrow, and on the third day I shall finish my work.' Yet I must be on my way today, tomorrow, and the next day; it is not right for a prophet to be killed anywhere except in Jerusalem.

"Jerusalem, Jerusalem! You kill the prophets, you stone the messengers God has sent you! How many times have I wanted to put my arms round all your people, just as a hen gathers her chicks under her wings, but you would not let me! And so your Temple will be abandoned. I assure you that you will not see me until the time comes when you say, 'God bless him who comes in the name of the Lord.'"

Death will not be the end

Jesus receives some sad news   John 11.1–16

Bethany was a village very near Jerusalem. When Jesus heard the news he was several days' walking distance away.

A man named Lazarus, who lived in Bethany, was ill. Bethany was the town where Mary and her sister Martha lived. (This Mary was the one who poured the perfume on the Lord's feet and wiped them with her hair; it was her brother Lazarus who was ill.) The sisters sent Jesus a message: "Lord, your dear friend is ill."

When Jesus heard it, he said, "The final result of this illness will not be the death of Lazarus; this has happened in order to bring glory to God, and it will be the means by which the Son of God will receive glory."

Jesus loved Martha and her sister and Lazarus. Yet when he received the news that Lazarus was ill, he stayed where he was for two more days. Then he said to the disciples, "Let us go back to Judaea."

"Teacher," the disciples answered, "just a short time ago the people there wanted to stone you; and are you planning to go back?"

Jesus said, "A day has twelve hours, hasn't it? So whoever walks in broad daylight does not stumble, for he sees the light of this world. But if he walks during the night he stumbles, because he has no light." Jesus said this and then added, "Our friend Lazarus has fallen asleep, but I will go and wake him up."

The disciples answered, "If he is asleep, Lord, he will get well."

Jesus meant that Lazarus had died, but they thought he meant natural sleep. So Jesus told them plainly, "Lazarus is dead, but for your sake I am glad that I was not with him, so that you will believe. Let us go to him."

Thomas (called the Twin) said to his fellow-disciples, "Let us all go with the Teacher, so that we may die with him!"

Jesus makes promises   John 11.17–27

When Jesus arrived, he found that Lazarus had been buried four days before. Bethany was less than three kilometres from Jerusalem, and many Judaeans had come to see Martha and Mary to comfort them over their brother's death.

When Martha heard that Jesus was coming, she went out to meet him, but Mary stayed in the house. Martha said to Jesus, "If you had been here, Lord, my brother would not have died! But I know that even now God will give you whatever you ask him for."

"Your brother will rise to life," Jesus told her.

"I know," she replied, "that he will rise to life on the last day."

Jesus said to her, "I am the resurrection and the life. Whoever believes in me will live, even though he dies; and whoever lives and believes in me will never die. Do you believe this?"

"Yes, Lord!" she answered. "I do believe that you are the Messiah, the Son of God, who was to come into the world."

Jesus weeps   John 11.28–37

After Martha said this, she went back and called her sister Mary privately. "The Teacher is here," she told her, "and is asking for you." When Mary heard this, she got up and hurried out to meet him. (Jesus had not yet arrived in the village, but was still in the place where Martha had met him.) The people who were in the house with Mary, comforting her, followed her when they saw her get up and hurry out. They thought that she was going to the grave to weep there.

Mary arrived where Jesus was, and as soon as she saw him, she fell at his feet. "Lord," she said, "if you had been here, my brother would not have died!"

Jesus saw her weeping, and he saw how the people who were with her were weeping also; his heart was touched, and he was deeply moved. "Where have you buried him?" he asked them.

"Come and see, Lord," they answered.

Jesus wept. "See how much he loved him!" the people said.

But some of them said, "He gave sight to the blind man, didn't he? Could he not have kept Lazarus from dying?"

Lazarus come out!　John 11.38–44

Deeply moved once more, Jesus went to the tomb, which was a cave with a stone placed at the entrance. "Take the stone away!" Jesus ordered.

Martha, the dead man's sister, answered, "There will be a bad smell, Lord. He has been buried four days!"

Jesus said to her, "Didn't I tell you that you would see God's glory if you believed?" They took the stone away. Jesus looked up and said, "I thank you, Father, that you listen to me. I know that you always listen to me, but I say this for the sake of the people here, so that they will believe that you sent me." After he had said this, he called out in a loud voice, "Lazarus, come out!" He came out, his hands and feet wrapped in grave clothes, and with a cloth round his face. "Untie him," Jesus told them, "and let him go."

The plot against Jesus　John 11.45–54

Many of the people who had come to visit Mary saw what Jesus did, and they believed in him. But some of them returned to the Pharisees and told them what Jesus had done. So the Pharisees and the chief priests met with the Council and said, "What shall we do? Look at all the miracles this man is performing! If we let him go on in this way, everyone will believe in him, and the Roman authorities will take action and destroy our Temple and our nation!"

One of them, named Caiaphas, who was High Priest that year, said, "What fools you are! Don't you realize that it is better for you to let one man die for the people, instead of having the whole nation destroyed?" Actually, he did not say this of his own accord; rather, as he was High Priest that year, he was prophesying that Jesus was going to die for the Jewish people, and not only for them, but also to bring together into one body all the scattered people of God.

From that day on the Jewish authorities made plans to kill Jesus. So Jesus did not travel openly in Judaea, but left and went to a place near the desert, to a town named Ephraim, where he stayed with the disciples.

Jesus goes to Jerusalem

It was coming up to the time when the Passover was celebrated. The Law said that every adult male Jew living within twenty-four kilometres of Jerusalem must attend and make sacrifices in the Temple. It was the aim of every Jew living anywhere in the world to do this at least once during their lives. Many others would come great distances, as Jesus had done when he was twelve years old. Often the journey was made several days before, to allow time to prepare for the feast.

Jesus warns his disciples what to expect   Luke 18.31–34

Jesus took the twelve disciples aside and said to them, "Listen! We are going to Jerusalem where everything the prophets wrote about the Son of Man will come true. He will be handed over to the Gentiles, who will mock him, insult him, and spit on him. They will whip him and kill him, but three days later he will rise to life."

But the disciples did not understand any of these things; the meaning of the words was hidden from them, and they did not know what Jesus was talking about.

Jesus' triumphant entry into Jerusalem   Mark 11.1–11

In the Old Testament, the prophets of Israel had not only spoken God's word but acted it out. There had been a prophecy, hundreds of years before, that the Messiah would ride into Jerusalem on a young donkey. This was the animal a king would be expected to ride when he went somewhere in peace.

As they approached Jerusalem, near the towns of Bethphage and Bethany, they came to the Mount of Olives. Jesus sent two of his disciples on ahead with these instructions: "Go to the village there ahead of you. As soon as you get there, you will find a colt tied up that has never been ridden. Untie it and bring it here. And if someone asks you why you are doing that, tell him that the Master needs it and will send it back at once."

So they went and found a colt out in the street, tied to the door of a house. As they were untying it, some of the bystanders asked them, "What are you doing, untying that colt?"

They answered just as Jesus had told them, and the men let them go. They brought the colt to Jesus, threw their cloaks over the animal, and Jesus got on. Many people spread their cloaks on the road, while others cut branches in the fields and spread them on the road. The people who were in front and those who followed behind began to shout, "Praise God! God bless him who comes in the name of the Lord! God bless the coming kingdom of King David, our father! Praise God!"

Jesus entered Jerusalem, went into the Temple, and looked round at everything. But since it was already late in the day, he went out to Bethany with the twelve disciples.

Jesus goes to the Temple   Mark 11.15–19

Around the Temple there were a number of courtyards. Anyone who was not a Jew was not allowed very far into the Temple area. One of the outer courtyards was used as a place for Gentiles (non-Jews) to pray and

think quietly. Some just used this as a shortcut between two parts of the city. A number of stalls had been set up in this area for Jews to buy animals for sacrifice. As Roman money could not be used for this, money-changers also set up stalls to exchange it for special Temple money.

When they arrived in Jerusalem, Jesus went to the Temple and began to drive out all those who were buying and selling. He overturned the tables of the money-changers and the stools of those who sold pigeons, and he would not let anyone carry anything through the temple courtyards. He then taught the people: "It is written in the Scriptures that God said, 'My Temple will be called a house of prayer for the people of all nations.' But you have turned it into a hideout for thieves!"

The chief priests and the teachers of the Law heard of this, so they began looking for some way to kill Jesus. They were afraid of him, because the whole crowd was amazed at his teaching.

When evening came, Jesus and his disciples left the city.

What right have you to do these things?   Mark 11.27–33

As Jesus was walking in the Temple, the chief priests, the teachers of the Law, and the elders came to him and asked him, "What right have you to do these things? Who gave you this right?"

Jesus answered them, "I will ask you just one question, and if you give me an answer, I will tell you what right I have to do these things. Tell me, where did John's right to baptize come from: was it from God or from man?"

They started to argue among themselves: "What shall we say? If we answer, 'From God,' he will say, 'Why, then, did you not believe John?' But if we say, 'From man...'" (They were afraid of the people, because everyone was convinced that John had been a prophet.) So their answer to Jesus was, "We don't know."

Jesus said to them, "Neither will I tell you, then, by what right I do these things."

The widow's offering   Mark 12.41–44

As Jesus sat near the temple treasury, he watched the people as they dropped in their money. Many rich men dropped in a lot of money; then a poor widow came along and dropped in two little copper coins, worth about a penny. He called his disciples together and said to them, "I tell you that this poor widow put more in the offering box than all the others.

262

For the others put in what they had to spare of their riches; but she, poor as she is, put in all she had—she gave all she had to live on."

Jesus talks about the destruction of the Temple
Mark 13.1–2

As Jesus was leaving the Temple, one of his disciples said, "Look, Teacher! What wonderful stones and buildings!"

Jesus answered, "You see these great buildings? Not a single stone here will be left in its place; every one of them will be thrown down."

6

How Jesus died

Crowds of people had followed Jesus. His closest disciples believed that he was the long-awaited Messiah. However, many of the things he did still surprised them. Everyone thought the Messiah would destroy their Roman rulers and make Israel a great country again. Instead, Jesus spoke about suffering and dying.

The people who found Jesus' attitude most difficult to understand were the religious leaders. Jesus had criticized many of them. He seemed to ignore many of the things they thought very important and when they challenged him in front of the people he made them look foolish. These men were very powerful and although the Romans ruled Palestine they allowed them to settle almost all religious matters.

Jesus' enemies move against him

The plot against Jesus   Matthew 26.1–5

Jerusalem was crowded with people who had come to celebrate the Passover. Many of them would have seen Jesus' work in other parts of the country and, much to the embarrassment of some of the Pharisees, they had given Jesus a hero's welcome to the city.

Jesus said to his disciples, "In two days, as you know, it will be the Passover Festival, and the Son of Man will be handed over to be crucified."

Then the chief priests and the elders met together in the palace of Caiaphas, the High Priest, and made plans to arrest Jesus secretly and put him to death. "We must not do it during the festival," they said, "or the people will riot."

Jesus in Bethany   Mark 14.3–9

It was the custom in Palestine when a guest arrived to put a small amount of perfume on their head. It was also the custom to pour perfume onto the bodies of the dead before burial.

Jesus was in Bethany at the house of Simon, a man who had suffered from a dreaded skin-disease. While Jesus was eating, a woman came in with an alabaster jar full of a very expensive perfume made of pure nard. She broke the jar and poured the perfume on Jesus' head. Some of the people there became angry and said to one another, "What was the use of wasting the perfume? It could have been sold for more than three hundred silver coins and the money given to the poor!" And they criticized her harshly.

But Jesus said, "Leave her alone! Why are you bothering her? She has done a fine and beautiful thing for me. You will always have poor people with you, and any time you want to, you can help them. But you will not always have me. She did what she could; she poured perfume on my body to prepare it ahead of time for burial. Now, I assure you that wherever the gospel is preached all over the world, what she has done will be told in memory of her."

Judas plots with the priests   Mark 14.10–11

Judas decided to betray Jesus to the chief priests. The Bible does not tell us much about Judas' reasons for doing this. But we do know that he regretted it later.

Then Judas Iscariot, one of the twelve disciples, went off to the chief priests in order to betray Jesus to them. They were pleased to hear what he had to say, and promised to give him money.

The Last Supper

This was the last meal Jesus was to have with the disciples and it was a very important one.

The upstairs room   Mark 14.12–16

On the first day of the Festival of Unleavened Bread, the day the lambs for the Passover meal were killed, Jesus' disciples asked him, "Where do you want us to go and get the Passover meal ready for you?"

Then Jesus sent two of them with these instructions: "Go into the city, and a man carrying a jar of water will meet you. Follow him to the house he enters, and say to the owner of the house: 'The Teacher says, Where is the room where my disciples and I will eat the Passover meal?' Then he will show you a large upstairs room, prepared and furnished, where you will get everything ready for us."

The disciples left, went to the city, and found everything just as Jesus had told them; and they prepared the Passover meal.

Jesus washes his disciples' feet   John 13.2, 4–17

In Palestine it was normally the job of the lowest servant to wash the guests' feet.

Jesus and his disciples were at supper... Jesus rose from the table, took off his outer garment, and tied a towel round his waist. Then he poured some water into a basin and began to wash the disciples' feet and dry them with the towel round his waist. He came to Simon Peter, who said to him, "Are you going to wash my feet, Lord?"

Jesus answered him, "You do not understand now what I am doing, but you will understand later."

Peter declared, "Never at any time will you wash my feet!"

"If I do not wash your feet," Jesus answered, "you will no longer be my disciple."

Simon Peter answered, "Lord, do not wash only my feet, then! Wash my hands and head, too!"

Jesus said, "Anyone who has had a bath is completely clean and does not have to wash himself, except for his feet. All of you are clean—all except one." (Jesus already knew who was going to betray him; that is why he said, "All of you, except one, are clean.")

268

After Jesus had washed their feet, he put his outer garment back on and returned to his place at the table. "Do you understand what I have just done to you?" he asked. "You call me Teacher and Lord, and it is right that you do so, because that is what I am. I, your Lord and Teacher, have just washed your feet. You, then, should wash one another's feet. I have set an example for you, so that you will do just what I have done for you. I am telling you the truth: no slave is greater than his master, and no messenger is greater than the one who sent him. Now that you know this truth, how happy you will be if you put it into practice!"

Jesus predicts that he will be betrayed   John 13.21–30

After Jesus had said this, he was deeply troubled and declared openly, "I am telling you the truth: one of you is going to betray me."

The disciples looked at one another, completely puzzled about whom he meant. One of the disciples, the one whom Jesus loved, was sitting next to Jesus. Simon Peter motioned to him and said, "Ask him whom he is talking about."

So that disciple moved closer to Jesus' side and asked, "Who is it, Lord?"

Jesus answered, "I will dip some bread in the sauce and give it to him; he is the man." So he took a piece of bread, dipped it, and gave it to Judas, the son of Simon Iscariot. As soon as Judas took the bread, Satan entered him. Jesus said to him, "Be quick about what you are doing!" None of the others at the table understood why Jesus said this to him. Since Judas was in charge of the money bag, some of the disciples thought that Jesus had told him to go and buy what they needed for the festival, or to give something to the poor.

Judas accepted the bread and went out at once. It was night.

Jesus, the way to the Father   John 14.1–14

Jesus told the disciples that by knowing him, they knew God.

"Do not be worried and upset," Jesus told them. "Believe in God and believe also in me. There are many rooms in my Father's house, and I am going to prepare a place for you. I would not tell you this if it were not so. And after I go and prepare a place for you, I will come back and take you to myself, so that you will be where I am. You know the way that leads to the place where I am going."

Thomas said to him, "Lord, we do not know where you are going; so how can we know the way to get there?"

Jesus answered him, "I am the way, the truth, and the life; no one goes to

the Father except by me. Now that you have known me," he said to them, "you will know my Father also, and from now on you do know him and you have seen him."

Philip said to him, "Lord, show us the Father; that is all we need."

Jesus answered, "For a long time I have been with you all; yet you do not know me, Philip? Whoever has seen me has seen the Father. Why, then, do you say, 'Show us the Father'? Do you not believe, Philip, that I am in the Father and the Father is in me? The words that I have spoken to you," Jesus said to his disciples, "do not come from me. The Father, who remains in me, does his own work. Believe me when I say that I am in the Father and the Father is in me. If not, believe because of the things I do. I am telling you the truth: whoever believes in me will do what I do—yes, he will do even greater things, because I am going to the Father. And I will do whatever you ask for in my name, so that the Father's glory will be shown through the Son. If you ask me for anything in my name, I will do it."

The promise of the Holy Spirit   John 14.15–31

"If you love me, you will obey my commandments. I will ask the Father, and he will give you another Helper, who will stay with you for ever. He is the Spirit who reveals the truth about God. The world cannot receive him, because it cannot see him or know him. But you know him, because he remains with you and is in you.

"When I go, you will not be left all alone; I will come back to you. In a little while the world will see me no more, but you will see me; and because I live, you also will live. When that day comes, you will know that I am in my Father and that you are in me, just as I am in you.

"Whoever accepts my commandments and obeys them is the one who loves me. My Father will love whoever loves me; I too will love him and reveal myself to him."

Judas (not Judas Iscariot) said, "Lord, how can it be that you will reveal yourself to us and not to the world?"

Jesus answered him, "Whoever loves me will obey my teaching. My Father will love him, and my Father and I will come to him and live with him. Whoever does not love me does not obey my teaching. And the teaching you have heard is not mine, but comes from the Father, who sent me.

"I have told you this while I am still with you. The Helper, the Holy Spirit, whom the Father will send in my name, will teach you everything and make you remember all that I have told you.

"Peace is what I leave with you; it is my own peace that I give you. I do not give it as the world does. Do not be worried and upset; do not be afraid. You heard me say to you, 'I am leaving, but I will come back to you.' If you loved me, you would be glad that I am going to the Father; for he is greater than I. I have told you this now before it all happens, so that when it does happen, you will believe. I cannot talk with you much longer, because the ruler of this world is coming. He has no power over me, but the world must know that I love the Father; that is why I do everything as he commands me.

"Come, let us go from this place."

The Lord's Supper   Mark 14.22–26

Mark tells the story of the Last Supper much more briefly. What Jesus told his followers to do is still done in churches today. The word "covenant" means an agreement—the agreement between God and man which is the story of the whole Bible.

While they were eating, Jesus took a piece of bread, gave a prayer of thanks, broke it, and gave it to his disciples. "Take it," he said, "this is my body."

Then he took a cup, gave thanks to God, and handed it to them; and they all drank from it. Jesus said, "This is my blood which is poured out for many, my blood which seals God's covenant. I tell you, I will never again drink this wine until the day I drink the new wine in the Kingdom of God."

Then they sang a hymn and went out to the Mount of Olives.

Deserted by everyone

Who will stand by Jesus?   Mark 14.27–31

Jesus said to them, "All of you will run away and leave me, for the scripture says, 'God will kill the shepherd, and the sheep will all be scattered.' But after I am raised to life, I will go to Galilee ahead of you."

Peter answered, "I will never leave you, even though all the rest do!"

Jesus said to Peter, "I tell you that before the cock crows twice tonight, you will say three times that you do not know me."

Peter answered even more strongly, "I will never say that, even if I have to die with you!"

And all the other disciples said the same thing.

Jesus prays in Gethsemane   Mark 14.32–42

Gethsemane was a garden in Jerusalem.

They came to a place called Gethsemane, and Jesus said to his disciples, "Sit here while I pray." He took Peter, James, and John with him. Distress and anguish came over him, and he said to them, "The sorrow in my heart is so great that it almost crushes me. Stay here and keep watch."

He went a little farther on, threw himself on the ground, and prayed that, if possible, he might not have to go through that time of suffering. "Father," he prayed, "my Father! All things are possible for you. Take this cup of suffering away from me. Yet not what I want, but what you want."

Then he returned and found the three disciples asleep. He said to Peter, "Simon, are you asleep? Weren't you able to stay awake even for one hour?" And he said to them, "Keep watch, and pray that you will not fall into temptation. The spirit is willing, but the flesh is weak."

He went away once more and prayed, saying the same words. Then he came back to the disciples and found them asleep; they could not keep their eyes open. And they did not know what to say to him.

When he came back the third time, he said to them, "Are you still sleeping and resting? Enough! The hour has come! Look, the Son of Man is now being handed over to the power of sinful men. Get up, let us go. Look, here is the man who is betraying me!"

The arrest of Jesus   Mark 14.43–52

In Palestine a kiss was a sign of greeting between friends as well as a sign of respect.

Jesus was still speaking when Judas, one of the twelve disciples, arrived. With him was a crowd armed with swords and clubs, and sent by the chief priests, the teachers of the Law, and the elders. The traitor had given the crowd a signal: "The man I kiss is the one you want. Arrest him and take him away under guard."

As soon as Judas arrived, he went up to Jesus and said, "Teacher!" and kissed him. So they arrested Jesus and held him tight. But one of those standing there drew his sword and struck at the High Priest's slave, cutting off his ear. Then Jesus spoke up and said to them, "Did you have to come with swords and clubs to capture me, as though I were an outlaw? Day after day I was with you teaching in the Temple, and you did not arrest me. But the Scriptures must come true."

Then all the disciples left him and ran away.

A certain young man, dressed only in a linen cloth, was following Jesus. They tried to arrest him, but he ran away naked, leaving the cloth behind.

Jesus before the Council   Mark 14.53–65

The words "the son of man" were used by some Jews to mean a special person sent by God. When Jesus says he is the "Son of Man" they call him a blasphemer (someone who insults God).

Then Jesus was taken to the High Priest's house, where all the chief priests, the elders, and the teachers of the Law were gathering. Peter followed from a distance and went into the courtyard of the High Priest's house. There he sat down with the guards, keeping himself warm by the fire. The chief priests and the whole Council tried to find some evidence against Jesus in order to put him to death, but they could not find any. Many witnesses told lies against Jesus, but their stories did not agree.

Then some men stood up and told this lie against Jesus: "We heard him say, 'I will tear down this Temple which men have made, and after three days I will build one that is not made by men.'" Not even they, however, could make their stories agree.

The High Priest stood up in front of them all and questioned Jesus, "Have you no answer to the accusation they bring against you?"

But Jesus kept quiet and would not say a word. Again the High Priest questioned him, "Are you the Messiah, the Son of the Blessed God?"

"I am," answered Jesus, "and you will all see the Son of Man seated on the right of the Almighty and coming with the clouds of heaven!"

The High Priest tore his robes and said, "We don't need any more witnesses! You heard his blasphemy. What is your decision?"

They all voted against him: he was guilty and should be put to death.

Some of them began to spit on Jesus, and they blindfolded him and hit him. "Guess who hit you!" they said. And the guards took him and slapped him.

Peter denies Jesus   Mark 14.66–72

Peter was still down in the courtyard when one of the High Priest's servant-girls came by. When she saw Peter warming himself, she looked straight at him and said, "You, too, were with Jesus of Nazareth."

But he denied it. "I don't know... I don't understand what you are talking about," he answered, and went out into the passage. Just then a cock crowed.

The servant-girl saw him there and began to repeat to the bystanders, "He is one of them!" But Peter denied it again.

A little while later the bystanders accused Peter again, "You can't deny that you are one of them, because you, too, are from Galilee."

Then Peter said, "I swear that I am telling the truth! May God punish me if I am not! I do not know the man you are talking about!"

Just then a cock crowed a second time, and Peter remembered how Jesus had said to him, "Before the cock crows twice, you will say three times that you do not know me." And he broke down and cried.

Jesus is taken to Pilate   Matthew 27.1–2, 11–14

The Council brought Jesus to Pontius Pilate, the Roman Governor. The members of the Council hoped that their accusations about Jesus would worry Pilate enough for him to sentence Jesus to death.

Early in the morning all the chief priests and the elders made their plans against Jesus to put him to death. They put him in chains, led him off, and handed him over to Pilate, the Roman governor…

Jesus stood before the Roman governor, who questioned him. "Are you the king of the Jews?" he asked.

"So you say," answered Jesus. But he said nothing in response to the accusations of the chief priests and elders.

So Pilate said to him, "Don't you hear all these things they accuse you of?"

But Jesus refused to answer a single word, with the result that the Governor was greatly surprised.

Jesus is sentenced to death   Mark 15.6–15

At every Passover Festival Pilate was in the habit of setting free any one prisoner the people asked for. At that time a man named Barabbas was in prison with the rebels who had committed murder in the riot. When the crowd gathered and began to ask Pilate for the usual favour, he asked them, "Do you want me to set free for you the king of the Jews?" He knew very well that the chief priests had handed Jesus over to him because they were jealous.

But the chief priests stirred up the crowd to ask, instead, for Pilate to set Barabbas free for them. Pilate spoke again to the crowd, "What, then, do you want me to do with the one you call the king of the Jews?"

They shouted back, "Crucify him!"

"But what crime has he committed?" Pilate asked.

They shouted all the louder, "Crucify him!"

Pilate wanted to please the crowd, so he set Barabbas free for them. Then he had Jesus whipped and handed him over to be crucified.

Judas' death   Matthew 27.3–7

When Judas, the traitor, learnt that Jesus had been condemned, he repented and took back the thirty silver coins to the chief priests and the elders. "I have sinned by betraying an innocent man to death!" he said.

"What do we care about that?" they answered. "That is your business!"

Judas threw the coins down in the Temple and left; then he went off and hanged himself.

The chief priests picked up the coins and said, "This is blood money, and it is against our Law to put it in the temple treasury." After reaching an agreement about it, they used the money to buy Potter's Field, as a cemetery for foreigners.

The soldiers make fun of Jesus   Mark 15.16–20

The soldiers took Jesus inside to the courtyard of the governor's palace and called together the rest of the company. They put a purple robe on Jesus, made a crown out of thorny branches, and put it on his head. Then they began to salute him: "Long live the King of the Jews!" They beat him over the head with a stick, spat on him, fell on their knees, and bowed down to him. When they had finished mocking him, they took off the purple robe and put his own clothes back on him. Then they led him out to crucify him.

Jesus is nailed to the cross   Luke 23.26, 32–43

The soldiers led Jesus away, and as they were going, they met a man from Cyrene named Simon who was coming into the city from the country. They seized him, put the cross on him, and made him carry it behind Jesus... Two other men, both of them criminals, were also led out to be put to death with Jesus. When they came to the place called "The Skull," they crucified Jesus there, and the two criminals, one on his right and the other on his left. Jesus said, "Forgive them, Father! They don't know what they are doing."

They divided his clothes among themselves by throwing dice. The people stood there watching while the Jewish leaders jeered at him: "He saved others; let him save himself if he is the Messiah whom God has chosen!"

The soldiers also mocked him: they came up to him and offered him cheap wine, and said, "Save yourself if you are the king of the Jews!"

Above him were written these words: "This is the King of the Jews."

One of the criminals hanging there hurled insults at him: "Aren't you the Messiah? Save yourself and us!"

The other one, however, rebuked him, saying, "Don't you fear God? You received the same sentence he did. Ours, however, is only right, because we are getting what we deserve for what we did; but he has done no wrong." And he said to Jesus, "Remember me, Jesus, when you come as King!"

Jesus said to him, "I promise you that today you will be in Paradise with me."

Jesus dies   Luke 23.44–49

It was about twelve o'clock when the sun stopped shining and darkness covered the whole country until three o'clock; and the curtain hanging in

the Temple was torn in two. Jesus cried out in a loud voice, "Father! In your hands I place my spirit!" He said this and died.

The army officer saw what had happened, and he praised God, saying, "Certainly he was a good man!"

When the people who had gathered there to watch the spectacle saw what happened, they all went back home, beating their breasts in sorrow. All those who knew Jesus personally, including the women who had followed him from Galilee, stood at a distance to watch.

Jesus is buried   Luke 23.50–56

The burial customs amongst the Jews in Palestine were different from our own. Ointment and perfume were put on the bodies. They were then wrapped in bandages along with certain spices and put in a burial place. Rich people often prepared tombs to be buried in; some of these were like caves, cut out of rock.

There was a man named Joseph from Arimathea, a town in Judaea. He was a good and honourable man, who was waiting for the coming of the Kingdom of God. Although he was a member of the Council, he had not agreed with their decision and action. He went into the presence of Pilate and asked for the body of Jesus. Then he took the body down, wrapped it in a linen sheet, and placed it in a tomb which had been dug out of solid rock and which had never been used. It was Friday, and the Sabbath was about to begin.

The women who had followed Jesus from Galilee went with Joseph and saw the tomb and how Jesus' body was placed in it. Then they went back home and prepared the spices and perfumes for the body.

On the Sabbath they rested, as the Law commanded.

The guard at the tomb   Matthew 27.62–66

The next day, which was a Sabbath, the chief priests and the Pharisees met with Pilate and said, "Sir, we remember that while that liar was still alive he said, 'I will be raised to life three days later.' Give orders, then, for his tomb to be carefully guarded until the third day, so that his disciples will not be able to go and steal the body, and then tell the people that he was raised from death. This last lie would be even worse than the first one."

"Take a guard," Pilate told them; "go and make the tomb as secure as you can."

So they left and made the tomb secure by putting a seal on the stone and leaving the guard on watch.

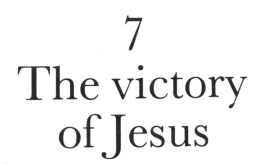

7
The victory
of Jesus

Jesus' followers were deeply shocked by his death. For hundreds of years the Jewish people had looked to "the one who was to come". The disciples believed they had found this person. They had left home and jobs to follow him.

Now, despite all he had done before, Jesus was dead and everyone knew about it. The men who had followed Jesus were now very upset. All their hopes were gone and they lived in fear of their lives. This did not seem at all like a victory.

The unbelievable surprise

The disciples really did not expect anything good to happen now.

The tomb is empty   Luke 24.1–12

Jesus had been taken from the cross and laid in the tomb on Friday evening. Saturday was the Sabbath and no contact with dead bodies was allowed on this day. The preparations on Friday had been very hurried, so at the first opportunity a group of women followers brought spices to anoint the body.

Very early on Sunday morning the women went to the tomb, carrying the spices they had prepared. They found the stone rolled away from the entrance to the tomb, so they went in; but they did not find the body of the Lord Jesus. They stood there puzzled about this, when suddenly two men in bright shining clothes stood by them. Full of fear, the women bowed down to the ground, as the men said to them, "Why are you looking among the dead for one who is alive? He is not here; he has been raised. Remember what he said to you while he was in Galilee: 'The Son of Man must be handed over to sinful men, be crucified, and three days later rise to life.'"

Then the women remembered his words, returned from the tomb, and told all these things to the eleven disciples and all the rest. The women were Mary Magdalene, Joanna, and Mary the mother of James; they and the other women with them told these things to the apostles. But the apostles thought that what the women said was nonsense, and they did not believe them. But Peter got up and ran to the tomb; he bent down and saw the linen wrappings but nothing else. Then he went back home amazed at what had happened.

Peter goes to see for himself   John 20.3–10

John tells us that another disciple went with Peter to find out what had really happened.

Then Peter and the other disciple went to the tomb. The two of them were running, but the other disciple ran faster than Peter and reached the tomb first. He bent over and saw the linen wrappings, but he did not go in. Behind him came Simon Peter, and he went straight into the tomb. He saw the linen wrappings lying there and the cloth which had been round Jesus' head. It was not lying with the linen wrappings but was rolled up by itself. Then the other disciple, who had reached the tomb first, also went in; he saw and believed. (They still did not understand the scripture which said that he must rise from death.) Then the disciples went back home.

Mary sees Jesus   John 20.11–18

Mary stood crying outside the tomb. While she was still crying, she bent over and looked in the tomb and saw two angels there dressed in white, sitting where the body of Jesus had been, one at the head and the other at the feet. "Woman, why are you crying?" they asked her.

She answered, "They have taken my Lord away, and I do not know where they have put him!"

Then she turned round and saw Jesus standing there; but she did not know that it was Jesus. "Woman, why are you crying?" Jesus asked her. "Who is it that you are looking for?"

She thought he was the gardener, so she said to him, "If you took him away, sir, tell me where you have put him, and I will go and get him."

Jesus said to her, "Mary!"

She turned towards him and said in Hebrew, "Rabboni!" (This means "Teacher.")

"Do not hold on to me," Jesus told her, "because I have not yet gone back up to the Father. But go to my brothers and tell them that I am returning to him who is my Father and their Father, my God and their God."

So Mary Magdalene went and told the disciples that she had seen the Lord and related to them what he had told her.

The report of the guards   Matthew 28.11–15

While the women went on their way, some of the soldiers guarding the tomb went back to the city and told the chief priests everything that had happened. The chief priests met with the elders and made their plan; they gave a large sum of money to the soldiers and said, "You are to say that his disciples came during the night and stole his body while you were asleep. And if the Governor should hear of this, we will convince him that you are innocent, and you will have nothing to worry about."

The guards took the money and did what they were told to do. And so that is the report spread round by the Jews to this very day.

The walk to Emmaus   Luke 24.13–35

It was about 11 kilometres from Emmaus to Jerusalem.

On that same day two of Jesus' followers were going to a village named Emmaus, about eleven kilometres from Jerusalem, and they were talking to each other about all the things that had happened. As they talked and discussed, Jesus himself drew near and walked along with them; they saw him, but somehow did not recognize him. Jesus said to them, "What are you talking about to each other, as you walk along?"

They stood still, with sad faces. One of them, named Cleopas, asked him, "Are you the only visitor in Jerusalem who doesn't know the things that have been happening there these last few days?"

"What things?" he asked.

"The things that happened to Jesus of Nazareth," they answered. "This man was a prophet and was considered by God and by all the people to be powerful in everything he said and did. Our chief priests and rulers handed him over to be sentenced to death, and he was crucified. And we had hoped that he would be the one who was going to set Israel free! Besides all that, this is now the third day since it happened. Some of the women of our group surprised us; they went at dawn to the tomb, but could not find his body. They came back saying they had seen a vision of angels who told them that he is alive. Some of our group went to the tomb and found it exactly as the women had said, but they did not see him."

Then Jesus said to them, "How foolish you are, how slow you are to believe everything the prophets said! Was it not necessary for the Messiah to suffer these things and then to enter his glory?" And Jesus explained to them what was said about himself in all the Scriptures, beginning with the books of Moses and the writings of all the prophets.

As they came near the village to which they were going, Jesus acted as if he were going farther; but they held him back, saying, "Stay with us; the day is almost over and it is getting dark." So he went in to stay with them. He sat down to eat with them, took the bread, and said the blessing; then he broke the bread and gave it to them. Then their eyes were opened and they recognized him, but he disappeared from their sight. They said to each other, "Wasn't it like a fire burning in us when he talked to us on the road and explained the Scriptures to us?"

They got up at once and went back to Jerusalem, where they found the eleven disciples gathered together with the others and saying, "The Lord is risen indeed! He has appeared to Simon!"

The two then explained to them what had happened on the road, and how they had recognized the Lord when he broke the bread.

The story is confirmed   Luke 24.36–49

While the two were telling them this, suddenly the Lord himself stood among them and said to them, "Peace be with you."

They were terrified, thinking that they were seeing a ghost. But he said to them, "Why are you alarmed? Why are these doubts coming up in your minds? Look at my hands and my feet, and see that it is I myself. Feel me, and you will know, for a ghost doesn't have flesh and bones, as you can see I have."

He said this and showed them his hands and his feet. They still could not believe, they were so full of joy and wonder; so he asked them, "Have you anything here to eat?" They gave him a piece of cooked fish, which he took and ate in their presence.

Then he said to them, "These are the very things I told you about while I was still with you: everything written about me in the Law of Moses, the writings of the prophets, and the Psalms had to come true."

Then he opened their minds to understand the Scriptures, and said to them, "This is what is written: the Messiah must suffer and must rise from death three days later, and in his name the message about repentance and the forgiveness of sins must be preached to all nations, beginning in Jerusalem. You are witnesses of these things. And I myself will send upon you what my Father has promised. But you must wait in the city until the power from above comes down upon you."

Jesus and Thomas   John 20.24–29

One of the twelve disciples, Thomas (called the Twin), was not with them when Jesus came. So the other disciples told him, "We have seen the Lord!"

Thomas said to them, "Unless I see the scars of the nails in his hands and put my finger on those scars and my hand in his side, I will not believe."

A week later the disciples were together again indoors, and Thomas was with them. The doors were locked, but Jesus came and stood among them and said, "Peace be with you." Then he said to Thomas, "Put your finger here, and look at my hands; then stretch out your hand and put it in my side. Stop your doubting, and believe!"

Thomas answered him, "My Lord and my God!"

Jesus said to him, "Do you believe because you see me? How happy are those who believe without seeing me!"

Jesus appears to the seven disciples   John 21.1–14

After this, Jesus appeared once more to his disciples at Lake Tiberias. This is how it happened. Simon Peter, Thomas (called the Twin), Nathanael (the one from Cana in Galilee), the sons of Zebedee, and two other disciples of Jesus were all together. Simon Peter said to the others, "I am going fishing."

"We will come with you," they told him. So they went out in a boat, but all that night they did not catch a thing. As the sun was rising, Jesus stood at the water's edge, but the disciples did not know that it was Jesus. Then he asked them, "Young men, haven't you caught anything?"

"Not a thing," they answered.

He said to them, "Throw your net out on the right side of the boat, and you will catch some." So they threw the net out and could not pull it back in, because they had caught so many fish.

The disciple whom Jesus loved said to Peter, "It is the Lord!" When Peter heard that it was the Lord, he wrapped his outer garment round him (for he had taken his clothes off) and jumped into the water. The other disciples came to shore in the boat, pulling the net full of fish. They were not very far from land, about a hundred metres away. When they stepped ashore, they saw a charcoal fire there with fish on it and some bread. Then Jesus said to them, "Bring some of the fish you have just caught."

Simon Peter went aboard and dragged the net ashore full of big fish, a hundred and fifty-three in all; even though there were so many, still the net did not tear. Jesus said to them, "Come and eat." None of the disciples dared ask him, "Who are you?" because they knew it was the Lord. So Jesus went over, took the bread, and gave it to them; he did the same with the fish.

This, then, was the third time Jesus appeared to the disciples after he was raised from death.

Many others see Jesus   1 Corinthians 15.3–7

In a letter written later by Paul to the church in a place called Corinth, he mentions other times when Jesus was seen after he was raised to life.

I passed on to you what I received, which is of the greatest importance: that Christ died for our sins, as written in the Scriptures; that he was buried and that he was raised to life three days later, as written in the Scriptures; that he appeared to Peter and then to all twelve apostles. Then he appeared to more than five hundred of his followers at once,

most of whom are still alive, although some have died. Then he appeared to James, and afterwards to all the apostles.

Jesus' last instructions Matthew 28.16–20

The eleven disciples went to the hill in Galilee where Jesus had told them to go. When they saw him, they worshipped him, even though some of them doubted. Jesus drew near and said to them, "I have been given all authority in heaven and on earth. Go, then, to all peoples everywhere and make them my disciples: baptize them in the name of the Father, the Son, and the Holy Spirit, and teach them to obey everything I have commanded you. And I will be with you always, to the end of the age."

Jesus is taken up to heaven Acts 1.6–11

When the apostles met together with Jesus, they asked him, "Lord, will you at this time give the Kingdom back to Israel?"

Jesus said to them, "The times and occasions are set by my Father's own authority, and it is not for you to know when they will be. But when the Holy Spirit comes upon you, you will be filled with power, and you will be witnesses for me in Jerusalem, in all Judaea and Samaria, and to the ends of the earth." After saying this, he was taken up to heaven as they watched him, and a cloud hid him from their sight.

They still had their eyes fixed on the sky as he went away, when two men dressed in white suddenly stood beside them and said, "Galileans, why are you standing there looking up at the sky? This Jesus, who was taken from you into heaven, will come back in the same way that you saw him go to heaven."

Jesus' followers make sense of it all

God always had a plan Ephesians 1.8–14

The early followers of Jesus soon realized that, from the very beginning, God had intended Jesus to live, die, and be raised to life.

In all his wisdom and insight God did what he had purposed, and made known to us the secret plan he had already decided to complete by means of Christ. This plan, which God will complete when the time is right, is to bring all creation together, everything in heaven and on earth, with Christ as head.

All things are done according to God's plan and decision; and God chose us to be his own people in union with Christ because of his own purpose, based on what he had decided from the very beginning. Let us, then, who were the first to hope in Christ, praise God's glory!

And you also became God's people when you heard the true message, the Good News that brought you salvation. You believed in Christ, and God put his stamp of ownership on you by giving you the Holy Spirit he had promised. The Spirit is the guarantee that we shall receive what God has promised his people, and this assures us that God will give complete freedom to those who are his. Let us praise his glory!

One in Christ   Ephesians 2.11–13

Remember, in the Old Testament the covenant was made between God and the Jews (Israelites). God's covenant is now open to all people, Jews and Gentiles.

You Gentiles by birth... remember what you were in the past. At that time you were apart from Christ. You were foreigners and did not belong to God's chosen people. You had no part in the covenants, which were based on God's promises to his people, and you lived in this world without hope and without God. But now, in union with Christ Jesus, you who used to be far away have been brought near by the sacrificial death of Christ.

God puts us right with him   Romans 3.22–26

God puts people right through their faith in Jesus Christ. God does this to all who believe in Christ, because there is no difference at all: everyone has sinned and is far away from God's saving presence. But by the free gift of God's grace all are put right with him through Christ Jesus, who sets them free. God offered him, so that by his sacrificial death he should become the means by which people's sins are forgiven through their faith in him. God did this in order to demonstrate that he is righteous.

The disciples are like new men

The coming of the Holy Spirit   Acts 2.1–13

"Pentecost" means "the fiftieth" and was the name given to the celebration held fifty days after the Passover. It was held in memory of the time when God gave Moses the Law on Mount Sinai. It also acted as a kind of harvest festival for the barley crop. Many Jews visited Jerusalem to share in this, but since the time of the apostles Christians have associated Pentecost with the following events.

When the day of Pentecost came, all the believers were gathered together in one place. Suddenly there was a noise from the sky which sounded like a strong wind blowing, and it filled the whole house where they were sitting. Then they saw what looked like tongues of fire which spread out and touched each person there. They were all filled with the Holy Spirit and began to talk in other languages, as the Spirit enabled them to speak.

There were Jews living in Jerusalem, religious men who had come from every country in the world. When they heard this noise, a large crowd gathered. They were all excited, because each one of them heard the believers speaking in his own language. In amazement and wonder they exclaimed, "These people who are talking like this are Galileans! How is it, then, that all of us hear them speaking in our own native languages? We are from Parthia, Media, and Elam; from Mesopotamia, Judaea, and Cappadocia; from Pontus and Asia, from Phrygia and Pamphylia, from Egypt and the regions of Libya near Cyrene. Some of us are from Rome, both Jews and Gentiles converted to Judaism, and some of us are from Crete and Arabia—yet all of us hear them speaking in our own languages about the great things that God has done!" Amazed and confused, they kept asking each other, "What does this mean?"

But others made fun of the believers, saying, "These people are drunk!"

Peter's message   Acts 2.14–15, 22–24, 32–33, 36–42

Then Peter stood up with the other eleven apostles and in a loud voice began to speak to the crowd: "Fellow-Jews and all of you who live in Jerusalem, listen to me and let me tell you what this means. These people are not drunk, as you suppose; it is only nine o'clock in the morning...

"Listen to these words, fellow-Israelites! Jesus of Nazareth was a man whose divine authority was clearly proven to you by all the miracles and wonders which God performed through him. You yourselves know this, for it happened here among you. In accordance with his own plan God had already decided that Jesus would be handed over to you; and you killed him by letting sinful men crucify him. But God raised him from death, setting him free from its power, because it was impossible that death should hold him prisoner...

"God has raised this very Jesus from death, and we are all witnesses to this fact. He has been raised to the right-hand side of God, his Father, and has received from him the Holy Spirit, as he had promised. What you now see and hear is his gift that he has poured out on us...

"All the people of Israel, then, are to know for sure that this Jesus, whom you crucified, is the one that God has made Lord and Messiah!"

When the people heard this, they were deeply troubled and said to Peter and the other apostles, "What shall we do, brothers?"

Peter said to them, "Each one of you must turn away from his sins and be baptized in the name of Jesus Christ, so that your sins will be forgiven; and you will receive God's gift, the Holy Spirit. For God's promise was made to you and your children, and to all who are far away—all whom the Lord our God calls to himself."

Peter made his appeal to them and with many other words he urged them, saying, "Save yourselves from the punishment coming on this wicked people!" Many of them believed his message and were baptized, and about three thousand people were added to the group that day. They spent their time in learning from the apostles, taking part in the fellowship, and sharing in the fellowship meals and the prayers.

Life among the believers   Acts 2.43–47

Many miracles and wonders were being done through the apostles, and everyone was filled with awe. All the believers continued together in close fellowship and shared their belongings with one another. They would sell their property and possessions, and distribute the money among all, according to what each one needed. Day after day they met as a group in the Temple, and they had their meals together in their homes, eating with glad and humble hearts, praising God, and enjoying the good will of all the people. And every day the Lord added to their group those who were being saved.

They could not be stopped

Peter orders a man to walk   Acts 3.1–10

One day Peter and John went to the Temple at three o'clock in the afternoon, the hour for prayer. There at the Beautiful Gate, as it was called, was a man who had been lame all his life. Every day he was carried to the gate to beg for money from the people who were going into the Temple. When he saw Peter and John going in, he begged them to give him something. They looked straight at him, and Peter said, "Look at us!" So he looked at them, expecting to get something from them. But Peter said to him, "I have no money at all, but I give you what I have: in the name of Jesus Christ of Nazareth I order you to get up and walk!" Then he took him by his right hand and helped him up. At once the man's feet and ankles became strong; he jumped up, stood on his feet, and started walking around. Then he went into the Temple with them, walking and jumping and praising God. The people there saw him walking and praising God, and when they recognized him as the beggar who had sat at the Beautiful Gate, they were all surprised and amazed at what had happened to him.

Peter's message in the Temple   Acts 3.11–19

As the man held on to Peter and John in Solomon's Porch, as it was called, the people were amazed and ran to them. When Peter saw the people, he said to them, "Fellow-Israelites, why are you surprised at this, and why do you stare at us? Do you think that it was by means of our own power or godliness that we made this man walk? The God of Abraham, Isaac, and Jacob, the God of our ancestors, has given divine glory to his Servant Jesus. But you handed him over to the authorities, and you rejected him in Pilate's presence, even after Pilate had decided to set him free. He was holy and good, but you rejected him, and instead you asked Pilate to do you the favour of turning loose a murderer. You killed the one who leads to life, but God raised him from death—and we are witnesses to this. It was the power of his name that gave strength to this lame man. What you see and know was done by faith in his name; it was faith in Jesus that has made him well, as you can all see.

"And now, my brothers, I know that what you and your leaders did to Jesus was due to your ignorance. God announced long ago through all the prophets that his Messiah had to suffer; and he made it come true in this way. Repent, then, and turn to God, so that he will forgive your sins."

Peter and John before the Council   Acts 4.1–22

Peter and John were still speaking to the people when some priests, the officer in charge of the temple guards, and some Sadducees arrived. They were annoyed because the two apostles were teaching the people that Jesus had risen from death, which proved that the dead will rise to life. So they arrested them and put them in jail until the next day, since it was already late. But many who heard the message believed; and the number of men grew to about five thousand.

The next day the Jewish leaders, the elders, and the teachers of the Law gathered in Jerusalem. They met with the High Priest Annas and with Caiaphas, John, Alexander, and the others who belonged to the High Priest's family. They made the apostles stand before them and asked them, "How did you do this? What power have you got or whose name did you use?"

Peter, full of the Holy Spirit, answered them, "Leaders of the people and elders: if we are being questioned today about the good deed done to the lame man and how he was healed, then you should all know, and all the people of Israel should know, that this man stands here before you completely well through the power of the name of Jesus Christ of Nazareth—whom you crucified and whom God raised from death. Jesus is the one of whom the scripture says,

'The stone that you the builders despised
    turned out to be the most important of all.'
Salvation is to be found through him alone; in all the world there is no
one else whom God has given who can save us.''

The members of the Council were amazed to see how bold Peter and
John were and to learn that they were ordinary men of no education.
They realized then that they had been companions of Jesus. But there
was nothing that they could say, because they saw the man who had been
healed standing there with Peter and John. So they told them to leave the
Council room, and then they started discussing among themselves.
"What shall we do with these men?" they asked. "Everyone in Jerusalem
knows that this extraordinary miracle has been performed by them, and
we cannot deny it. But to keep this matter from spreading any further
among the people, let us warn these men never again to speak to anyone
in the name of Jesus."

So they called them back in and told them that on no condition were they
to speak or to teach in the name of Jesus. But Peter and John answered
them, "You yourselves judge which is right in God's sight—to obey you
or to obey God. For we cannot stop speaking of what we ourselves have
seen and heard." So the Council warned them even more strongly and
then set them free. They saw that it was impossible to punish them,
because the people were all praising God for what had happened. The
man on whom this miracle of healing had been performed was over forty
years old.

Miracles and wonders   Acts 5.12–16

Many miracles and wonders were being performed among the people by
the apostles. All the believers met together in Solomon's Porch. Nobody
outside the group dared to join them, even though the people spoke
highly of them. But more and more people were added to the group—a
crowd of men and women who believed in the Lord. As a result of what
the apostles were doing, sick people were carried out into the streets and
placed on beds and mats so that at least Peter's shadow might fall on
some of them as he passed by. And crowds of people came in from the
towns around Jerusalem, bringing those who were ill or who had evil
spirits in them; and they were all healed.

The apostles are arrested   Acts 5.17–35, 38–39

The "angel of the Lord" appeared in Old Testament times (page 136).
Now God was at work again—the news of this "new life" was spreading
fast.

296

Then the High Priest and all his companions, members of the local party of the Sadducees, became extremely jealous of the apostles; so they decided to take action. They arrested the apostles and put them in the public jail. But that night an angel of the Lord opened the prison gates, led the apostles out, and said to them, "Go and stand in the Temple, and tell the people all about this new life." The apostles obeyed, and at dawn they entered the Temple and started teaching.

The High Priest and his companions called together all the Jewish elders for a full meeting of the Council; then they sent orders to the prison to have the apostles brought before them. But when the officials arrived, they did not find the apostles in prison, so they returned to the Council and reported, "When we arrived at the jail, we found it locked up tight and all the guards on watch at the gates; but when we opened the gates, we found no one inside!" When the chief priests and the officer in charge of the temple guards heard this, they wondered what had happened to the apostles. Then a man came in and said to them, "Listen! The men you put in prison are in the Temple teaching the people!" So the officer went off with his men and brought the apostles back. They did not use force, however, because they were afraid that the people might stone them.

They brought the apostles in, made them stand before the Council, and the High Priest questioned them. "We gave you strict orders not to teach in the name of this man," he said; "but see what you have done! You have spread your teaching all over Jerusalem, and you want to make us responsible for his death!"

Peter and the other apostles replied, "We must obey God, not men. The God of our ancestors raised Jesus from death, after you had killed him by nailing him to a cross. God raised him to his right-hand side as Leader and Saviour, to give the people of Israel the opportunity to repent and have their sins forgiven. We are witnesses to these things—we and the Holy Spirit, who is God's gift to those who obey him."

When the members of the Council heard this, they were so furious that they wanted to have the apostles put to death. But one of them, a Pharisee named Gamaliel, who was a teacher of the Law and was highly respected by all the people, stood up in the Council. He ordered the apostles to be taken out for a while, and then he said to the Council, "Fellow-Israelites, be careful what you do to these men... do not take any action against these men. Leave them alone! If what they have planned and done is of human origin, it will disappear, but if it comes from God, you cannot possibly defeat them. You could find yourselves fighting against God!"

8

Belief in Jesus spreads around the world

Up to this point in the Bible God had spoken mainly to the Jewish or Israelite people. We have seen how this took place through people like Abraham and Jacob, then through Moses and the prophets, and most fully, through Jesus.

Peter and the apostles saw Jesus as the long-awaited Messiah, and their first task was to convince their fellow-Jews of this. Jerusalem therefore became, for a while, the centre of the church. Then they realized that the message of Jesus was for everyone. God was calling them to spread his message throughout the world.

This, of course, meant travel and in the first century that was not easy. But things were not as bad as they had been. In the past any kind of travel was slow and dangerous, but the apostles' message came at a time when safe transport and reliable communication were just beginning. The fear of wars was gone, as a long period of peace began under Roman rule. The threat of attack by bandits was less as Roman soldiers patrolled. The normal problem of crossing miles of difficult country was made easier by the famous Roman roads. The language barrier was broken as merchants following the Romans carried the Greek language across their empire.

A new apostle is called

Saul tries to destroy the church   Acts 8.1–3

When the New Testament writers use the word "church" they do not mean a building, but the people who believe in and worship Jesus

Christ. Saul was a Pharisee. He was sure that the church was wrong and should be destroyed.

Stephen was killed by the authorities because of his beliefs.

That very day the church in Jerusalem began to suffer cruel persecution. All the believers, except the apostles, were scattered throughout the provinces of Judaea and Samaria. Some devout men buried Stephen, mourning for him with loud cries.

But Saul tried to destroy the church; going from house to house, he dragged out the believers, both men and women, and threw them into jail.

Drama on the road to Damascus   Acts 9.1–19

In the meantime Saul kept up his violent threats of murder against the followers of the Lord. He went to the High Priest and asked for letters of introduction to the synagogues in Damascus, so that if he should find there any followers of the Way of the Lord, he would be able to arrest them, both men and women, and bring them back to Jerusalem.

As Saul was coming near the city of Damascus, suddenly a light from the sky flashed round him. He fell to the ground and heard a voice saying to him, "Saul, Saul! Why do you persecute me?"

"Who are you, Lord?" he asked.

"I am Jesus, whom you persecute," the voice said. "But get up and go into the city, where you will be told what you must do."

The men who were travelling with Saul had stopped, not saying a word; they heard the voice but could not see anyone. Saul got up from the ground and opened his eyes, but could not see a thing. So they took him by the hand and led him into Damascus. For three days he was not able to see, and during that time he did not eat or drink anything.

There was a Christian in Damascus named Ananias. He had a vision, in which the Lord said to him, "Ananias!"

"Here I am, Lord," he answered.

The Lord said to him, "Get ready and go to Straight Street, and at the house of Judas ask for a man from Tarsus named Saul. He is praying, and in a vision he has seen a man named Ananias come in and place his hands on him so that he might see again."

Ananias answered, "Lord, many people have told me about this man and about all the terrible things he has done to your people in Jerusalem. And he has come to Damascus with authority from the chief priests to arrest all who worship you."

The Lord said to him, "Go, because I have chosen him to serve me, to make my name known to Gentiles and kings and to the people of Israel. And I myself will show him all that he must suffer for my sake."

So Ananias went, entered the house where Saul was, and placed his hands on him. "Brother Saul," he said, "the Lord has sent me—Jesus himself, who appeared to you on the road as you were coming here. He sent me so that you might see again and be filled with the Holy Spirit." At once something like fish scales fell from Saul's eyes, and he was able to see again. He stood up and was baptized; and after he had eaten, his strength came back.

Saul changes sides   Acts 9.19–31

Saul stayed for a few days with the believers in Damascus. He went straight to the synagogues and began to preach that Jesus was the Son of God.

All who heard him were amazed and asked, "Isn't he the one who in Jerusalem was killing those who worship that man Jesus? And didn't he come here for the very purpose of arresting those people and taking them back to the chief priests?"

But Saul's preaching became even more powerful, and his proofs that Jesus was the Messiah were so convincing that the Jews who lived in Damascus could not answer him.

After many days had gone by, the Jews met together and made plans to kill Saul, but he was told of their plan. Day and night they watched the city gates in order to kill him. But one night Saul's followers took him and let him down through an opening in the wall, lowering him in a basket.

Saul went to Jerusalem and tried to join the disciples. But they would not believe that he was a disciple, and they were all afraid of him. Then Barnabas came to his help and took him to the apostles. He explained to them how Saul had seen the Lord on the road and that the Lord had spoken to him. He also told them how boldly Saul had preached in the name of Jesus in Damascus. And so Saul stayed with them and went all over Jerusalem, preaching boldly in the name of the Lord. He also talked and disputed with the Greek-speaking Jews, but they tried to kill him. When the believers found out about this, they took Saul to Caesarea and sent him away to Tarsus.

And so it was that the church throughout Judaea, Galilee, and Samaria had a time of peace. Through the help of the Holy Spirit it was strengthened and grew in numbers, as it lived in reverence for the Lord.

The Gentiles are told the good news

After his conversion to belief in Jesus as the Messiah, Saul, or Paul as he became known, went on three great missionary journeys. He preached about Jesus and started churches in many important towns and cities. During these journeys he had many adventures. Here we are told about some of them.

Thrown into prison   Acts 16.16–40

One day as we were going to the place of prayer, we were met by a slave-girl who had an evil spirit that enabled her to predict the future. She earned a lot of money for her owners by telling fortunes. She followed Paul and us, shouting, "These men are servants of the Most High God! They announce to you how you can be saved!" She did this for many days, until Paul became so upset that he turned round and said to the spirit, "In the name of Jesus Christ I order you to come out of her!" The spirit went out of her that very moment.

When her owners realized that their chance of making money was gone, they seized Paul and Silas and dragged them to the authorities in the public square. They brought them before the Roman officials and said, "These men are Jews, and they are causing trouble in our city. They are teaching customs that are against our law; we are Roman citizens, and we cannot accept these customs or practise them." And the crowd joined in the attack against Paul and Silas.

Then the officials tore the clothes off Paul and Silas and ordered them to be whipped. After a severe beating, they were thrown into jail, and the jailer was ordered to lock them up tight. Upon receiving this order, the jailer threw them into the inner cell and fastened their feet between heavy blocks of wood.

About midnight Paul and Silas were praying and singing hymns to God, and the other prisoners were listening to them. Suddenly there was a violent earthquake, which shook the prison to its foundations. At once all the doors opened, and the chains fell off all the prisoners. The jailer woke up, and when he saw the prison doors open, he thought that the prisoners had escaped; so he pulled out his sword and was about to kill himself. But Paul shouted at the top of his voice, "Don't harm yourself! We are all here!"

The jailer called for a light, rushed in, and fell trembling at the feet of Paul and Silas. Then he led them out and asked, "Sirs, what must I do to be saved?"

They answered, "Believe in the Lord Jesus, and you will be saved—you and your family." Then they preached the word of the Lord to him and to all the others in his house. At that very hour of the night the jailer took them and washed their wounds; and he and all his family were baptized at once. Then he took Paul and Silas up into his house and gave them some food to eat. He and his family were filled with joy, because they now believed in God.

The next morning the Roman authorities sent police officers with the order, "Let those men go."

So the jailer told Paul, "The officials have sent an order for you and Silas to be released. You may leave, then, and go in peace."

But Paul said to the police officers, "We were not found guilty of any crime, yet they whipped us in public—and we are Roman citizens! Then they threw us in prison. And now they want to send us away secretly. Not likely! The Roman officials themselves must come here and let us out."

The police officers reported these words to the Roman officials; and when they heard that Paul and Silas were Roman citizens, they were afraid. So they went and apologized to them; then they led them out of the prison and asked them to leave the city. Paul and Silas left the prison and went to Lydia's house. There they met the believers, spoke words of encouragement to them, and left.

In Athens Acts 17.16–34

While Paul was waiting in Athens for Silas and Timothy, he was greatly upset when he noticed how full of idols the city was. So he held discussions in the synagogue with the Jews and with the Gentiles who worshipped God, and also in the public square every day with the people who happened to pass by. Certain Epicurean and Stoic teachers also debated with him. Some of them asked, "What is this ignorant show-off trying to say?"

Others answered, "He seems to be talking about foreign gods." They said this because Paul was preaching about Jesus and the resurrection. So they took Paul, brought him before the city council, the Areopagus, and said, "We would like to know what this new teaching is that you are talking about. Some of the things we hear you say sound strange to us, and we would like to know what they mean." (For all the citizens of Athens and the foreigners who lived there liked to spend all their time telling and hearing the latest new thing.)

Paul stood up in front of the city council and said, "I see that in every way you Athenians are very religious. For as I walked through your city and looked at the places where you worship, I found an altar on which is written, 'To an Unknown God'. That which you worship, then, even though you do not know it, is what I now proclaim to you. God, who made the world and everything in it, is Lord of heaven and earth and does not live in man-made temples. Nor does he need anything that we can supply by working for him, since it is he himself who gives life and breath and everything else to everyone. From one man he created all races of mankind and made them live throughout the whole earth. He himself fixed beforehand the exact times and the limits of the places where they would live. He did this so that they would look for him, and perhaps find him as they felt about for him. Yet God is actually not far from any one of us; as someone has said,

'In him we live and move and exist.'
It is as some of your poets have said,
'We too are his children.'
Since we are God's children, we should not suppose that his nature is anything like an image of gold or silver or stone, shaped by the art and skill of man. God has overlooked the times when people did not know him, but now he commands all of them everywhere to turn away from their evil ways. For he has fixed a day in which he will judge the whole world with justice by means of a man he has chosen. He has given proof of this to everyone by raising that man from death!"

When they heard Paul speak about a raising from death, some of them made fun of him, but others said, "We want to hear you speak about this again." And so Paul left the meeting. Some men joined him and believed, among whom was Dionysius, a member of the council; there was also a woman named Damaris, and some other people.

The riot in Ephesus   Acts 19.21–41

In many of the areas Paul visited the people worshipped idols.

Paul made up his mind to travel through Macedonia and Achaia and go on to Jerusalem. "After I go there," he said, "I must also see Rome." So he sent Timothy and Erastus, two of his helpers, to Macedonia, while he spent more time in the province of Asia.

It was at this time that there was serious trouble in Ephesus because of the Way of the Lord. A certain silversmith named Demetrius made silver models of the temple of the goddess Artemis, and his business brought a great deal of profit to the workers. So he called them all together with others whose work was like theirs and said to them, "Men, you know that our prosperity comes from this work. Now, you can see and hear for yourselves what this fellow Paul is doing. He says that man-made gods are not gods at all, and he has succeeded in convincing many people, both here in Ephesus and in nearly the whole province of Asia. There is the danger, then, that this business of ours will get a bad name. Not only that, but there is also the danger that the temple of the great goddess Artemis will come to mean nothing and that her greatness will be destroyed—the goddess worshipped by everyone in Asia and in all the world!"

As the crowd heard these words, they became furious and started shouting, "Great is Artemis of Ephesus!" The uproar spread throughout the whole city. The mob seized Gaius and Aristarchus, two Macedonians who were travelling with Paul, and rushed with them to the theatre. Paul himself wanted to go before the crowd, but the believers would not let him. Some of the provincial authorities, who were his friends, also sent him a message begging him not to show himself in the theatre. Meanwhile the whole meeting was in an uproar: some people were shouting one thing, others were shouting something else, because most of them did not even know why they had come together. Some of the people concluded that Alexander was responsible, since the Jews made him go up to the front. Then Alexander motioned with his hand for the people to be silent, and he tried to make a speech of defence. But when they recognized that he was a Jew, they all shouted together the same thing for two hours: "Great is Artemis of Ephesus!"

At last the town clerk was able to calm the crowd. "Fellow-Ephesians!" he said. "Everyone knows that the city of Ephesus is the keeper of the temple of the great Artemis and of the sacred stone that fell down from heaven. Nobody can deny these things. So then, you must calm down and not do anything reckless. You have brought these men here even though they have not robbed temples or said evil things about our goddess. If Demetrius and his workers have an accusation against anyone, we have the authorities and the regular days for court; charges can be made there. But if there is something more that you want, it will have to be settled in a legal meeting of citizens. For after what has happened today, there is the danger that we will be accused of a riot. There is no excuse for all this uproar, and we would not be able to give a good reason for it." After saying this, he dismissed the meeting.

Paul continues his work from prison

Despite what happened in Ephesus, it was back in Jerusalem that Paul faced the greatest opposition. Paul had been released from prison but he was not free for long.

Arrested in the Temple   Acts 21.27—22.5

Some Jews stirred up the whole crowd and seized Paul. "Men of Israel!" they shouted. "Help! This is the man who goes everywhere teaching everyone against the people of Israel, the Law of Moses, and this Temple. And now he has even brought some Gentiles into the Temple and defiled this holy place!" (They said this because they had seen Trophimus from Ephesus with Paul in the city, and they thought that Paul had taken him into the Temple.)

Confusion spread through the whole city, and the people all ran together, seized Paul, and dragged him out of the Temple. At once the Temple doors were closed. The mob was trying to kill Paul, when a report was sent up to the commander of the Roman troops that all Jerusalem was rioting. At once the commander took some officers and soldiers and rushed down to the crowd. When the people saw him with the soldiers, they stopped beating Paul. The commander went over to Paul, arrested him, and ordered him to be bound with two chains. Then he asked, "Who is this man, and what has he done?" Some in the crowd shouted one thing, others something else. There was such confusion that the commander could not find out exactly what had happened, so he ordered his men to take Paul up into the fort. They got as far as the steps with him, and then the soldiers had to carry him because the mob was so wild. They were all coming after him and screaming, "Kill him!"

As the soldiers were about to take Paul into the fort, he spoke to the commander: "May I say something to you?"

"You speak Greek, do you?" the commander asked. "Then you are not that Egyptian fellow who some time ago started a revolution and led four thousand armed terrorists out into the desert?"

Paul answered, "I am a Jew, born in Tarsus in Cilicia, a citizen of an important city. Please let me speak to the people."

The commander gave him permission, so Paul stood on the steps and motioned with his hand for the people to be silent. When they were quiet, Paul spoke to them in Hebrew:

"My fellow-Israelites, listen to me as I make my defence before you!" When they heard him speaking to them in Hebrew, they became even quieter; and Paul went on:

"I am a Jew, born in Tarsus in Cilicia, but brought up here in Jerusalem as a student of Gamaliel. I received strict instruction in the Law of our ancestors and was just as dedicated to God as are all of you who are here today. I persecuted to the death the people who followed this Way. I arrested men and women and threw them into prison. The High Priest and the whole Council can prove that I am telling the truth. I received from them letters written to fellow-Jews in Damascus, so I went there to arrest these people and bring them back in chains to Jerusalem to be punished.

Paul faces a furious crowd   Acts 22.17–29

Paul told them how Jesus had spoken to him and then told them what had happened in Jerusalem.

It was against the law for a soldier to bind a Roman citizen without trial, and a serious offence to whip them. The commander could have been severely punished for doing this.

"While I was praying in the Temple, I had a vision, in which I saw the Lord, as he said to me, 'Hurry and leave Jerusalem quickly, because the people here will not accept your witness about me.' 'Lord,' I answered, 'they know very well that I went to the synagogues and arrested and beat those who believe in you. And when your witness Stephen was put to death, I myself was there, approving of his murder and taking care of the cloaks of his murderers.' 'Go,' the Lord said to me, 'for I will send you far away to the Gentiles.' "

The people listened to Paul until he said this; but then they started shouting at the top of their voices, "Away with him! Kill him! He's not fit to live!" They were screaming, waving their clothes, and throwing dust up in the air. The Roman commander ordered his men to take Paul into the fort, and he told them to whip him in order to find out why the Jews were screaming like this against him. But when they had tied him up to be whipped, Paul said to the officer standing there, "Is it lawful for you to whip a Roman citizen who hasn't even been tried for any crime?"

When the officer heard this, he went to the commander and asked him, "What are you doing? That man is a Roman citizen!"

So the commander went to Paul and asked him, "Tell me, are you a Roman citizen?"

"Yes," answered Paul.

The commander said, "I became one by paying a large amount of money."

"But I am one by birth," Paul answered.

At once the men who were going to question Paul drew back from him; and the commander was frightened when he realized that Paul was a Roman citizen and that he had put him in chains.

Paul gets his enemies quarrelling   Acts 22.30—23.11

Paul had been arrested by the commander of the Roman troops in Jerusalem.

The commander wanted to find out for certain what the Jews were accusing Paul of; so the next day he had Paul's chains taken off and ordered the chief priests and the whole Council to meet. Then he took Paul and made him stand before them.

Paul looked straight at the Council and said, "My fellow-Israelites! My conscience is perfectly clear about the way in which I have lived before God to this very day." The High Priest Ananias ordered those who were standing close to Paul to strike him on the mouth. Paul said to him, "God will certainly strike you—you whitewashed wall! You sit there to judge me according to the Law, yet you break the Law by ordering them to strike me!"

The men close to Paul said to him, "You are insulting God's High Priest!"

Paul answered, "My fellow-Israelites, I did not know that he was the High Priest. The scripture says, 'You must not speak evil of the ruler of your people.'"

When Paul saw that some of the group were Sadducees and the others were Pharisees, he called out in the Council, "Fellow-Israelites! I am a Pharisee, the son of Pharisees. I am on trial here because of the hope I have that the dead will rise to life!"

As soon as he said this, the Pharisees and Sadducees started to quarrel, and the group was divided. (For the Sadducees say that people will not rise from death and that there are no angels or spirits; but the Pharisees believe in all three.) The shouting became louder, and some of the teachers of the Law who belonged to the party of the Pharisees stood up and protested strongly: "We cannot find anything wrong with this man! Perhaps a spirit or an angel really did speak to him!"

The argument became so violent that the commander was afraid that Paul would be torn to pieces. So he ordered his soldiers to go down into the group, get Paul away from them, and take him into the fort.

That night the Lord stood by Paul and said, "Don't be afraid! You have given your witness for me here in Jerusalem, and you must also do the same in Rome."

The plot against Paul's life   Acts 23.12—24

The next morning some Jews met together and made a plan. They took a vow that they would not eat or drink anything until they had killed Paul.

There were more than forty who planned this together. Then they went to the chief priests and elders and said, "We have taken a solemn vow together not to eat a thing until we have killed Paul. Now then, you and the Council send word to the Roman commander to bring Paul down to you, pretending that you want to get more accurate information about him. But we will be ready to kill him before he ever gets here."

But the son of Paul's sister heard about the plot; so he went to the fort and told Paul. Then Paul called one of the officers and said to him, "Take this young man to the commander; he has something to tell him." The officer took him, led him to the commander, and said, "The prisoner Paul called me and asked me to bring this young man to you, because he has something to say to you."

The commander took him by the hand, led him off by himself, and asked him, "What have you got to tell me?"

He said, "The Jewish authorities have agreed to ask you tomorrow to take Paul down to the Council, pretending that the Council wants to get more accurate information about him. But don't listen to them, because there are more than forty men who will be hiding and waiting for him. They have taken a vow not to eat or drink until they have killed him. They are now ready to do it and are waiting for your decision."

The commander said, "Don't tell anyone that you have reported this to me." And he sent the young man away.

Then the commander called two of his officers and said, "Get two hundred soldiers ready to go to Caesarea, together with seventy horsemen and two hundred spearmen, and be ready to leave by nine o'clock tonight. Provide some horses for Paul to ride and get him safely through to the governor Felix."

Paul appeals to the Emperor   Acts 25.9–12

Paul arrived safely in Caesarea, where the Romans had their headquarters, and was tried by the governor Felix. The case dragged on for a long time. Felix was eventually recalled to Rome and replaced by a new governor called Festus.

But Festus wanted to gain favour with the Jews, so he asked Paul, "Would you be willing to go to Jerusalem and be tried on these charges before me there?"

Paul said, "I am standing before the Emperor's own court of judgement, where I should be tried. I have done no wrong to the Jews, as you yourself well know. If I have broken the law and done something for which I deserve the death penalty, I do not ask to escape it. But if there is no truth in the charges they bring against me, no one can hand me over to them. I appeal to the Emperor."

Then Festus, after conferring with his advisers, answered, "You have appealed to the Emperor, so to the Emperor you will go."

The journey to Rome

It was a very long way from Jerusalem to Rome. For a long time Paul had wanted to go to Rome. However, the circumstances in which he now sets off are rather different from those he would have planned. Other surprises were to follow.

Paul sets sail   Acts 27.1–12

When it was decided that we should sail to Italy, they handed Paul and some other prisoners over to Julius, an officer in the Roman regiment called "The Emperor's Regiment." We went aboard a ship from Adramyttium, which was ready to leave for the seaports of the province of Asia, and we sailed away. Aristarchus, a Macedonian from Thessalonica, was with us. The next day we arrived at Sidon. Julius was kind to Paul and allowed him to go and see his friends, to be given what he needed. We went on from there, and because the winds were blowing against us, we sailed on the sheltered side of the island of Cyprus. We crossed over the sea off Cilicia and Pamphylia and came to Myra in Lycia. There the officer found a ship from Alexandria that was going to sail for Italy, so he put us aboard.

We sailed slowly for several days and with great difficulty finally arrived off the town of Cnidus. The wind would not let us go any further in that direction, so we sailed down the sheltered side of the island of Crete, passing by Cape Salmone. We kept close to the coast and with great difficulty came to a place called Safe Harbours, not far from the town of Lasea.

We spent a long time there, until it became dangerous to continue the voyage, for by now the Day of Atonement was already past. So Paul gave them this advice: "Men, I see that our voyage from here on will be dangerous; there will be great damage to the cargo and to the ship, and loss of life as well." But the army officer was convinced by what the captain and the owner of the ship said, and not by what Paul said. The harbour was not a good one to spend the winter in; so most of the men were in favour of putting out to sea and trying to reach Phoenix, if possible, in order to spend the winter there. Phoenix is a harbour in Crete that faces south-west and north-west.

The ship is carried along by a fierce storm   Acts 27.13–38

A soft wind from the south began to blow, and the men thought that they could carry out their plan, so they pulled up the anchor and sailed as close as possible along the coast of Crete. But soon a very strong wind—the one called "North-easter"—blew down from the island. It hit the ship, and since it was impossible to keep the ship headed into the wind, we gave up trying and let it be carried along by the wind. We got some shelter when we passed to the south of the little island of Cauda. There, with some difficulty, we managed to make the ship's boat secure. They pulled it aboard and then fastened some ropes tight round the ship. They were afraid that they might run into the sandbanks off the coast of Libya, so they lowered the sail and let the ship be carried by the wind. The violent storm continued, so on the next day they began to throw some of the ship's cargo overboard, and on the following day they threw part of the ship's equipment overboard. For many days we could not see the sun or the stars, and the wind kept on blowing very hard. We finally gave up all hope of being saved.

After the men had gone a long time without food, Paul stood before them and said, "Men, you should have listened to me and not have sailed from Crete; then we would have avoided all this damage and loss. But now I beg you, take heart! Not one of you will lose his life; only the ship will be lost. For last night an angel of the God to whom I belong and whom I worship came to me and said, 'Don't be afraid, Paul! You must stand before the Emperor. And God in his goodness to you has spared the lives of all those who are sailing with you.' So take heart, men! For I trust in God that it will be just as I was told. But we will be driven ashore on some island."

It was the fourteenth night, and we were being driven about in the Mediterranean by the storm. About midnight the sailors suspected that we were getting close to land. So they dropped a line with a weight tied to it and found that the water was forty metres deep; a little later they did the same and found that it was thirty metres deep. They were afraid that the ship would go on the rocks, so they lowered four anchors from the back of the ship and prayed for daylight. Then the sailors tried to escape from the ship; they lowered the boat into the water and pretended that they were going to put out some anchors from the front of the ship. But Paul said to the army officer and soldiers, "If the sailors don't stay on board, you have no hope of being saved." So the soldiers cut the ropes that held the boat and let it go.

Just before dawn, Paul begged them all to eat some food: "You have been waiting for fourteen days now, and all this time you have not eaten anything. I beg you, then, eat some food; you need it in order to survive. Not even a hair of your heads will be lost." After saying this, Paul took some bread, gave thanks to God before them all, broke it, and began to eat. They took heart, and every one of them also ate some food. There was a total of 276 of us on board. After everyone had eaten enough, they lightened the ship by throwing all the wheat into the sea.

Abandon ship! Acts 27.39–44

When day came, the sailors did not recognize the coast, but they noticed a bay with a beach and decided that, if possible, they would run the ship aground there. So they cut off the anchors and let them sink in the sea, and at the same time they untied the ropes that held the steering oars. Then they raised the sail at the front of the ship so that the wind would blow the ship forward, and we headed for shore. But the ship hit a sandbank and went aground; the front part of the ship got stuck and could not move, while the back part was being broken to pieces by the violence of the waves.

The soldiers made a plan to kill all the prisoners, in order to keep them from swimming ashore and escaping. But the army officer wanted to save Paul, so he stopped them from doing this. Instead, he ordered all the men who could swim to jump overboard first and swim ashore; the rest were to follow, holding on to the planks or to some broken pieces of the ship. And this was how we all got safely ashore.

On Malta Acts 28.1–10

When we were safely ashore, we learnt that the island was called Malta. The natives there were very friendly to us. It had started to rain and was cold, so they lit a fire and made us all welcome. Paul gathered up a bundle of sticks and was putting them on the fire when a snake came out on account of the heat and fastened itself to his hand. The natives saw the snake hanging on Paul's hand and said to one another, "This man must be a murderer, but Fate will not let him live, even though he escaped from the sea." But Paul shook the snake off into the fire without being harmed at all. They were waiting for him to swell up or suddenly fall down dead. But after waiting for a long time and not seeing anything unusual happening to him, they changed their minds and said, "He is a god!"

Not far from that place were some fields that belonged to Publius, the chief official of the island. He welcomed us kindly and for three days we were his guests. Publius' father was in bed, sick with fever and dysentery. Paul went into his room, prayed, placed his hands on him, and healed him. When this happened, all the other sick people on the island came and were healed. They gave us many gifts, and when we sailed, they put on board what we needed for the voyage.

In Rome   Acts 28.16–25

When we arrived in Rome, Paul was allowed to live by himself with a soldier guarding him.

After three days Paul called the local Jewish leaders to a meeting. When they had gathered, he said to them, "My fellow-Israelites, even though I did nothing against our people or the customs that we received from our ancestors, I was made a prisoner in Jerusalem and handed over to the Romans. After questioning me, the Romans wanted to release me, because they found that I had done nothing for which I deserved to die. But when the Jews opposed this, I was forced to appeal to the Emperor, even though I had no accusation to make against my own people. That is why I asked to see you and talk with you. As a matter of fact, I am bound in chains like this for the sake of him for whom the people of Israel hope."

They said to him, "We have not received any letters from Judaea about you, nor have any of our people come from there with any news or anything bad to say about you. But we would like to hear your ideas, because we know that everywhere people speak against this party to which you belong."

So they fixed a date with Paul, and a large number of them came that day to the place where Paul was staying. From morning till night he explained to them his message about the Kingdom of God, and he tried to convince them about Jesus by quoting from the Law of Moses and the writings of the prophets. Some of them were convinced by his words, but others would not believe. So they left, disagreeing among themselves.

Looking backward and forward

Paul had founded many churches during his missionary journeys and he kept in touch by writing letters to them. They were addressed to groups rather than individuals and answered many of the questions the early Christians had about their faith. A number of these letters are included in the Bible and they tell us a great deal about Paul and the first Christian churches.

Paul's suffering   2 Corinthians 11.24–29

Five times I was given the thirty-nine lashes by the Jews; three times I was whipped by the Romans; and once I was stoned. I have been in three shipwrecks, and once I spent twenty-four hours in the water. In my many travels I have been in danger from floods and from robbers, in danger from fellow-Jews and from Gentiles; there have been dangers in the cities, dangers in the wilds, dangers on the high seas, and dangers from false friends. There has been work and toil; often I have gone without sleep; I have been hungry and thirsty; I have often been without enough food, shelter, or clothing. And not to mention other things, every day I am under the pressure of my concern for all the churches. When someone is weak, then I feel weak too; when someone is led into sin, I am filled with distress.

A vision of Jesus in heaven   Revelation 1.10–18

Like Jesus, many of the apostles were eventually killed because powerful men saw their teaching as a threat. But Jesus had risen and they did not see death as the end. John was imprisoned on an island called Patmos. Here he had a number of visions, which he wrote down in order to help others who were suffering.

On the Lord's day the Spirit took control of me, and I heard a loud voice, that sounded like a trumpet, speaking behind me. It said, "Write down what you see, and send the book to the churches in these seven cities: Ephesus, Smyrna, Pergamum, Thyatira, Sardis, Philadelphia, and Laodicea."

I turned round to see who was talking to me, and I saw seven gold lampstands, and among them there was what looked like a human being, wearing a robe that reached to his feet, and a gold belt round his chest. His hair was white as wool, or as snow, and his eyes blazed like fire; his feet shone like brass that has been refined and polished, and his voice sounded like a roaring waterfall. He held seven stars in his right hand, and a sharp two-edged sword came out of his mouth. His face was as bright as the midday sun. When I saw him, I fell down at his feet like a dead man. He placed his right hand on me and said, "Don't be afraid! I am the first and the last. I am the living one! I was dead, but now I am alive for ever and ever. I have authority over death and the world of the dead."

Worshipping Jesus in heaven
Revelation 4.1–6, 8–11; 5.11–14

A lamb was the animal that the Jews usually sacrificed for the people's sins. Jesus is often referred to as the "Lamb of God".

At this point I had another vision and saw an open door in heaven. And the voice that sounded like a trumpet, which I had heard speaking to me before, said, "Come up here, and I will show you what must happen after this." At once the Spirit took control of me. There in heaven was a throne with someone sitting on it. His face gleamed like such precious stones as jasper and carnelian, and all round the throne there was a rainbow the colour of an emerald. In a circle round the throne were twenty-four other thrones, on which were seated twenty-four elders dressed in white and wearing crowns of gold. From the throne came flashes of lightning, rumblings, and peals of thunder. In front of the throne seven lighted torches were burning, which are the seven spirits of God. Also in front of the throne there was what looked like a sea of glass, clear as crystal.

Surrounding the throne on each of its sides, were four living creatures... Each one of the four living creatures had six wings, and they were covered with eyes, inside and out. Day and night they never stop singing:
    "Holy, holy, holy, is the Lord God Almighty,
        who was, who is, and who is to come."

The four living creatures sing songs of glory and honour and thanks to the one who sits on the throne, who lives for ever and ever. When they do so, the twenty-four elders fall down before the one who sits on the throne, and worship him who lives for ever and ever. They throw their crowns down in front of the throne and say,
    "Our Lord and God! You are worthy
        to receive glory, honour, and power.
    For you created all things,
        and by your will they were given existence and life."

Again I looked, and I heard angels, thousands and millions of them! They stood round the throne, the four living creatures, and the elders, and sang in a loud voice:
    "The Lamb who was killed is worthy
        to receive power, wealth, wisdom, and strength,
        honour, glory, and praise!"
And I heard every creature in heaven, on earth, in the world below, and in the sea—all living beings in the universe—and they were singing:
    "To him who sits on the throne and to the Lamb,
        be praise and honour, glory and might,
        for ever and ever!"
The four living creatures answered, "Amen!" And the elders fell down and worshipped.

A prayer of praise Jude 24 and 25

To him who is able to keep you from falling, and to bring you faultless and joyful before his glorious presence—to the only God our Saviour, through Jesus Christ our Lord, be glory, majesty, might, and authority, from all ages past, and now, and for ever and ever! Amen.

Index of Jesus' miracles

Name of miracle	Reference	Page
The wedding in Cana	John 2.1–12	191
A man with an evil spirit	Mark 1.21–28	191
Many diseases cured	Mark 1.29–34	194
Jesus heals a dreaded skin-disease	Mark 1.40–45	194
Jesus heals a paralysed man	Mark 2.1–12	195
Jesus heals a blind beggar	Luke 18.35–43	196
Jairus' daughter	Mark 5.21–63	202
Jesus feeds five thousand men	Mark 6.30-44	204
Jesus walks on water	Mark 6.45–52	204
A woman's faith	Mark 7.24–30	206
The Roman officer's servant	Luke 7.1–10	206
The widow's son	Luke 7.11–17	207
Jesus heals a man born blind	John 9.1–11	211
Jesus heals on the Sabbath	Luke 13.10–17	247
Lazarus come out!	John 11.38–44	257

Index of Jesus' parables

Name of parable	Reference	Page
The parable of the lost sheep	Luke 15.1–7	214
The parable of the lost coin	Luke 15.8–10	215
The parable of the lost son	Luke 15.11–32	215
The parable of the weeds	Matt 13.24–30	217
The parable of the mustard seed	Matt 13.31–32	217
The parable of the yeast	Matt 13.33	218
The parable of the hidden treasure	Matt 13.44	218
The parable of the fine pearl	Matt 13.45–46	218
The parable of the net	Matt 13.47–50	218
The parable of the growing seed	Mark 4.26–29	218
The parable of the fig tree which did not grow fruit	Luke 13.6–9	219
The parable of the great feast	Luke 14.15–24	219
The parable of the sower	Luke 8.4–15	220
The parable of the ten girls	Matt 25.1–13	220
The parable of the three servants	Matt 25.14–30	221
Watchful servants	Luke 12.35–40	222
The parable of the tenants in the vineyard	Luke 20.9–15	223
The parable of the friend at midnight	Luke 11.5–8	223
The parable of the widow and the judge	Luke 18.1–8	223
The parable of the Pharisee and the tax collector	Luke 18.9–14	224
The parable of the unforgiving servant	Matt 18.21–35	224
The parable of the rich fool	Luke 12.13–21	225
The rich man and Lazarus	Luke 16.19–31	226
The parable of the two sons	Matt 21.28–32	228
The parable of the good Samaritan	Luke 10.25–37	228
The story of the final judgement	Matt 25.31–46	229

Index of Bible references

OLD TESTAMENT

Genesis
1.1—2.3 *19*
2.8–9, 15–17 *22*
3.1–13, 22–23 *22*
4.2–7 *24*
4.8–14, 16 *24*
6.5–8 *25*
6.9–22 *25*
7.1–5, 7–10, 11–24 *27*
8.1–22 *29*
9.8–17 *30*
12.1–7 *31*
22.1–18 *32*
24.1–28 *34*
25.24–34 *36*
27.1–41 *37*
28.11–22 *41*
32.24–31 *41*
37.1–35 *42*
41.17–46 *44*
43.29–34 *46*
44.1–34 *47*
45.1–20, 25–28 *48*
46.5–7 *48*

Exodus
1.1–14 *50*
1.15–22 *51*
2.1–10 *51*
2.11–25 *52*
3.1–17 *54*
4.10–16 *54*
5.1–9 *55*
12.1–14 *58*
12.37–42 *59*
14.5–31 *59*
15.1–3 *61*
16.2–3, 9–16 *61*
17.1–6 *65*
19.16–20 *65*
20.1–17 *66*
32.1–20 *67*

Leviticus
19.1, 13–18 *66*

Deuteronomy
6.1–9, 12–15 *139*
34.1–12 *70*

Joshua
1.1–9 *72*
6.1–7, 12–13, 15–16,
 20 *73*
24.14–24 *74*

Judges
6.1–16 *76*
6.25–32 *77*
7.1–21 *77*

Ruth
1.1–19 *86*
2.1–3, 14–16 *87*
4.13–22 *87*

1 Samuel
1.9–20 *80*
1.24–28 *81*
3.1–21 *81*
8.1–22 *83*
10.17–25 *84*
16.1–13 *89*
17.2–11 *90*
17.12–40 *90*
17.41–54 *92*
17.55—18.5 *94*
18.6–16 *94*
20.1–23 *95*
20.24–41 *96*
26.1–25 *97*
28.3–25 *98*
31.1–6 *100*

2 Samuel
1.17–27 *101*
11.1–5 *102*
11.6–13 *103*
11.14–21, 25–27 *103*
12.1–15 *105*
15.1–6, 12 *106*
15.13–23 *106*

16.15–20, 23 *108*
17.1–14 *108*
17.15–23 *109*
17.24, 27–29 *110*
18.1–18 *110*
18.19–33 *111*

1 Kings
2.1–4 *113*
3.5–15 *113*
3.16–28 *113*
4.20–21, 29–30,
 32–34 *114*
5.1–5 *115*
6.1, 7, 15, 19, 21–22,
 38 *115*
10.1–9 *115*
10.14–15 *114*
18.20–39 *118*
19.1–18 *120*
19.19–21 *122*
21.1–24, 27–29 *122*

2 Kings
2.1–13 *124*
5.1–14 *125*
22.1–13 *138*
23.1–6 *140*

Ezra
1.1–4 *158*
3.1–7 *159*
4.4–5 *159*

Nehemiah
2.1–8 *160*
2.11–20 *161*
4.1–23 *162*
6.1–14 *164*
6.15–16 *165*
8.1–3, 5–8 *165*
9.1, 38 *165*

Psalms
15 *128*
84.1–2, 10–12 *117*
126.1–3 *159*

Isaiah
6.1–8 *134*
11.1–9 *137*
36.1–2, 13–21 *135*
37.21–37 *136*
40.1–8 *150*
53.7–12 *150*

Jeremiah
1.4–10 *141*
7.1–11 *142*
31.31–34 *142*
52.3–11 *144*

Ezekiel
1.1, 3–9, 22–28 *145*
1.28—2.5 *147*
34.11–15 *147*
37.1–14 *148*

Daniel
3.1–2, 5–6, 8, 12,
 19–25 *152*
5.1–12 *154*
5.13–31 *155*
6.1–22 *156*
7.1, 9–10, 13–14 *151*

Hosea
11.1–4 *129*

Amos
5.10–15, 21–24 *127*
8.4–10 *127*

Jonah
1.1–6 *129*
1.7–17 *130*
2.10 *130*
3.1–10 *131*
4.1–11 *131*

Micah
6.6–8 *128*

Haggai
1.2–9 *160*

NEW TESTAMENT

Matthew
2.1–12 *178*
2.13–15 *179*
2.16 *179*
2.19–23 *179*
3.4–6, 13–17 *187*
4.1–11 *187*
5.13 *232*
5.14–16 *232*
5.21–26 *233*
5.38–42 *233*
5.43–48 *233*
6.1–4 *235*
6.5–15 *236*
6.19–21 *236*
6.24–34 *236*
7.1–6 *237*
7.7–12 *237*
7.13–14 *238*
7.15–20 *238*
7.21–23 *238*
7.24–27 *238*
7.28–29 *239*
9.9–13 *197*
9.35–38 *197*
13.24–30 *217*
13.31–32 *217*
13.33 *218*
13.44 *218*
13.45–46 *218*
13.47–50 *218*
15.10–20 *240*
16.13–20 *248*
16.21–28 *249*
18.21–35 *224*
21.28–32 *228*
22.15–22 *246*
22.23–33 *240*
22.34–40 *246*
23.1–7 *240*
23.23–26 *241*
25.1–13 *220*
25.14–30 *221*
25.31–46 *229*
26.1–5 *265*
27.1–2 *277*
27.3–7 *279*
27.11–14 *277*
27.62–66 *282*
28.11–15 *285*
28.16–20 *290*

Mark
1.14–20 *188*
1.21–28 *191*
1.29–34 *194*
1.35–39 *194*
1.40–45 *194*
2.1–12 *195*
2.18–20 *198*
3.7–12 *198*
3.13–19 *198*
3.31–35 *199*
4.26–29 *218*
4.35–41 *199*
5.21–43 *202*
6.1–6 *201*
6.6–11 *203*
6.30–44 *204*
6.45–52 *204*
6.53–56 *206*
7.24–30 *206*
9.2–13 *249*
9.33–37 *252*
9.38–41 *252*
10.13–16 *253*
10.17–31 *253*
10.35–45 *254*
11.1–11 *260*
11.15–19 *261*
11.27–33 *262*
12.41–44 *262*
13.1–2 *264*
14.3–9 *266*
14.10–11 *266*
14.12–16 *268*
14.22–26 *272*
14.27–31 *273*
14.32–42 *273*
14.43–52 *275*
14.53–65 *276*
14.66–72 *276*
15.6–15 *277*
15.16–20 *280*

Luke
1.26–38 *172*
1.39–45 *172*
1.46–56 *174*
1.57–66 *170*
1.67–80 *171*
2.1–7 *174*
2.8–20 *175*

2.21 *179*
2.22–38 *182*
2.41–52 *183*
3.2–7 *186*
7.1–10 *206*
7.11–17 *207*
7.18–28, 31–35 *208*
7.36–50 *209*
8.1–3 *201*
8.4–8 *220*
8.11–15 *220*
9.57–58 *201*
10.25–37 *228*
11.5–8 *223*
12.13–21 *225*
12.35–40 *222*
13.6–9 *219*
13.10–17 *247*
13.31–35 *255*
14.7–14 *210*
14.15–24 *219*
15.1–7 *214*
15.8–10 *215*
15.11–32 *215*
16.19–31 *226*
18.1–8 *223*
18.9–14 *224*
18.31–34 *260*
18.35–43 *196*
19.1–10 *210*
20.9–15 *223*
23.26, 32–43 *280*
23.44–49 *280*
23.50–56 *282*
24.1–12 *283*
24.13–25 *285*
24.36–49 *287*

John
2.1–12 *191*
3.1–17 *241*
4.1–26 *242*
8.2–11 *243*
9.1–11 *211*
11.1–16 *255*
11.17–27 *256*
11.28–37 *256*
11.38–44 *257*
11.45–54 *257*
13.2, 4–17 *268*
13.21–30 *269*

14.1–14 *269*
14.15–31 *271*
20.3–10 *284*
20.11–18 *284*
20.24–29 *287*
21.1–14 *288*

Acts
1.6–11 *290*
2.1–13 *291*
2.14–42 *292*
2.43–47 *294*
3.1–10 *294*
3.11–19 *295*
4.1–22 *295*
5.12–16 *296*
5.17–35, 38–39 *296*
8.1–3 *298*
9.1–19 *299*
9.19–31 *300*
16.16–40 *302*
17.16–34 *304*
19.21–41 *305*
21.27—22.5 *306*
22.17–29 *308*
22.30—23.11 *309*
23.12–24 *309*
25.9–12 *310*
27.1–12 *311*
27.13–38 *312*
27.39–44 *313*
28.1–10 *313*
28.16–25 *315*

Romans
3.22–26 *291*

1 Corinthians
15.3–7 *288*

2 Corinthians
11.24–29 *315*

Ephesians
1.8–14 *290*
2.11–13 *291*

Jude
24, 25 *317*

Revelation
1.10–18 *316*
4.1–6, 8–11 *316*
5.11–14 *316*